5 Editors Tackle the 12 Fatal Flaws of Fiction Writing

by C. S. Lakin
with
Linda S. Clare, Christy Distler,
Robin Patchen,
and Rachel Starr Thomson

The Writer's Toolbox Series

5 EDITORS TACKLE THE 12 FATAL FLAWS OF FICTION WRITING by C. S. Lakin, with Linda S. Clare, Christy Distler, Robin Patchen, and Rachel Starr Thomson

UBIQUITOUS PRESS

Morgan Hill, CA

The Writer's Toolbox Series

Praise for *5 Editors Tackle the 12 Fatal Flaws of Fiction Writing*

"Concise, informative, and easy to understand, this book should be on every writer's bookshelf. Fiction writers will benefit from the expertise, examples, and tips found in this twelve-step editing guide. Perfect for aspiring writers still learning the craft or established authors who want to brush up on their skills."

—Cheryl Kaye Tardif, international best-selling author and book publisher

"This is a wonderful resource for writers who want to avoid these common mistakes in their manuscript, or correct them if they sneak in. Five talented editors discuss the most common flaws they see in manuscripts, including ways to fix or avoid them. I highly recommend it for any writer."

—Richard Mabry, award-winning author of medical suspense

"*The 12 Fatal Flaws of Fiction Writing* is not your average resource that merely *tells* you how to fix flawed writing mechanisms. It's a practical guide that truly *shows* you how to find your story through a balance of techniques. This book belongs on the top of your writing toolbox, where it'll turn you from a storyteller to a storyshower, encouraging you to develop your trademark style, and get raving—not scathing—reviews."

—Garry Rodgers, best-selling crime writer and retired homicide detective

"C.S. Lakin is the go-to person for improving your fiction writing, and her Writer's Toolbox Series is filled to the hilt with the essential tools you need to write clearly and effectively and, overall, become a better fiction writer. *5 Editors Tackle the 12 Fatal Flaws of Fiction Writing* is a must-have addition to every writer's library."

—Bryan Hutchinson, author of *Writer's Doubt: The #1 Enemy of Writing*

Table of Contents

Introduction

Fiction writers often struggle to improve their craft. They want to write better, more effectively. Tell a stronger, more evocative story. But oftentimes what a writer envisions in her mind doesn't come across on the page.

The biggest challenge can come from the inability to see what *isn't* working. The prose feels off. The scene just isn't gelling. The dialogue sounds stilted or clunky. Writers consult their stack of reference books or jump online and search for answers on blog posts. They may even travel long distances to attend workshops and conferences to get to the heart of their problems.

But even then, the solutions are often elusive.

What writers need are not more books and instructors telling them what to do and how to do it. They need examples. And not just examples of great fiction writing. They need examples of weak, flawed writing too.

What helps writers most is to read passages that demonstrate flawed writing, then be shown revisions that target specific flaws and offer clear, effective solutions to those problems.

12 Fatal Flaws

When working on a manuscript, editors mark up and revise sections to show writing clients what's not working, why, and how these passages might be rewritten. We believe this is the best way to help writers identify their specific weaknesses, as well as learn how to get mastery over them.

Not every writer can afford to hire an editor to point out a manuscript's flaws. And wouldn't it be better for writers to arm themselves with the knowledge and skills needed to avoid succumbing to these writing flaws in the first place? We think so.

That's why we five editors put together a year-long course online—on the Live Write Thrive blog—specifically aimed at tackling the most problematic issues we see day in and day out as we edit and critique manuscripts. While there are undoubtedly more than twelve "fatal flaws" of fiction writing, we set out to examine in depth the most troublesome and ubiquitous of these.

We refer to these issues as fatal flaws because of their potential to cause "novel failure." Any one of these twelve flaws, if prevalent in a novel or other work of fiction, can be a writer's undoing. And because there is no one way to fix each flaw, we've created multiple examples to expose each one, using passages written in a variety of genres, points of view, and writing styles. We feel this wide assortment of more than sixty examples provides just the help writers need.

In addition to being editors, we are all novelists—who struggle with these fiction flaws like any other author. We hope that by sharing our decades of experience as writers as well as book editors, we might help you seek and destroy the fatal flaws in your writing.

How to Best Benefit from This Book

As you read each entry, try to identify what's wrong in the Before passage. Consider jotting down your observations in a notebook, paying special attention to the sections that apply most to your own writing issues. If you have a print copy, you may want to mark up these sections.

Pay attention to how the fatal flaw is presented and what solutions are offered to fix it. At the end of each chapter you'll find a checklist of the points covered—what you need to search for in your scenes or stories to ferret out the fatal flaw. You'll also get a bonus passage to work on, to help you test what you've learned (with a sample "correct" passage provided on the next page). We suggest you copy and print out these passages and work on them before peeking at the sample solution on the following page.

Every writer has a unique style and approach to fiction writing, so we hope that by reviewing a wide spectrum of examples, you will be able to spot potential weaknesses in your writing and fix them.

So as we tackle the twelve fatal flaws of fiction writing, jump in and take them on with us. If you're still having problems with specific flaws, consider hiring an editor with fiction-writing experience to help you home in on your weak areas and give you the skills to self-edit your work effectively. There's no reason any writer should have to experience novel failure.

So let's start tackling.

Fatal Flaw #1: Overwriting

Repetition. Redundancy. Useless words.

All fiction writers fall into the trap of overwriting. We're lured by the desire to be clear and thorough in our descriptions. To make sure the reader gets what we're trying to say. We think if we pack our sentences full of words, we'll get the point across. We'll convey the right emotion and, in turn, evoke the emotional response we long for in our readers.

But however logical that seems, the odd truth is that, more often than not, less is more. Plot and character motivation can come across more strongly and effectively with fewer words. Carefully chosen words. Just the right words put down just the right way.

We tend to underestimate our readers' ability to fill in blanks. We tend to get too close to what we are writing to see it clearly. We tend to doubt our own writing ability—and so we overwrite.

Gushing Is Fine . . . in a First Draft

Some writers find it helpful to gush onto the page in a first draft and worry about the cleanup later. Go ahead and do that. It's a good way to keep the creative juices flowing and get the story out in some form. But too often writers get attached to what they've written. The sentences harden into concrete seconds after they appear on the page or computer screen. It takes courage and stalwart determination to be a brutal self-editor and hack away at those sentences.

While some writers "underwrite" (a flaw we'll cover later in this book), most writers fall victim to overwriting. Overwriting is probably the most common flaw of fiction writing, and its tentacles reach into every aspect of a writer's story: narrative, dialogue, action, and internalizing. Like a contagion, it infects our scenes so they die a slow (or quick) death.

But good news! There is an antidote. The formula is one part determination, two parts knowledge, three parts diligence, and four parts mercilessness. Once you learn to detach emotionally from the words you write, the battle is half won.

Every word counts in your story. Every word has weight. It's heartbreaking to launch your story into a sea of readers and watching it sink before it clears the harbor. So before you break that bottle of champagne over the bow, learn to identify the symptoms of overwriting. Then, with cutlass in hand, hack away. The examples in this chapter will show you how.

Editor:
Rachel Starr Thomson

The Forest for the Trees

When you put pen to paper, it's fully possible to underwrite. To fail to say what you meant to say. But just as possible, and more common, is *overwriting*—the tendency to say too much, in too many words, and crowd out the forest for the trees.

Overwriting takes many forms. Wordiness. Vagueness. Redundancy. Convolution. Pushing metaphors so far beyond the breaking point that they cease to be enlightening and become ridiculous instead.

In all forms, overwriting loses the forest for the trees. Readers get so snarled up in excessive words, tangled sentences, and overdone diction that the big picture is lost.

It's not fun to read. And often, it's not fun to write.

If your words feel forced or unnatural while you're writing them, you might be falling into this trap. It often happens when we try to "sound like real writers," or want to come across as particularly smart or poetic. In those cases we lose our own voices for something artificial.

Finding the Forest

You correct overwriting by letting go of your commitment to every individual tree, leaf, and branch and rediscovering the forest instead. Where's the heart of the scene? The point of the dialogue? The voice of the character?

Some say Michelangelo carved his famous *David* sculpture by chipping away everything that didn't look like David. That's how you cure overwriting.

See if you can catch the overwriting in this passage. What would you chip away?

Before:

As the sun was sinking down far below the edge of the purple, colorful horizon at the edge of the world, Jenny raised her wineglass to her ruby red lips and sighed sadly at seeing the day end. "It's over," she breathed.

Behind her, her impossibly handsome Italian boyfriend, Calvino, pushed his chair away from the table where they had been eating dinner like a panther slinking through the shadows of a dark night in Africa. She was just thinking he had been sitting there too long and wondered when he would come to join her by the edge of the expansive gold-rimmed balcony with its fluted decorations patterned after a famous architect from 1743.

He started to come toward her, and she waited for a long, interminable minute, staring at the purple sunset clouds, until he walked across the balcony, approached her shoulder, and bent down slightly so he could whisper in her ear. "It's never really over," he murmured.

Did this passage make you gag? It should have. Let's take a look at the revision.

After:

As the sun sank below the purple horizon, Jenny raised her wineglass to her lips and sighed at seeing the day end. "It's over."

Behind her, Calvino pushed his chair away from the dinner table. *It's about time,* she thought. She glimpsed his dark Italian features from the corner of her eye as he approached her on the gold-rimmed balcony.

"It's never really over," he whispered in her ear.

In this example, the edited version is far shorter—and more focused.

It cuts redundant language, so "As the sun was sinking down far below the edge of the purple, colorful horizon at the edge of the world" becomes "As the sun sank below the purple horizon."

It cuts a lot of the small in-between actions that can clutter prose: "She was thinking and wondering"; "he started to come toward her"; "he walked, approached, and bent down."

6

The rewritten version also implies the relationship between the two characters through their actions and words rather than explaining it outright. It cuts details that are irrelevant to the scene (the eighteenth-century architect) and a simile that, in the end, added nothing to the character or the moment.

By cutting all these examples of wordiness, we end up with a sharper scene—one that is focused on the forest. On the tension between the characters. On the lament over the end of the day and the promise of something more to come. Many a tree is gone, but the view is clearer.

Extrapolate that first example over the course of an entire scene, or an entire chapter, and you can see why overwriting can be such a problem—and why learning to cut back, *to focus on the scene you actually want your readers to see,* can go a long way toward creating a sharper, more vivid, and memorable story.

Editor:
Linda S. Clare

The Devil's in the Details

The world is full of details—and good writers notice them perpetually. Yet when you introduce your created world to readers, it's easy to get carried away. Overwriting, or including too many details, can derail your scenes and lose readers. As Rachel said in the opening section, writers need to learn how to hack away the unnecessary to create a sharp, vivid story. Yes, stories need details, but which ones should a writer include in her scenes? How do you decide?

You Are the Manager

As a fiction writer, you are a manager. You hold the power to guide your readers, managing their attention and memory. By stressing a certain detail or event, you are sending the message "Pay attention to this. Remember this."

If you attempt to write a scene that includes a blow-by-blow account of what is happening, it may mirror real life, but readers will not know which details matter to the story and which are incidental. If you overload readers with stimuli, they won't know what to pay attention to and what to ignore. To use Rachel's metaphor, pointing out every leaf will steal the view of the forest. If you understand this, it's easier to remind yourself to write only what the readers need to know, with a few "extra sprinkles" of concrete sensory detail to help make the scene believable.

Write the Right Details

Details are vital to believability. If you only paint your scene in general or vague words, readers are less likely to remain engaged.

So how do you know what to include and what to leave out? Think of your story as a road that runs through a city. There are lots of other roads, but only this road leads readers to their destination: the story outcome. Along the way readers might smell the air or see the trees whizzing past, but they keep their eyes on the road.

The extra details you provide should add to the experience of the story in a sensory-emotional way. They also need to be connected to what your main character is after, whether it's a new love, a killer, or a pot of gold. All other details are of little importance to the story and usually can be safely eliminated.

Leave Out the Boring Stuff

Elmore Leonard famously said, "I try to leave out the parts readers skip." Many times these "boring" bits fall into the categories of stage directions. Stage directions that mimic real life can be insufferable for readers.

For instance, let's say you write a scene about a meeting your character must attend. In real life these meetings are often long and boring and filled with missteps. There's a computer glitch, or someone is late. People drone on and on.

You get the idea. The key to writing a scene showing a boring or otherwise mundane situation is to give the reader the *feeling* of boring or repetitive without actually making readers suffer through the *actual boring thing*.

The Rule of Three

Something I call the Rule of Three can be helpful in deciding how much detail to include. In general, give readers three details of something important that you need them to remember. These should be concrete and sensory—meaning they are connected in some way with the five senses and/or are very specific (e.g., a cherry-red Camaro instead of a red car). You can also use the Rule of Three to give the illusion of a boring or unimportant action or dialogue.

For instance, if your scene is about a child whining in the grocery store, you can give the illusion of this with just three lines or exchanges of dialogue:

"Mommy, can I have that Sugary Cereal?"

"No, you can have plain Cheerios."

"But all the kids get Sugary Cereal!"

"No, not all kids get it. Besides, you're not all kids."

"Whhhhyyyy can't I have it, Mommy? Pleeeaaassse?"

"I said no and that's that."

We understand that these types of exchanges typically go on and on. But to force your readers to endure the real-life version is cruel and will drive them away. The above example is plenty for readers to get the idea.

See if you can spot the overwriting in the following passage.

Before:

Tiffany decided to encourage the design team to continue to keep up their good job. They had been working hard and accomplished a lot. That was part of her job—encouraging her team.

"Now, team," she told them at the meeting that had just started at three o'clock in the afternoon in the large corner office of their building, "we have just come up with a lot of exciting ideas for you to work on. I know you are already working hard and staying late, and I'm not looking to add to your workload. Therefore, I've asked Bill from Merchandising to join us to share something we've been working on. We've developed a new strategy for our product offering that will be better for our business and make better use of the talent on this team. I know you are all very talented, and I want to encourage you. But we aren't using everyone's talents to the full or in the best way."

Bill came in and said hi to everyone. Then he plugged in his laptop and a PowerPoint presentation came up on the screen. He pressed buttons and skipped through some of the slides until he came to the ones he wanted to show everyone.

"Here are some key facts that Tiffany and I wanted to share with you." A chart showed that the number of styles from Women's Apparel had increased on average 15 percent season to season. Another graph showed their best-selling products had the highest out-of-stocks. The last graph showed that margins had been on a straight-line decline for the past few years.

Tiffany thought Bill's presentation was well done. He really focused on the things that her team needed to pay attention to, such as which styles had increased in sales and which were their best-selling items.

Tiffany said, "This analysis shows we're making a lot more stuff every year. But, we're not making enough of the best stuff to satisfy demand. And despite all our hard work, we aren't making money. The big conclusion? More stuff doesn't mean better business. We need to make fewer, better things that sell. And that means a more manageable workload for you."

Heads nodded all around.

Was that as painful for you to read as it was for me to write? Compare it with this much more focused and tight version.

After:

Tiffany encouraged her design team to keep up their good job. They'd been working hard and accomplished a lot.

"Now, team," she told them at the three o'clock meeting, "we've just come up with a lot of exciting ideas. You're already working hard and staying late, and I'm not looking to add to your workload. I've asked Bill from Merchandising to share. We've developed a new strategy that will be better for everyone and utilize your talents more effectively.

Bill greeted the group and brought up his presentation on the screen. "Here are some key facts." He pointed to a series of graphs. Women's Apparel styles had an average 15 percent increase, best-selling products had the highest out-of-stock rate, and margins had been on a straight-line decline for the past few years.

Tiffany nodded and smiled at Bill. His presentation really focused on the things that her team needed to pay attention to.

She said, "We're making a lot more stuff every year, but we're not making enough of the best stuff to satisfy demand. And despite all our hard work, we aren't making money. We need to make fewer, better things that sell. And that means a more manageable workload for you."

Heads nodded all around.

The first thing you may notice is that the second version is far less wordy. Once we know what the scene is about, it's not necessary to keep repeating words such as *analysis, encouragement,* or *products.* The people in the scene get it, and so do we.

And what about those boring missteps as Bill fumbles with his computer? Those details might make for a comedy scene, but if they're not central to the story, why torture readers? You might be able to use a bit of this if you put it into Tiffany's head: *That Bill! Why can't he get his act together?* But in this example, the writer was only being faithful to nonessential details.

When you write scenes, do you worry that readers will not see the exact thing you imagine? If so, you may want to loosen your hold on the reins. As long as the story moves and is dramatizing the action, you can safely allow readers to imagine these details any way they wish.

Repetition, Redundancy, and Overused Punctuation—Oh My!

The first time I heard the phrase "write tight" was in high school English class. Our teacher returned our short stories and called me to her desk when class ended. "I love your story line," she said. "But you need to write tighter. I want you to go back through your story and cut out anything that's repetitive or not necessary. Don't use an entire paragraph to say what you can say with a sentence or two. And lay off the dashes."

I no longer have that short story, nor do I remember the entire story line, but I haven't forgotten the writing style I'd used. Three of its problems were repetition, redundancy, and overused punctuation. Just what are these three writing faux pas?

Repetition is "the act of saying or doing something again." When applied to language, it becomes *redundancy*, or "the act of using a word, phrase, etc., that repeats something else and is therefore unnecessary." In fiction, this takes several forms.

- Repeating a certain word or phrase—*just, very, he turned, she went*
- Repeating a word structure—*looked, stared, peered*
- Repeating character traits—continually referring to a character's hair or eye color
- Repeating character actions—*he scratched his beard* or *she bit her lip*
- Adding an unnecessary word to modify a verb—stood *up*, collaborated *together*, screamed *loudly*.

Repetition and redundancy weakens your writing. And weak writing doesn't captivate readers.

Now let's look at punctuation. Really, any punctuation marks can be overused. (Well, except probably the period—I have yet to hear an editor advise, "Go easy with the periods. You're using too many.") These are the common culprits:

- Exclamation point (!): Used to indicate yelling (in dialogue) or extreme emotion (in narrative). Don't use more than one (!!), and don't use it in conjunction with a question mark (!?). Publishers tend to discourage its use (some want no more than two or three exclamation points in an entire manuscript). Why? The exclamation point encourages weaker writing, since the author can use it alone to indicate emotion. Instead, stronger dialogue or narrative will better convey that emotion.

- Question mark (?): Used to punctuate a question. Don't use more than one (??), and don't use it in conjunction with an exclamation point (?!).

- Em dash (—): Used in several ways, including to offset information, to show an interruption in speech, or to show a sudden break in thought. Most editors recommend using em dashes sparingly (not a problem since commas often produce the same sentence flow).

- Ellipses (. . .): Used to show trailing off of words (in dialogue) or of an idea (in narrative), or to show hesitation in dialogue. Ellipses fall into the same category as exclamation points and em dashes—use them judiciously.

There are instances when an exclamation point, an em dash, or ellipses is the best punctuation to convey the appropriate intensity or flow. The key is to use them so their effect is not lost in repetition.

Take a look at these Before and After passages and see if you can pick out the issues noted above.

Before:
I'd just about fallen asleep when I heard the sound—a sound I'd never wanted to hear. It sounded like a thud and loud shuffling noise downstairs. I sat up in the dark and just listened silently as I chewed my lip. Throwing the covers back, I stood

up and found my way through the darkness to the door. I stopped, opened the unlatched door, and peered out into the blackness of the hallway . . .

There was the sound again!! Had someone broken into the house?!

I slipped out into the hallway and moved slowly through the dark, finding my way to top of the stairs. My whole body shook—trembling like I never had before. What if someone had broken in??

There was the sound again!! I stopped at the stairs and peered down into the blackness below. Listening silently, I bit my lip. I started down the steps, taking one step at a time . . .

Suddenly I heard a cat's yowl, and my cat came running up the steps. I went down a few more steps and looked over the railing into the living room. In the dim light streaming inside through the front window, I could see the papers of my research report on the floor by the coffee table.

It had only been the cat!

A bit too much? Try this rewrite.

After:

Wait, what was that? I listened, unable to move or even breathe. Although on the edge of sleep, I'd heard something. A thud and scuffling downstairs. I sat up and threw the covers back, then slid out of bed. Cracking the unlatched door another inch, I peered into the darkness of the hallway. Maybe my imagination was too overactive.

The sound came again, this time resembling the shuffling of papers. Had someone broken into the house?

I crept down the hallway and stopped at the top of the stairs. My heart pounded as I grasped the banister with a trembling hand. After a few moments, I descended the steps.

A yowl pierced the silence, and my cat tore up the stairs.

I blew out a breath, still shaking despite my relief, and padded down the stairs until I could see into the living room below. In the dim light that streamed through the front window, my textbooks and the papers of my research report lay strewn next to the coffee table.

Crazy cat.

So what's wrong with the Before passage (hint: a lot, and I won't list them all)? Let's break it down:

Repetition:

- Forms of *sound* are used five times.

- *Darkness, blackness,* and *dark* are used to convey the same meaning.

- *Shook* and *trembling* are used in the same sentence.

- *Peered* is used twice.

- *Found my way* and *finding my way* were used.

Redundancy:

- Problem: *just about.* Fix: *about* (better yet, reword the sentence).

- Problem: *just listened silently.* Fix: *listened* (*just* isn't necessary, and of course we're silent when we listen).

- Problem: *stood up.* Fix: *stood* (*up* isn't necessary).

- Problem: the character chews her lip and then bites her lip. Fix: delete repetition

- Problem: *streaming inside through.* Fix: *streamed through* (*inside* isn't necessary).

Overused Punctuation:

- Double exclamation marks, double question marks, and combined question mark and exclamation mark are used.

- Em dash used where a comma would be appropriate.

- Ellipses used where a period would be appropriate.

Everyone has a different writing style. Some authors write tighter than others, and that's to be expected. Just remember that when a facet of writing is overused—whether it be words or phrases, character traits or actions, or punctuation—it loses its impact. If you weed out repetition and redundancy and choose punctuation carefully, you'll love the improvement you see.

The Perils of Purple Prose

What do you want people to experience when they read your novel? Do you want them to marvel at your fabulous writing skills? Are you hoping they'll be impressed by your outstanding grasp of grammar? Perhaps you want to dazzle them with your exceptional vocabulary?

Or do you want them to experience a story?

Truth is, oftentimes you can either impress people with your prose or you can tell them a story, but you can't do both. So many of my editing clients' manuscripts are so filled with flowery language that the meaning is lost. I find myself offering the same advice over and over—my take on Nike's slogan: *Just say it.*

Throw Away Your Thesaurus

Okay, don't throw it away, but hide it in the far corner of a cabinet. Focus not on how to impress your reader but on what your character actually sounds like. We'll talk about character voice in our chapter on POV, but suffice it to say, a thirteen-year-old girl won't sound much like a New York City taxi driver. Your characters might speak in long, complex sentences or with a more straightforward style, but I bet, in real life, none of them speaks in purple prose.

Let's look at a Before and an After passage. The genre: contemporary fiction. The character: a twenty-eight-year-old schoolteacher.

Before:
The tempest bore down, the sky temporarily the victor in its ever-present battle with the verdant fields below, enraging lands and inciting them to bombard their treasures skyward. And I, the lowly pawn in this game not of kings and conquering foes but of sky and earth, sought refuge in my humble home. My paternal figure had commanded me when

I'd first taken possession of the modest abode that in the miniscule space beneath the risers would I find shelter from the storm, so there now I went, huddled astride cardboard receptacles filled with the paraphernalia of my fleeting existence.

Ah, what future could there be for me now? Perhaps in the Immortal's perfect knowledge, He had been right to close my eyes to what lay ahead. Had I but known this torrent was bearing down, would I have had the courage to go forth? Yet as the whirlwind neared, I surrendered to myriad misgivings about my present circumstances. Would that there had been a beau, one true amour, to live out these last few moments of breath. Alas, alone I reclined and wondered—might there be some purpose in this storm?

Say what? Okay, shake that off and take a look at the revision.

After:

If I had known that the tornado blowing through that May afternoon would be nothing compared to the storm brewing in its aftermath, I might never have left my shelter. Maybe that's one of God's greatest gifts—shielding our eyes from the future. There's a stretch of highway west of Oklahoma City where I swear it's so flat and straight you can see all the way to Amarillo. If we could see that far into the future, we'd never hit the gas. In the same way, if I could've seen what lay ahead for me, I might still be hiding in that closet.

But God's so much smarter than I am. Think what I would have missed.

Obviously, I wasn't thinking about my future when I was crouched in the closet beneath my stairs. Well, not beyond wondering if there would be a future. Tornadoes will do that to you.

As you may have noticed, the passage hasn't been just edited, it's been rewritten. The more purple the prose, the less of it you get to keep during your rewriting process. And in this case, the prose was beyond repair.

What did I do to repair it? First, I considered who the POV character was. In the first passage, we can deduce that she's most likely a woman, based on her desire for "a beau, my one true amour," but what else can we learn about her? Hmm . . . she has an extensive vocabulary. That's about it.

In the After segment, you can hear the character's voice. Your paragraphs should sound like your characters' voices and reflect your writing style. Personality on the page—that's what you're looking for.

Next, let's consider the genre. Did the Before passage scream contemporary fiction to you? Didn't think so.

Consider the Circumstances

Another thing to consider when looking at your favorite "purple prose" passages—what are the circumstances? From the Before passage, we can deduce that a dangerous storm is on its way, and our POV character is in its path, afraid for her life. So, put yourself in our schoolteacher's shoes. You're about to be hurled by an F4 all the way to Kansas (and you're not wearing your ruby slippers). Would your thoughts mirror those in the Before segment? Mine wouldn't either. (Having lived through a similar circumstance, my thoughts were more like, "Please don't let it hit us. Please don't let it hit us . . ." but that would get boring after a few paragraphs.)

Finally, think about what you're trying to accomplish with your scene. In this case, these are the first few paragraphs of a novel, so it's important that they set the right tone—for both the novel and the character.

Taking into account the character, the genre, the circumstances, and the author's purpose for the scene, the rewritten passage conveys language that should better appeal to readers and make them want to read more. Avoid purple prose. Nobody loves a smarty-pants.

Editor:
C. S. Lakin

How Novelists Can Say More with Less

Less is more. More impacting. More riveting. More intriguing. Throughout history, marriages have failed and wars have been won or lost over a mere word or two. Jesus said, "Let your yes mean yes and your no mean no." Simply stated, as was his style.

I often share with my clients something my eleventh-grade English teacher used to spout frequently: "Say what you mean. Don't say what you don't mean."

The best way to say what you mean is to use only the words you need—the most appropriate words for your context—and discard the rest. Think of the pages of your novel as expensive real estate. Writers who want to write well should aim to be as picky about the words they string together as the foods they eat or the clothes they wear. Pickier.

Bogging Down Your Writing Is a Bad Thing

Your novel's pacing will be greatly affected by word choice. If you bog down your sentences with unnecessary words, your scenes will drag. In addition, using boring, flat, or weak verbs and adjectives will make the reading dull, no matter how exciting your plot might be.

Take a look at this Before passage and see if you can spot some of the problems. Then read my revision and compare.

Before:
Suddenly, lightning struck!!! It was so loud and noisy, Debby screamed and lost hand control of her drinking glass, spilling it and shattering it on the Italian stone coffee table. Somehow, the power was gone, a blackout took place, and Debby trembled as she fearfully listened to the thunder rolling in louder in waves than usual. She felt it was so loud, the house began to shake. As if being in the middle of an earthquake. She began to cry and instantly the danger passed and everything was calm.

21

Debby was still frozen, too afraid to move much. She slowly turned her head to the left and then to the right as she focused her attention on what was going on through the front room window. She heard the sound of a loud vehicle idling outside of her home and that sound grew louder. Approaching the window with caution, she slowly pulled the left curtain open. Her eyes widened as she saw an old run-down rusty car parked out in front of her house. It showed no headlights . . . just sitting and idling with an ominous sound coming from its tailpipe.

A cold draft suddenly made Debby tremble greatly as she began to see what was starting to materialize. Two red beams of light, very small, like tiny eyes, began to glow from within the car where the driver was sitting on the front seat. The glow grew brighter and then she realized suddenly that they were indeed eyes and they were gazing right at her!!! Debby started to gasp for breath and she felt her heart was suddenly stricken with intense pain as if there was a tight grip of a fist around it . . . tightening. As her pain grew, her body began to crouch forward, nearly ripping the curtain off its rod.

Was that exhausting to read? Try this.

After:

Without warning, lightning struck. Debby screamed and dropped her glass, which shattered on the Italian stone coffee table. The lights flickered out, and she trembled as thunder shook the house as if an earthquake rolled under it. Then, the night quieted, except for the patter of heavy rain and the murmur of distant thunder.

Debby froze, trembling. She turned and peered through the front room window. A motor idled on the street. With barely a touch, she pulled the curtain aside. A badly damaged black-and-white patrol car sat parked in front of her house, headlights off, no red-and-blue flashing lights. An ominous sound came from its tailpipe.

A cold draft tickled Debby's neck as she watched two red beams of light, like eyes, glow inside the dark car where a driver sat. The glow grew brighter and Debby gasped. They *were* eyes—and they were gazing right at her.

A stab of pain made Debby clutch her chest. With a cry, she buckled with her fist entangled in the curtain and fell to the floor, the fluttering cloth covering her face like a shroud of death.

The first thing you probably noticed is the word count dropped by about a third. Think about ditching adverbs and replacing weak verbs with stronger ones. As Christy discussed, avoid excessive punctuation, such as multiple exclamation marks.

A great way to seek and destroy extraneous words and passages is to use Word's Find and Replace. Search for *it was, there were, ing,* and *ly*. Often a word ending in *ing* will reveal a wordy phrase, and *ly* will catch adverbs (we'll cover pesky adverbs in a later chapter).

Overall, take the time to consider each word you use and see if you can't come up with a better word, maybe one more colorful or descriptive. A phrase like "It was interesting and I liked it" is not interesting, and readers won't like it. Write in your unique style and genre, but do it well.

Think of rewriting as creating a reduction sauce. The more you can eliminate those words and phrases that are not rich in flavor, the less you will have in the end. Which is more. And more, in most cases, is better.

In Conclusion . . .

Overwriting is by far the worst offender of all the fatal flaws. As you go through your scenes, challenge every word and phrase. Keep in mind the objectives of your scene and your big picture—your premise and the story you are telling. Remember that overwriting doesn't pertain to just the little bits of punctuation and the words making up a sentence. It can also manifest on the macro level, by cluttering your story with unnecessary actions and dialogue that do nothing to advance or reveal key points of character and plot.

When checking your scenes for overwriting, try not to narrow your focus such that you only see the trees. Step back and scan the forest. Sometimes that means entire scenes should be cut. The key to conquering overwriting is to be brutal. Don't get overly attached to your words. Be willing to sacrifice some on the altar of clarity and effectiveness. Repeat this mantra in your head when you find yourself hesitating to "kill your darlings": *Less is more . . . Less is more . . .*

Fatal Flaw #1 Checklist

Go through your scenes and look for these types of overwriting:

- Boring and/or excessive details and descriptions

- Extraneous words that aren't needed and don't add anything to your story

- Vague words and phrases. Look for *it was* and *there were* and replace with strong nouns and verbs.

- Repetition and redundancy. Don't use the same adjectives or nouns multiple times in close proximity. Don't use two descriptors that essentially mean the same thing (such as "he was smart and intelligent").

- Purple prose in narrative and character voice

- Excessive punctuation

- Character traits or actions that don't convey anything helpful

Your Turn: Try to spot and fix all the overwriting you can find in this passage. An example of a revision is on the next page (no peeking!). There isn't one correct way to rewrite a passage, so your final version may be different from the revision provided. The key is to test yourself to see if you've nailed Fatal Flaw #1.

The caller stared at the ~~dead~~ cell phone ~~for a beat~~ before tossing it hard on the counter. ~~Somehow, at that moment, there was no concern at all if it smashed into tiny bits.~~ Intense irritation ~~was sprouting like an unrelenting weed and had no intention of stopping until it took over the caller entirely. The extra energy searched frantically for an appropriate, or inappropriate, release on the~~ world. Soon, an explosion of emotions would be ~~imminent and~~ deadly.

"Tomorrow? I can't wait until tomorrow. I need to do something now. ~~No, right this second.~~" For some reason, sweat poured from the caller's brow ~~like a faucet~~. On a high from the night before, the caller paced around the kitchen ~~in mad circles. Going around and around, getting dizzy but unable to stop.~~ The hardened heart in the caller's chest raced ~~with full force like a thoroughbred at the track~~. A complete conversation was brewing inside of a shattered mind, although only one side of it rang aloud in the empty room.

"Action. I need to take action. He wants me to wait. Ha! Of course he does. I can't wait. ~~There's no time. Not a minute to waste.~~ Why is he making me wait?" The caller's head shook in disbelief. "I didn't want this to happen. I tried to stop it. I have no choice now. I must ~~take action. Action. Action. All I can do is~~ take action." The caller was going crazy, about to spin out of control ~~mentally,~~ when a crash against the window froze the caller, forcing reality back to his mind.

"Whoa, that was a bird." A deep breath later and the caller regained control.

Suddenly the caller grabbed a short glass and threw in a few ice cubes, then he searched the refrigerator for a beer. It was in a row of five in plain sight and never far from reach, as it always was.

25

Revision of the Previous Passage:

Jared stared at the dead cell phone for a beat before tossing it on the counter. Irritation stabbed him. He knew that he'd soon explode with rage, and the results would be deadly.

"Tomorrow? I can't wait until tomorrow. I need to do something now." Sweat poured from his brow. On a high from the night before, he paced the kitchen, getting dizzy but unable to stop. His heart raced as the prior conversation brewed in his shattered mind.

"I need to take action. He wants me to wait. But there's not a minute to waste. Why is he making me wait?" He shook his head in disbelief. "I didn't want this to happen. I tried to stop it. But I have no choice now."

A crash against the window made him freeze, stopping his flood of manic thoughts.

"Whoa. A bird."

He grabbed a glass and threw in a few ice cubes, then searched the refrigerator for a beer.

Fatal Flaw #2: Nothin' Happenin'

As writers, we may find ourselves asking, "Why is it so hard to *start?*"

And we don't just mean the writing part. That's hard too, as our prolific Facebook activity log, empty coffeepot, and suspiciously clean piles of laundry will attest. (Nobody can houseclean like a procrastinating writer.) We mean actually starting the story.

Long explanations. Chapters of backstory. Characters sitting and thinking—about the past, the present, the future. Actions that lead nowhere. Weather.

Oh, the weather.

When we consider the immensity of history, information, and world creation most writers are trying to fit into two hundred or more pages, it's not surprising we need to work up to our stories. But readers won't toil through pages of preparation, information, or meditation before the story really begins. They need to engage, to get immersed in the action and become intimate with the characters quickly. Some say within the first page.

So when you edit, it's time to take a hard look at your opening. Begin *in media res*—get to the good part. Engage readers right away through dialogue and relevant action, all of it building up the scene's purpose. Raise questions. Use characters and emotion to invest actions with meaning. Stir up tension. Intrigue. Mystery. Excitement.

Find where your story begins, and do as the king in Wonderland once told Alice: begin there.

Along with showing you what and how to delete, the examples in this chapter will help you identify the place where your story truly begins and give techniques to immerse your readers from the very first sentence.

Even if it begins with the weather.

Editor:
Rachel Starr Thomson

Nothin' Happenin': Finding Your Story

Openings are a science unto themselves, be they openings for an entire book, for a chapter, or for a scene. One principle, however, is generally agreed upon: it is best to open with something happening.

We might take a cue from the Bible here: "In the beginning," we are told, "God created the heavens and the earth."

We can surmise that, in fact, God did several other things before he created. That he took some time to think, to plan, to survey the darkness and the deep—whatever was in existence at that time—or whatever other wonderful things might have gone on in the cosmic brooding that preceded creation. But the Book opens with action.

Getting to the Story

Because our stories don't actually spring full-fledged from our pens or keyboards, we writers need time to ease into them, and so a lot of our drafts open in one of these ways:

- With a lot of description, most often of the weather.

- With backstory or explanation of what's about to happen.

- With a character thinking or reminiscing. (This does not qualify as "something happening." In fact, the state of thinking can be notably less active and interesting than even the weather.)

- With a character doing a lot of mundane things before getting to anything pertinent to the story.

And then, finally, we write our way up to where the story really takes off—several paragraphs or even whole chapters after we begin.

The problem here is that while we are getting warmed up, readers are trying to enter the story world—and if they can't get in soon enough, if the opening bores them or feels irrelevant or rambling, they are liable to move on before we do. All the way to a different book.

Take this opening for a suspense novel:

Before:

It was a gray, rainy day. The drizzle had started that morning and not ceased. By now puddles had formed around the storm drains and headlights glared off the wet pavement. The clouds overhead were thick and flat like a heavy blanket lying over the entire city, with no break anywhere for the sun to come through, even though it was only midafternoon.

Cars passed by in single file, following each other too closely and honking when the traffic got tighter. Skyscrapers rose on every side, their sides gleaming black and mirroring the traffic flow. On the corner of Smyth and Davidson, patrons snaked out the door of the local Starbucks, some shielding their heads with umbrellas while others pulled collars up and shivered in the dampness. Across the street was a drugstore, and a lone homeless man sat by a fire hydrant on the corner, his cardboard sign waterlogged and its markered plea for help running down in black streaks.

It was the kind of day that was typical in the Midwest in March. It made people unhappy, depressed, wishing they were at home watching TV instead of going to work, driving through town, dealing with one more gray day after a long and oppressive winter.

The winter days never seemed to end. Daylight Savings Time had cut the days off at their knees all the way back in November, and ever since it was one dark, cold, snowy, damp, drizzly day after another. Eventually winter started to lighten into spring, but it was March spring—the kind that's so cold and damp and dark in its own right that it hardly seems like an improvement.

Casey Miller's gun hand shook as she stared down at the body, rain-soaked and pale on the sidewalk.

After:

> Casey Miller's gun hand shook as she stared down at the body, rain-soaked and pale on the sidewalk.

The Before example isn't bad writing. It's got some vivid images, in fact, and mood-setters. *But the story does not start until Casey Miller looks down on that body,* and readers are unlikely to stick with a page-and-a-quarter's worth of description long enough to get there. Can some of the setting details be included after the fact? Sure. In fact, if you open with something happening, you can cut back to scene details to create contrast and make the ugly opening words starker:

> Casey Miller's gun hand shook as she stared down at the body, rain-soaked and pale on the sidewalk.
> Skyscrapers rose into a heavy, clouded sky all around them; patrons, holding umbrellas or pulling up their collars against the cold rain, snaked out the door of the Starbucks across the street. Cars passed in single file, honking impatiently, splashing the rain in the gutters.
> No one else saw him.
> He was dead, and only she could see.

In place of remarks about the weather, we now have two characters—one alive, one dead—a vivid setting, and a mystery. All in less time than the Before passage took to describe March in the city. We've found the story. And more importantly, so have our readers.

Editor:
Linda S. Clare

How to Get Readers into Your Story—and How to Keep Them There

In the opening of many novels, we see a character alone on stage, riding a train, plane, car, or donkey. Many times this character is gazing out a window (unless, of course, she's riding the donkey), thinking. Some call this "driving to the story."

As Rachel already pointed out, thinking does not qualify as something happening. Not only that, but many times this type of "sittin' and thinkin'" scene is so loaded with backstory that readers don't know when the real story begins—or worse, they don't care.

The Wilson Principle

To hook your readers and get the story going quickly, your POV character needs someone to interact with. If you write only her thoughts, she has no one who will disagree with her. There is no variety or stimulating action. While it can sometimes work, writers risk losing readers' interest by taking such an approach.

In the movie *Castaway*, Tom Hanks finds himself marooned on a desert island. He has no one to talk to, no one to interact with. That's why he invents Wilson, the volleyball. He draws a face on the ball and gives him some seaweed hair. Voilà! Tom Hanks's character has a sidekick.

In the film, Wilson becomes someone for Hanks to confide in and get angry at. Wilson sets off a range of emotions in Hanks. In your novel, getting at least one more character on stage with your POV character gives this same advantage. Readers are enlivened through the possibilities of dialogue, body language, and physical action. You can sprinkle a touch of backstory here, but when your character is not alone, you no longer must rely so heavily on character memories, which, especially in your chapter 1, have little significance to readers.

When you write a scene, note the number of other characters on stage. People are the usual choice to join your character, but pets or

31

even a personified volleyball can provide a way to include dialogue and action in the scene. Use the Wilson Principle to keep your audience engaged.

Create a Red Wine Disaster

Another way to get your readers into the story is to open the scene *just before the conflict heats up*. If you picture a lady wearing a white evening gown, sitting alone in a restaurant, you might not be very interested. If the same lady orders red wine—still not very unusual. But what if the steward trips as he's bringing the wine glass on a tray? Now you might be mildly interested, especially if the waiter bobbles it around. If the wine arcs out of the glass, you suspect something is going to happen. And if the wine heads directly toward the white gown, you know there will be conflict and tension (and a wine-stained dress!).

The real action starts just before the wine hits the dress. Readers won't know how this woman will react, and they'll read to find out. Beginning your scenes *just before something big occurs* will tantalize readers to keep reading.

You might think readers would want to know as much as you do about the character as soon as possible, but the opposite is generally true. Readers are willing to trade information for excitement, for the "what will happen next?" feeling. You can use the Red Wine Rule to keep much of the action out of your character's head (and memories) and act out that action directly onstage.

A word about dreams: Many writers start a novel based on a powerful dream. That's fine, but when you allow your *character* to chronicle a dream, you force readers back into the character's head. If you must include a dream, keep it as brief as possible and try to have your character tell someone about it rather than simply narrating to readers.

The "No Crystal Ball" Rule

Another way writers lose their readers is by interrupting the action and inserting knowledge the POV character cannot possibly know. You can spot this flaw by looking for some future time reference: "Later, Meg would realize she already knew him." Or "In a few moments, Sylvia would learn just how much she hated broccoli."

This kind of foreknowledge is meant to add tension, but in reality it only yanks readers out of the real-time scene. If you wish to foreshadow knowledge the character will later learn, use hints of body language or show the character trying to pinpoint why something seemed familiar, ominous, or surprising. Readers would rather "live" the story as it unfolds. Use the "No Crystal Ball" rule to stay in the moment. (We'll be looking at this in depth in the chapter on POV Violations.)

Now let's look at an example of overwriting that breaks all three of my "rules":

Before:

Sylvia O'Grady shifted uncomfortably on her seat. She could see her reflection in the train's windows, her dark hair silhouetted by a setting sun and the rolling hills of Central California whizzing past outside. Madeira and scrub oaks dotted the golden landscape—so very different from her hometown in Indiana. She sighed—she'd likely never see the Midwest again. But no one in California would have to know about her impediment either.

She'd grown up with three brothers, and she knew how to defend herself. Tom, Sam, and Harry had always protected her, but they were all off fighting in Woodrow Wilson's war. Her mother had cried the day her sons enlisted in the US Army. Sylvia had cried too, but made sure they didn't see her. Tom especially was quick to call her a sissy. After all, he was a Golden Gloves champion in the welterweight division. Sylvia had learned from Tom how to throw a mean right hook, which came in handy when mean old Johnny Smith had pulled her pigtails in Miss Dodge's third-grade class.

All the O'Gradys had attended the same one-room school, unless Papa needed them to help out with the harvest. Then Tom and Sam would be absent for a couple of weeks, until all the hay was baled and bucked. Papa had only finished third grade himself, so getting an education wasn't a top priority.

As the train pulled into the station, Sylvia would soon learn that getting an education and teaching her new students at Dullsville Primary School were two completely different things.

The first thing you might notice about the admittedly poor example is there's no dialogue. No one else interacts with Sylvia as she reminisces. Now let's look at another version:

After:

Sylvia O'Grady shifted uncomfortably on her seat. She could see her reflection in the train's windows, her dark hair silhouetted by a setting sun and the rolling hills of Central California whizzing past outside. She felt a tap on her shoulder.

"'Scuse me, miss, is this seat taken?" A tall, lanky young man with the brightest blue eyes stood in the aisle.

"No. I mean, please thit down." Her cheeks flamed. She wasn't even in Dullsville yet, and already her secret was out.

"Thanks." The stranger sat beside her and extended a hand. "Roberts," he said. His smile was wide and easy. "Greg Roberts. And you are?"

She couldn't keep her gaze off him, but she concentrated on keeping the lisp out of her speech. "S-s-sylvia. S-s-sylvia O'Grady." It sounded more like a hiss, and spittle flew from her lips. She gasped and held her handkerchief to her mouth. The man must think her an animal.

But Mr. Roberts's eyes twinkled. "I'm pleased to meet you, Sylvia O'Grady. Where are you headed?"

Now Sylvia could smile. "Dullsville. What a name for a town!" She pointed out the train's window, where madeira and scrub oaks dotted the golden landscape.

"I agree. And what will you do there? I doubt you would ever be considered dull."

"That remains to be seen." Sylvia chuckled. "I hope to teach third grade. Where are you going?"

"A teacher, eh? A fine occupation." Mr. Roberts stretched his long legs into the train car aisle. "I'm a salesman, pots and pans mainly. But I'm starting over in Marysville. Not many seem to need new cookware back in Indiana these days."

Sylvia clapped her hands. "Indiana. I was raised there. What a coin-*th*idence." She winced. That darned lisp. She'd likely never see the Midwest again either, but she kept it to herself. "My three brothers and I all grew up on our farm."

Mr. Roberts swiveled to face her. "Are your brothers older or younger?"

"Older." Sylvia bit her lip. She didn't want to sound impertinent, but she was so curious. "Begging your pardon. You look very healthy, Mr. Roberts. Why hasn't Uncle Sam gotten hold of you?"

He looked puzzled and then slapped his knee. "Oh! You mean the war. Well, see, I had to look after my dear mother, God rest her soul." He shook his head. "You don't know how I've longed to join up and knock the stuffing out of some Kraut."

"But if your mother has passed, couldn't you enlist?"

He seemed taken aback, but then pointed to his eyes. "It's the old peepers, I'm afraid. Put a rifle in my hand, and I can't hit the broad side of a barn."

"My papa's eyes have grown so dim, he makes Mama do all the hunting these days."

Mr. Roberts leaned close—so close she felt heat creep up her neck. "But I'll wager he's very proud of his daughter the teacher."

Sylvia turned away. If only it were true.

The second version cuts out the backstory and replaces it with a live-action scene. By getting Mr. Roberts on stage right away with Sylvia, we employ both the Wilson Principle and the Red Wine Rule. By sticking to the moment ("No Crystal Ball"), we're able to act out the scene with lots of dialogue. Readers still learn the important background info—that she has a lisp, that she is a teacher, and that the story takes place in Central California during World War I.

Spend some time examining your scenes for these infractions, and see if you can't employ any or all of these three rules to help you avoid this fatal flaw.

In Medias Res: Cutting to the Chase

In medias res. If you've been writing for some time now, chances are you've heard at least one seasoned writer or editor tout its importance. Or maybe not. The first time I heard the phrase was when I joined a critique group and one of the members commended my novel's first scene with, "Nice use of *in medias res.*" *Wait. In medias what?* Off I headed to Google for an explanation.

Latin for "in the midst of things," *in medias res* refers to the literary technique of starting the story in the middle of the action instead of using descriptive narrative to provide background and build up to the action. It's the principle we've been discussing in this section, and it matters so much because we only get one chance to make a first impression. If our story doesn't capture readers' attention in the initial few pages (some say in the very first page), many readers simply won't read on. Even if the story's pace and action pick up soon after, it won't matter, because we've already lost our reader.

So what grabs a reader's attention? Dialogue and action, to name two. Yes, description is also important—it embellishes with setting and often-needed background. But in most cases, description can be interspersed throughout the story. Dialogue breaks up the narrative and provides pertinent information without dumping it on the reader all at once. And by starting in the middle of the action, questions are posed and tension is built, making the reader ask questions. Readers want those questions answered, so they continue reading.

Let's take a look at two versions of the same story beginning, with one passage starting with descriptive narrative and one passage starting *in medias res.*

Before:
I followed Mother and Daddy toward the administration building of Covington Hall. The boarding school, which sat on two acres of land in the small town of Covington, Connecticut, consisted of nine dark red brick buildings, all with black roofs

and white window frames. The administration building was the largest of the nine and had two rows of ten nine-paned windows across the front on the second and third stories. The first story had two large dark wood doors in the center and four nine-paned windows on either side of them. At the two front corners of the building were thick white pillars that went from the ground to the roof, and a white sign that read "Covington Hall" in black uppercase letters hung above the door. Cobbled walkways wound around the campus, leading to each of the buildings, and tall trees stood intermingled with them.

I didn't want to be at boarding school, but I'd made the mistake of being with a girl I hardly knew when she decided to take her dad's Mercedes and go joyriding. It wouldn't have been so bad, except she didn't know how to drive and crashed it into our town's burgundy and gold sign that read *Welcome to Ellington*. Her dad blamed me, saying I'd talked her into joyriding, and since he was one of the town's three lawyers, no one was about to deny that. I got dubbed the town troublemaker, and my mother decided I should go to boarding school.

After:

I crossed my arms and blew my breath out as I followed Mother and Daddy toward Covington Hall. The three-story brick administration building with its two massive white pillars blocked the early morning sunlight, intensifying the chill in the air. Fitting, since the school's pretentious appearance made it feel just that—cold.

"Covington Hall is one of the best boarding schools in New England." Mother looked back at me as she held Daddy's arm. She stopped, turning around, and swiped her shoulder-length hair behind her ear. "Don't slouch, Cassandra. And don't look so surly. Your past actions are behind us now, and attending Covington is your chance for a new start. Let's make a good first impression, yes?"

Next to her, Daddy tried to smile. "Your mother's right, Cassie-girl. Switching schools always takes some getting used to, but you've always handled change well." He glanced around at the historic buildings, cobbled walkways, and autumn-bronzed trees that stretched around us. "You'll make new friends—"

"Who won't land you in the back of a police car," Mother cut in.

Daddy sighed. "And this'll soon feel like home. I know you'll do well here."

His words were probably meant to ease his own doubts as much as they were meant to comfort me. By the sadness that pinched his eyebrows above his wire-rimmed glasses, he didn't want me to attend boarding school any more than I did—which was not at all. But then again, I could have a good time anywhere. Covington Hall was about to meet its match.

The Before passage gives more description but less essential information. It explains the school's aesthetics and what the character (name and gender yet unknown) did to end up there, but there's little tension, no action aside from three people walking, and no dialogue to break up the narrative. Read on? Maybe, but only if the action picks up *real* soon.

The After passage provides more significant information that will entice readers. Cassandra has gotten herself in enough trouble to end up at boarding school, which will pique the reader's interest. What did she *do*? The After passage also adds two more attention-grabbers—dialogue that gives her a name (making her more real) and shows the tension in her relationship with her parents, and the tension that mounts with her challenge to the school. More questions abound: What's the deal with her and her parents? Clearly, her interaction with her father is different from her interaction with her mother, but why? And just what does she have in store for the school?

Intersperse description to ground the story's setting and situation, and continue to do that as the story plays out. But above all, engage the reader early on. We have the rest of the story to add embellishment.

Think of *in medias res* as getting to the good part. As fiction writers, we can grab our readers' attention right away by opening with action and dialogue that will build tension and get readers asking questions and wondering what will happen next.

Action That Matters

It's very important that our readers understand exactly what's going on at every moment in our story. So we must tell the reader everything that ever happened that led to this scene, whatever it is. That's the only way the reader will get it, right?

Not exactly.

It's not that your reader doesn't care about that stuff. Oh, wait. Yes, that's exactly what it is. Unless it affects the story, your reader doesn't care. *Not one bit.*

As you've learned so far in this chapter, your scenes should begin when the action begins. That's a tough thing to determine, though. I'm acting right now by typing these words on the page, and I promise you, there isn't a soul alive who wants a play-by-play of my typos. So how do you know when the scene should begin?

Determine Your Scene's Purpose

There are lots of ways to think about where to start a scene, but first consider what the purpose of the scene is. What is it you *need* the reader to learn? Everything in the scene should lead up to that, beginning from the very first sentence.

In the paragraphs that follow, I'm setting up a scene in which my POV character returns home after six years, to her grandmother's house. She has spoken with her grandmother over the years, but she hasn't been able to get in touch with her since her baby was born two weeks before. The purpose of this scene is first to establish how Rae feels about her grandmother and how badly she needs the old woman's help. The twist of the scene is that Gram isn't there, and Rae has no idea where she is.

Before:

By the time my flight arrived at Kennedy, my nerves were frazzled. Nine hours in the air, and my travel day was just getting started. I stopped at the rest room and changed little Johnny's diaper. I'd fed him on the flight, so we should have a few hours before he needed to eat again. I grabbed my suitcase from baggage claim, then pulled it to the shuttle stop, where we sat beside a businessman on one side and a woman with two little kids on the other. The older of the two kids, a girl of about eight, kept peeking at Johnny. She reached for him a couple of times, but I asked her not to touch. It was hard enough keeping a two-week-old healthy without her dirty little fingers on him.

Finally, we made it to the bus station, where we boarded a bus to Boston. Four hours later, at South Station, we waited a half an hour, during which time I fed the baby and changed him again, then boarded a bus to New Hampshire.

By the time we reached Manchester, we were both exhausted. We took a taxi to a hotel, where I paid the clerk in cash. We slept late the next day. Then we hired another taxi, which took us to a car dealership I remembered from my youth. I bought an old sedan for five thousand dollars, then went to Walmart and purchased a car seat, more formula, some diapers, and a box of granola bars.

It was after dinnertime by the time we hit the road again. The closer we got to my hometown, the more I looked forward to seeing my grandmother. I hadn't been home in six years, and I couldn't wait. Gram was the only person in the world— except for my infant son—who truly loved me. I imagined her wrinkly hands on my cheeks, her sparkling blue eyes welcoming me home. I'd probably scare the old woman to death, pulling in at this late hour. Well, that's what she got for not charging her cell phone. I'd tried to warn her we were coming.

We drove to Nutfield, passed through town, and turned onto the driveway of my childhood home. The first thing I noticed was that the porch light was off. Gram never turned that off. No lights shone from inside the house, either. The place looked deserted.

Admit it. You skimmed, didn't you? If you think reading it was hard, you should've tried writing it. When I get bored writing, I know it's bad.

What's wrong with it? There's lots of action. My poor heroine gets no rest—I'm tired just thinking about doing all that travel with a two-week-old baby. But while there's a lot of action, nothing is happening that moves the story forward.

I can think of a couple of ways to fix this. I could try to infuse the passage with emotion. If I add enough internal conflict, I might be able to get away with it.

After:

> We'd been traveling for two days by the time Johnny and I crossed into Nutfield. Planes, trains, and automobiles—literally. Not to mention a taxi that stunk of body odor, and that cheap hotel—the only one that agreed to my cash-up-front, no ID requirement. Just Johnny, me, and the varmints that called it home. All I could think about now was my comfortable bed and my beautiful grandmother.
>
> No idea why Gram hadn't answered the phone. I'd been calling for days. She'd probably forgotten to charge it. A little senility, nothing major. Gram was my rock. My comfort. As soon as we stepped into her house, she'd wrap us in her wrinkled arms and make everything all right.
>
> But when I turned down the driveway to my childhood home, the place looked deserted.

I hope you found that segment a little less yawn-inducing. How'd I do it? I used that magic button in the top right-hand corner of my keyboard. It's called "Delete." I summed up all that travel in a few sentences and added some sensory details to give the reader an idea of the type of travel Rae had experienced—no five-star hotels for her. I also upped the tension with a few well-placed phrases, such as "cash-up-front, no ID." I hope that makes the reader wonder what's going on.

I introduced her desire to see her grandmother and showed the reader her expectations for that reunion. More tension comes into play with that sentence fragment: "A little senility, nothing major." Do you get the sense Rae is trying to convince herself? Are you as sure as Rae that Gram is fine?

Because of what Rae has invested in her grandmother and her childhood home, when the house is dark, the reader feels that sense of unease. When Rae steps inside, will Gram be there with open arms?

The After segment is 268 fewer words than the "Before," and it tells readers everything they need to know to set up this scene. Don't be afraid to hack away at your details and explanations. Your readers will be glad you did.

Handling Backstory in Dialogue in Your Opening Pages

So many new writers start their books with pages—even chapters—of backstory. They want to tell the reader all about the creation of their fantasy world. Or they want to make sure readers understand every nuance of Mexican politics in 1956 because it will be critical to the plot on page 103. They want to make sure the reader understands every feature of time travel or cloning in the year 2133.

Then their editor suggests that instead of including all this material in the opening chapters of their book, they should just reveal the backstory through dialogue. *Aha*, the author thinks, *dialogue—of course!* After all, as we've already seen in this chapter, dialogue is a great way to open *in media res* and cut to the good stuff. But instead of jettisoning their precious descriptions and explanations, they essentially put quotation marks around the same ponderous material.

Problem solved, right? Wrong.

None of your characters should talk like the narrator. And readers still don't want a backstory dump—even in dialogue. Often the attempt to stuff backstory into dialogue results in long, tedious monologues instead of more believable two-way conversation.

Before:

Debby started panicking. "You know, John, that we can't send people back in time without the right amount of energy, and even though we've done an excellent job in extracting energy from dark matter, as our last two experiments attest, I fear that there isn't enough to get Colleen into the past and out of danger. Just look at the flux capacitor levels—the microcosm indicator is off as well, and it needs to be at 90 percent for a guaranteed trip. The flux capacitor is crucial for making a time jump, and needs to be at about 92 percent efficiency to work well. Also you need to contact Clare and Silas and make sure they can divert another 38 gigawatts of energy to the main frame so in one hundred hours she can make her jump back to the present. The main frame can handle up to 50 gigawatts, so that shouldn't be a problem."

Whew, did you find that tedious to read?

To make matters worse, these types of monologues often take place in the middle of important action—and readers aren't going to believe a character will stop and give a lecture when bullets are flying or buildings are blowing up around her. Backstory, even in "active" dialogue, stops the present action.

After:

> Debby frowned at the bank of blinking lights. "We don't have enough energy here for Colleen to make the jump."
>
> "What can we do?" John asked.
>
> An alarm sounded, and Debby hit the panel to the left to silence it. "Don't know." She glanced at the flux capacitor level and shook her head. It was nowhere near the 90 percent she needed. "I think you need to contact Clare and Silas. Maybe they can divert more energy."
>
> "How much do we need?" John asked.
>
> Debby did some quick calculations. "At least another 89 gigawatts."
>
> "All right." John jumped out of his chair. "I'll contact them—if I can find them."

In this example, we assume that John and Debby already know a great deal of the backstory and pertinent information because they are in the story. Even if I want to make sure that the reader is clear about time travel, a cumbersome description like this one only slows the action.

Readers Don't Really Need to Know It All

Have faith in your characters, and even more faith in your readers. Allow the reader to enjoy the journey. It can be more fun to discover the world and plot along with the heroine than to have it all explained. When dialogue sums everything up, the reader may wonder why he should bother to read on.

Use a limited amount of shorthand that your readers will understand to convey what is going on. Use the characters to convey their expertise in their own proprietary language, which can add depth to a character and give a sense of what's going on.

Make the notes for your world; do the research. Become the expert in your field of study and of the world you are developing. But don't build a time machine piece by piece through your dialogue.

Another disadvantage of placing every bit of information in the beginning of your novel or story via dialogue is that by chapter 4, you'll have nothing left to reveal.

If the situation has been explained, and you, the author, feel it's all been said, your dialogue may then become sterile, stiff, and unnatural sounding. You know that your characters must speak to one another, but if their situation as well as the plot has already been outlined, there is little reason to advance the plot through the conversations.

Here are some things you can do to avoid dumping too much backstory in your dialogue:

- Jettison all the dense backstory paragraphs at the beginning of your novel's scenes.

- Explain in common, character-driven language some finer points of the plot via dialogue.

- Trust your reader to pick up on gestures, expressions, and atmosphere as substitutes for direct (and long) explanations.

- Don't explain everything—only bring in bits that are essential, are interesting, and advance the plot.

- Don't build a time machine all in one monologue.

Readers don't spend as much time as they used to "getting into" a novel or story. It is your job to put the reader into the action and create intimacy with your characters as quickly as possible. The rest will follow.

In Conclusion . . .

Take some time to look at your novel (or short story) opening, as well as your scene openings. Consider how and where you are showcasing your POV character. Is she doing boring, passive things?

Thinking a lot without being shown in action? Are you intruding as the author to foreshadow things that will occur later, things your character can't know?

One of the best ways to avoid the fatal flaw of Nothin' Happenin' is to choose strong moments in which to bring your character onstage. If you plan ahead, knowing the high moment you are building to, you can get your character into the action just before conflict starts.

We're tempted to explain in detail our backstory, character motivation and reasoning, and what our setting and characters look like. But no one wants a truckload of information dumped at the start of a story. Readers want to be swept away, transported—not buried under a ton of rock.

We'll be looking hard at backstory and how to "show, don't tell" later in this book, which will complement what you've learned about Fatal Flaw #2. But for now, remember RUE: Resist the Urge to Explain. Especially in your scene openings.

Fatal Flaw #2 Checklist

**Go through your scenes and look for these signs of Nothin'
Happenin' in your openings:**

- Frontloading the beginning of scenes with explanation and
  backstory

- Having more than a few lines of summarizing action instead of
  showing it

- Not starting in the middle of something happening

- Starting a scene in action, then stopping to go into lengthy
  explanations before returning to the action

- Including a lot of unimportant details about character, setting,
  and situation instead of letting the scene unfold in present
  action

- Having the character think for a long time without doing
  anything

- Starting with a lot of weather description written in omniscient
  POV

- Showing the character doing mundane or unimportant things
  like waking up and brushing her teeth

- Foreshadowing what hasn't happened yet and what the POV
  character can't know ("Little did Margo know, an hour from
  now she would get in a car accident")

- Dumping a lot of explanation and backstory into the opening
  dialogue

Your Turn: Try to spot and fix the problems in this opening novel passage. An example of a revision is on the next page (no peeking!). There isn't one correct way to rewrite a passage, so your final version may be different from the revision provided. The key is to test yourself to see if you've nailed Fatal Flaw #2.

Alma Rodriguez clutched the counter of the galley with both hands as the aircraft lurched and shook. She had experienced turbulence during her two years as a flight attendant, but this felt ominous—like the plane would fall apart at any moment. Was her overactive imagination at work again? She steadied herself, stepped out of the galley, and checked down the aisle for any trouble. Except for two passengers staring back at her, their faces flushed with dwindling fear, all seemed well.

Returning to her tasks, Alma peeked through the porthole of the galley door on South Air's Flight 223 as it headed to Mexico City from JFK International. She suddenly remembered something her botany teacher in high school told the class.

"The stinging nettle is frequently called the endearing thug of the plant world," Miss Ralston had said all those years ago. A senior in high school in her new home town of Albany, New York, Alma sat up straighter, riveted as her teacher waxed eloquent.

"When it invades, it spreads rapidly, stifles the countryside, and drives away other plants. If not managed, this invasive weed soon dominates and wipes out precious, low-lying wildflowers. The leaves and stems of the stinging nettle bear many hairs that cause a painful sting when touched. But the stinging nettle produces larval food for several species of butterflies, and it has been effectively used by humans for both nourishment and medicine."

My God, that reminds me of my aunt Elena, Alma thought. That day in botany class, Alma had decided to remove herself from her aunt's domination as soon as she became an adult. She would establish her own identity, travel the world—maybe she would even date someone from another part of the earth. This had become her mantra. And now here she was—a flight attendant for a big airline, and finally seeing the world. Just as she had dreamed.

Born in Ixtapa, Alma was raised by her grandmother at Las Palmas, an old plantation that had been passed down through generations, until her aunt—her dead mother's only sister—returned to Cuba when Alma was only eight, bringing with her a stronghold that both choked and stifled her niece. After high school graduation, Alma cast aside all pressures to go to college, get married to a local man, and have children; instead, she passionately pursued her dream. Now her destinations ranged from Paris, France, to Athens, Greece. Life was exciting. But now, thinking of Mexico, she felt a twinge of nostalgia. Would her grandmother still be alive?

And would she welcome me in, after what I did to shame her? Alma thought as she balanced a tray loaded with cups, spoons, and cream and sugar in one hand and hefted a coffeepot in the other.

"Would you like a cup of coffee before we land, sir?" she asked the first passenger in the row.

Revision of the Previous Passage:

Alma Rodriguez clutched the counter of the galley with both hands as the aircraft lurched and shook. She had experienced turbulence during her two years as a flight attendant, but this felt ominous—as if the plane might fall apart at any moment. She steadied herself, stepped out of the galley, and scanned the aisles. Except for two passengers staring back at her, their faces flushed with dwindling fear, all seemed well.

Returning to her tasks, Alma peeked through the porthole of the galley door on South Air's Flight 223 as it headed to Mexico City from JFK International. The warm sunlight on her face immediately calmed her. She hated clear air turbulence—something she wouldn't readily admit to the other flight attendants.

Alma grabbed two bags of coffee from a drawer below the counter, filled both coffeepots, and listened as hot liquid trickled down through the ground coffee. Its rich aroma wafted through the air, and she thought about the last time she'd been to Mexico—almost ten years ago.

Born in Ixtapa, Alma was raised by her grandmother at Las Palmas, an old plantation that had been passed down through generations. After high school graduation, Alma cast aside all pressures to go to college, get married to a local man, and have children; instead, she passionately pursued her dream. Now her destinations ranged from Paris, France, to Athens, Greece. Life was exciting. But thinking of Mexico, she felt a twinge of nostalgia. Would her grandmother still be alive?

And would she welcome me in, after what I did to shame her? Alma shook off the worry as she balanced a tray loaded with cups, spoons, and cream and sugar in one hand and hefted a coffeepot in the other.

"Would you like a cup of coffee before we land, sir?" she asked the first passenger in the row.

Fatal Flaw #3: Weak Construction

We've all been there. Writing our scenes in a white-hot heat. Never has our prose been more passionate. Never have we been so alive.

Surely this is the best thing we have ever written.

But then comes editing, and we discover we've transgressed. In our speed we grew careless, perhaps lazy. Our writing is vague and confused. In places it's (horrors) boring. Even we can't tell who is talking in that conversation or why we should care.

Weak construction sneaks in at the level of words and sentences, and like termites in a wood-frame house can bring the whole structure down. It comes in the form of passive voice, of *ing* verbs, of dangling modifiers. ("Yawning widely, the book was abandoned for another six-hour Netflix binge.") It makes a swamp of our beautifully imagined worlds and drowns our dialogue in banality.

In this chapter, we break down the problem of weak construction into its parts and examine them under a microscope. How do we find dangling participles? What will turn the vague swamp into a seaside resort of clarity and color? What details should be included, and what details need to go?

We'll take a special look at weak construction in dialogue, and we'll single out some of the most ubiquitous words and sentence structures that make trouble.

But it's not all bad news. In fact, this might be the most transformative part of the editing task. Every instance of weak construction is an opportunity to bring new, vivid life to every sentence and paragraph of the story, because we are not just cutting and hacking; we are replacing and rewriting—bringing in fresh phrasing, vivid nouns, active verbs, sparkling dialogue, and details that bring our worlds and our words to life.

Let's get started!

Editor:
Rachel Starr Thomson

Building Blocks: Avoiding Weak Sentence Construction

Annie Dillard wrote that one who wants to be a writer should like sentences. In reality, I think, most of us write because we have stories to tell, but the love of words (and sentences, and paragraphs) must come into play, or else we would all be making movies instead of writing books.

Along the way we learn that not every sentence is created equal. That our words and how we string them together will give life to the stories we tell or drain them dry.

Fortunately, while natural talent and a good ear certainly help, good sentence writing is not some mystical skill that only the most devoted Jedi will ever attain. This fatal flaw is all about weak sentence construction—or, more specifically, how to avoid it.

To Be Inging, There Was Passive Vagueness

Okay, that nonsense subhead was fun to write. I admit it. Let's watch its parts in action:

Before:
> The ramshackle mansion was being built on a hilltop. In the trees birds were singing and the leaves were rustling under a sky that was sunny and clouds that were puffy and white. Nails were hammered sharply into boards while bricks were laid. It was a beautiful, pristine day. The work was coming along. Filling the air, the sounds of construction were encouraging. Laying aside his tool, he knew the workers were waiting for him.

After:
> Garth stood on the hilltop, arms folded, and gazed at the workers and the ramshackle mansion rising at their hands. The striking, churning, buzzing sounds of construction drowned

52

out the songs of birds in the trees. Dark-skinned slaves hammered nails into boards and laid bricks one by one as the sun shone on them from a pristine blue sky.

He set aside his hammer, encouraged by their progress. The workers awaited him.

The main problems of the Before paragraph can be broken down as follows:

- Overuse of "be" verbs (be, being, been, is, am, are, was, and were)

- Overuse of the past progressive (aka past continuous) tense—the "ing" verbs

- Overuse of the passive voice

- Vague descriptors

I use the word *overuse* when addressing these problems because "be" verbs, past progressive, and passive voice all have their place in our writing. Artists will use all shades, not only primary colors. But overuse—or just plain bad use—of any of these is death on vivid storytelling.

To Be or Not to Be

The eight forms of the verb "be"—otherwise known as state-of-being verbs—are useful, necessary little words without which English would hardly function. It's a great mistake to try to excise them from our writing completely. (And contrary to legend, the use of a "be" verb does not automatically constitute passive voice.)

In storytelling, however, the state-of-being verbs can be a problem because they do just that: they state being. They do not show action. They do not move, act, or describe. They are just there. And nine times out of ten, they can be replaced by a stronger verb.

So rather than "She was at home," you might try "She waited at home," or "She stayed at home," or "She twiddled her thumbs at home, wishing with all her might that she were somewhere else." A "sky that was sunny" becomes "a sunny sky," and "clouds that were puffy" become "puffy clouds." "There was a man on the hill" becomes "A man stood on the hill." Word count drops, rhythm improves, and images grow vivid.

The "be" verbs also act as helpers for past progressive verbs. Rather than simply stating that an action happened, a past progressive (or past continuous) verb traces its action—it shows that is "is happening." So in the Before paragraph we see "was being," "were singing," "were rustling," "was coming."

At times you may want to stress the continuation of an action. In that case past progressive is fine. But normally, the simple past form of the verb will be more effective: sang, rustled, came, encouraged, waited.

The forms of "be" show up again in the use of passive voice. This is actually the biggest problem with the Before paragraph, far outweighing the others. Reading it, you might wonder, "Who the heck are these people? There's no one in this scene!"

The mansion might be raised by phantoms for all we can see.

The ramshackle mansion was being built . . . by whom? Nails were hammered sharply into boards . . . by whom? Bricks were laid . . . by whom? Who was encouraged by the sounds of construction? Who lays aside his hammer? There isn't a single *actor* in the whole paragraph; instead, every noun is *acted upon*. That is the difference between passive and active voice.

Passive Voice Does Have a Place

Even passive voice has its place in fiction. But active voice acts, and that makes it by far the stronger mode of construction. The After passage has people doing real things.

Which brings us, finally, to the problem of vagueness. Passive voice and state-of-being verbs contribute to making a scene vague. So does past progressive tense with its tendency to suggest that nothing is ever really finished or going anywhere definite.

The more general the wording, the less vivid it will be. The more concrete and specific, the more vivid. Specifics make a movie out of mud. In the next section of this chapter, we'll dive into the Vague Swamp—and explore how to re-create it as something vivid—more deeply.

Avoiding the Vague Swamp

More than likely, the fictional world you've created for your novel exists in your mind as fully imagined. This means you've assigned a myriad of details to it—far too many to write down in any one scene.

However, the details you do share with readers will muddy drastically if you employ words that aren't precise. Using vague or generalized words to describe your world takes away from the experience you wish readers to have.

We can divide "Vague Swamp" words into three general categories: intensifiers, diminishers, and vague-aries. These words are nouns or modifiers (adjectives or adverbs) that are meant to give a word more precise meaning but actually do little to define the object. Intensifier examples include *very, really, mostly, many, large, a lot, huge*. Diminishers: *small, tiny, little, some*. Vague-aries: *something, situation, circumstance, thing, stuff, problem*.

Let's look at how a writing sample with intensifiers, diminishers, and vague-aries might be rewritten to tighten the prose and give readers a more precise picture.

Before:

James tried to explain how he had managed to get out of the situation. A large cat had taken some of his stuff, and now he had a huge problem. "I can't go to work without certain things," he told his boss.

"It's the little things that have me worried," the boss said. "The small stuff is getting out of hand."

"Well, there are a lot of things I worry about too. In fact, I've got a big payment coming up. You have to let me do my shift today." James rubbed the large bruise on his knee. "Besides, you haven't tangled with this cat. He's the biggest one I've ever seen. And he loves to steal stuff."

The boss laughed. "Who ever heard of a cat burglar who was a real cat? I think you're blowing the situation out of control."

"It's true, I swear. Just give me a tiny bit of leeway here. I can't come into work without my stuff!"

"Sorry, James. You've given some excuses, but this one takes the cake. Go find someone else to con."

James hung up the phone. Outside, that large cat was walking away, his last pair of socks in Kitty's petite jaws.

After:

James didn't know how else to explain why he was late to work. Who would believe a raccoon-sized cat had taken his last pairs of his socks? "I can't go to work without my argyle socks," he told his boss on the phone.

"You've been late too often," his boss said. "The three consecutive tardies?"

"Things have been hard lately. And I know it's a lot to ask, but I've got a five-thousand-dollar payment coming up. You have to let me do my shift today." James rubbed the fist-sized bruise on his knee. "Besides, you haven't tangled with this cat. He's the size of a raccoon! And he loves to steal clothing."

"Who ever heard of a cat burglar who was a real cat?" The boss laughed. "I think you're blowing the missing-socks caper out of proportion."

"It's true, I swear. Just give me a pass this time. I can't come into work without my argyle socks."

"Sorry, James. You've given three excuses, but this one takes the cake. Go con the CEO."

James hung up the phone. Outside, that criminal cat was walking away, James's last pair of argyle socks in his kitty-sized jaws.

As you can see, it's much easier to picture a scene that uses specific words. But you can also overdo specifics.

Example:

From her cordovan leather chair, Darla glanced out the bay window and gasped. That same forest-green 1967 Ford Mustang convertible had circled Fantasy Drive three times. The dyed-blond hairs on her neck raised, but it was too early to call the Los Angeles Police Department. She kept her right hand hovering over her iPhone 6, in case that Ford Mustang convertible rounded Fantasy Drive's corner again.

In this case too many specifics weigh down the prose. With so much repetitive detail, readers will get the idea the writer doesn't think they're very smart.

Rewrite:

From her leather chair, Darla glanced out the window and gasped. That same forest-green 1967 Ford Mustang convertible had circled Fantasy Drive several times now. The hairs on her neck raised, but it was too early to call the police. She kept her hand hovering over her cell, in case that Mustang rounded the corner again.

In the rewrite, I purposely kept some details and eliminated others based upon how important the detail was to the scene's overall purpose and action. It makes no difference to readers whether Darla's hair is blond or dyed or which hand hovers over the phone. In much the same way, one could argue for keeping the police location, but I'd recommend at least shortening it to LA Police or LAPD.

It's important that your scenes are believable to readers. If you litter your scenes with vague or generalized words from the Vague Swamp, you automatically limit readers' ability to recreate the scene you have imagined and immerse themselves in your world. The fiction writer's ability to create a "vivid and continuous dream"—as John Gardner famously advises—directly influences how fully readers experience any scene.

Keeping It Real—Weak Construction in Dialogue

Strong dialogue is crucial. In fact, according to a literary agent I met at a writers' conference this last summer, it's one of the first things an agent evaluates when reading a manuscript.

Dialogue gives a quick yet solid indication of a writer's abilities. Strong dialogue keeps a story interesting by revealing characters' traits, advancing the plot, and breaking up narrative with action that clearly describes what's happening. Conversely, weak dialogue results in shallow characters with no individuality, a dragging plot, and an ambiguous, unsatisfying story. Even the best plot won't hold a reader's interest if the writer lacks the ability to create good dialogue.

While we have devoted a whole chapter to flawed dialogue construction later, it's important to consider here how dialogue can contribute to overall weak construction.

Consider this Before passage:

Before:
Moments later, Mother, Daddy, and I sat down on leather chairs in the headmaster's office.

"Mr. and Mrs. Peterson. Cassandra," he began slowly. "Welcome to Covington Hall."

"Thank you, Mr. Smith," she answered primly. "We are happy to be here."

"Yes. We believe this is the best school for Cassie," he confirmed.

"Indeed. Cassandra has always been an excellent student," she added quickly. "She is looking forward to being a student here at Covington Hall."

"And we are looking forward to having her as a student here," he agreed.

"Yes. She will fit in well with the other students here," she assured us. "We have several students here who have well-above-average intelligence who previously made poor decisions. I am happy to say that these students have excelled and showed exemplary behavior here at Covington."

"And that is what we want for her," she said. "A new start."

I crossed my arms and let my breath out without making a sound. Apparently, no one thought it was in any way important to ask what I wanted.

My first thoughts? Blah blah blah. Everybody sounds the same (like a monotone robot)—and who's saying what? Besides Cassandra, there are two men and two women in the room. While readers might be able to decipher who's speaking by what's said, if they need to make an effort to figure it out, they're going to give up on the story. Then there's Talking Head Syndrome (all talking, no action—which we'll look at in great detail later on).

Finally, the use of superfluous dialogue tags and adverbs ending in *ly* seriously bog down the reading. Few readers are going to stick it out through this version of the story; reading isn't supposed to be so complicated yet so boring that it hurts.

After:

Moments later, Mother, Daddy, and I sat down on leather chairs in the headmaster's office.

Headmaster Smith observed me with his tiny eyes and pointed nose, reminding me of a gaunt, balding mole. He then nodded at Mother and Daddy. "Mr. and Mrs. Peterson. Cassandra. Welcome to Covington Hall."

"Thank you, Mr. Smith," Mother said. Even without looking at her, I could tell she wore a sickening-sweet smile. "We're happy to be here."

Daddy took my hand in his. "We truly believe this is the best school for Cassie."

"Cassandra has always been an excellent student." Mother rested her gaze on me and snapped her shoulders back. When I followed her cue and sat up straighter, she returned her attention to Headmaster Mole. "She's looking forward to being a student here."

The headmaster's tall assistant clasped her hands at her narrow waist as she stood behind him. She attempted a thin-lipped smile, although it looked more like she'd just sucked a lemon. "Cassandra should fit in quite nicely here. We have several students with well-above-average intelligence who previously made poor decisions. I'm happy to say these students have excelled and showed exemplary behavior here at Covington Hall."

Mother beamed at them. "That's exactly what we want for her. A new start."

I let my breath out without making a sound. Apparently, no one thought what I wanted mattered.

What's different this time? Um, well . . . *everything*. Here's a list:

- Action accompanies the dialogue. The characters are actually *doing* things, not just speaking—and in their actions, we get a much better idea of who they are, physically and personally. Action moves the story forward.

- The dialogue isn't stilted or monotone. Contractions are used where appropriate, and the characters don't all sound the same. Just like real people, characters are all different; their "voices" should reflect that.

- It's obvious who's speaking. Instead of using the vague pronouns *he* and *she*, both of which could indicate more than one of the characters, names are given. A scene with two characters generally requires only sporadic use of names, but a scene with multiple speakers quickly becomes confusing if the author doesn't delineate who's speaking.

- Finally, the story flows so much better without the repeated dialogue tags and adverbs ending in *ly*. Nowadays, most editors recommend *said* as the dialogue tag of choice (if a tag is necessary—many times they're not since action or other dialogue makes it clear who's speaking). That doesn't mean writers should never use other tags, but *said* keeps the dialogue transparent by allowing the reader to skim over it, concentrating on what's being said instead of how it's being said. Omitting the *ly* adverbs supports transparency in the same way and also encourages the writer to show emotion through dialogue and action instead of telling it with words.

Learning to write strong dialogue takes work, but it's worth the effort. If you're struggling with this, mindfully listen to how people speak in everyday situations, and read dialogue aloud after it's been written. Then evaluate.

Does it sound natural or stilted? Do characters have their own voice? Does it flow well and sound transparent, or do dialogue tags and adverbs bog it down? Does it complement the action, and does the action complement it?

Rewrite as necessary—and love the stronger dialogue that results.

Memo from the Department of Redundancy Department

"We get it."

I type those words often in my clients' manuscripts. And when I see a lot of redundancy in their manuscripts, I've been known to simply type "DRD" in the comment box. Department of Redundancy Department—a great Monty Python phrase.

So many writers fall into this trap. They think of a few different ways to say the same thing, and they seem to like every one of their choices. I know this, because they leave them all in.

The quickest way to slow down your manuscript is to be redundant. It's boring, it's overwriting, and it's weak.

How do we clean up our sloppy prose so it's both clear and riveting?

Exactly What Are You Trying to Say?

What do you want your reader to learn from this passage? What tone do you hope to convey, and what emotions do you want to elicit? Keeping those ideas in mind, ensure that every word in your passage matches your goals.

In the following paragraph, my POV character has just returned home after many years away. It's the middle of the night, and her grandmother, who lives in the house, doesn't know she's coming. Rae has just pulled into the driveway and is surprised to find the house dark—that's what I want my reader to learn. There is an element of danger in my book, so I want the reader to pick up on some suspense. And I want my reader to feel Rae's emotions—eagerness to see her grandmother, worry about her grandmother's health, and beneath that, an underlying fear.

Before:

Allowing my gaze to wander over the property, I took in the house, the barn, the woods, the yard, and the driveway slowly. I wondered why the light wasn't on on the porch and no light fell onto the surrounding ground. Turning around, I looked at the road from which I'd come and looked at the trees, which stood high above my head all around me. Gazing at the car, I looked into the backseat, and I saw my son, sleeping in his car seat, relaxed in repose, his eyes closed and his mouth moving as if he were dreaming of warm milk. I turned back to the house, to that dark porch, and those black windows where no lights had been lit, no life lighting its interior as if all the brightness had seeped out, the darkness had crept in, and there was no joy in there at all. Worriedly, I moved cautiously, keeping my feet from tripping on the gravel driveway, then turning slowly, I walked up the walkway to the dark porch. I lifted my hand, knocking gently on the door. Unfortunately, no light lit within the darkened residence, and nobody answered the door.

I knocked again worriedly and hoped my grandmother would come quickly. The baby was in the car and would wake up soon. And I needed Gram's help with him. Mostly, though, I really wanted to feel my grandmother's arms around me, to hug her and hold her tight, to see that she was all right, knowing she was healthy despite the fact that the house was dark. I was hoping Gram would make everything all better for me.

Riveting, right? Did you see all those redundancies? Let me point out a few. She "allowed her gaze to wander" and then "took in." Later, we have, "Gazing . . . I looked . . . and I saw." And in that same sentence, the baby is "sleeping . . . relaxed in repose . . . his eyes closed . . . dreaming." Then there's the "dark porch . . . black windows where no lights had been lit, no life lighting its interior . . . all the brightness had seeped out, the darkness had crept in . . . ."

If I were editing this, I would highlight all of that and type "DRD" in the comment balloon.

As if the redundancies aren't bad enough, I counted ten adverbs. That's probably ten too many. This is another form of redundancy: using multiple adverbs or adjectives where one strong verb would do the job.

I hope you got the point of the passage—that the house is dark and Rae is worried about it. Did you feel nervous or fearful? Did the

63

tone seem suspenseful to you? Probably not—due to all the redundancies (and a generous sprinkling of *ing* verbs, our old friends from the previous sections of the chapter). Let's see if we can fix it.

After:

I stepped out of my car and breathed in the familiar scents of forest and fall. The leaves, still green, rustled in the slight breeze. But the house—why was it so dark? When I was a kid, Gram had always left the porch light on. Maybe she'd gotten out of the habit. Maybe her senility was worse than I'd thought.

No, Gram would be fine. As soon as she saw us, she'd wrap us in those wrinkly arms and pull us inside. She'd make a pot of tea and tell me to drink up, because the chamomile would help me sleep.

I gazed at Johnny, asleep in his car seat. Gram would love him. And Johnny and I would be safe here, at least for a little while.

A car passed by on the street behind me, and I whipped around to watch its lights fade in the surrounding forest. Nothing to worry about. Julien didn't know where I was—not yet anyway.

I lifted Johnny out of the car and started for the house. Once we got inside with Gram, everything would be all right.

Better, I hope. I eliminated the redundancies and the telling words—*saw, looked, wondered,* etc. I kept (and added) some important details and dumped the unimportant ones. I tried to use more straightforward verbs—fewer *ing* words. I had her react to the car driving by to hint at her fear. I added the bit about Gram hugging her and making the tea because I want the reader to feel eager for Rae to see Gram and nervous that there's something wrong. Is it better? I think so.

Don't Fall into the Modifier Trap

A discussion of weak writing wouldn't be complete without a look at misplaced modifiers and dangling participles, so before we wrap up this fatal flaw, let's take a look at these . . . whatever they are.

You may have heard of these terms, and you might even know what they are. But even being in the know doesn't ensure writers will catch these traps of weak construction.

Here's the problem with modifiers. We know what *we* mean when we put our thoughts into words. Sometimes, though, what we mean to say isn't what's actually written. Misplaced modifiers and badly placed participial phrases are often the result of quick writing. The challenge is in locating and rewriting these sentences.

Okay, What's a Modifier?

A modifier, simply put, is something that modifies. It's a word or phrase that modifies (affects, changes) another word. In the phrase "blue ball," the adjective *blue* modifies the noun *ball*. Writers sometimes stick those modifiers in the wrong place in a sentence.

Take a look at these lines and see if you can identify the problem:

- This morning I chased a dog in my pajamas. (Did the dog dress himself?)

- I sold a desk to a lady that had broken legs. (Poor woman; how will she carry that desk?)

- We sat on the porch listening to the birds sing while playing cards. (Wow, talented birds.)

- She saw several whales on vacation in Mexico. (Do whales take vacations?)

The 12 Fatal Flaws of Fiction Writing

It's easy for these modifiers to slip into the wrong place in our fiction passages, so it's important to watch for them.

What's a Participle?

What is a participle? It's a verb or a noun that gets turned into an adjective. Participles can be in the present tense or the past tense, and the present participle always ends with *ing*. For example, "sing" is a verb, and "singing" is its present participle.

There is nothing wrong with beginning sentences with these words, but watch what happens when close attention isn't being paid to the subject of the phrase:

- Floating downstream, the day seemed so peaceful.

- Beating me at cards, my fun evening with my friends cost me my week's wages.

- Turning the doorknob, the noises in the creepy room scared me.

You'd have a strange story with days that float down streams, evenings that can play cards, and noises that can turn doorknobs.

Before:

Dirk Matsen managed to escape from the borrowed truck before it sank and swam to the riverbank. His water-soaked clothes dragging, they impeded his slippery climb up the steep bank until flopping onto the hard ground. Groaning and creaking, Dirk watched the car slip under the dirty, opaque water. Huffing and puffing, the murky cold water made him struggle for breath. Where was the other car? The other driver? Had he just been run off the road by a ghost, or was there someone else trapped underwater?

Did you notice the problems?

How do these sentences sneak in? Often, they are buried in the middle of a paragraph or a description that surrounds the offending sentence with additional context and meaning. This is a reflection of lazy writing as well as fast writing.

As we crank out our scenes at furious rates, we lose contact with individual sentences and depend on context, general understanding, or the reader to make sense of our words. But every sentence matters, and constructing each one with care leads us to stronger, more understandable writing.

After:

> Dirk Matsen pushed open the door and escaped from the borrowed truck before it sank in the murky cold water. With tired arms, he swam to the riverbank. His water-soaked clothes felt like heavy weights, but he finally pulled himself over the steep slippery bank and flopped onto the hard ground. He looked up and watched as the car, groaning and creaking, slipped under the dirty, opaque water.
>
> Matsen sat on the bank, huffing and wheezing as he looked around. Where was the other car? The other driver? Had he just been run off the road by a ghost, or was someone else trapped underwater?

By eliminating the participial phrases and fixing the misplaced modifier in the passage, readers shouldn't have any trouble understanding what I'm trying to say.

Often, oddly placed modifiers are the result of telling action rather than showing action. Think about how to show by asking yourself questions. How did the driver swim to shore? What was he thinking? Was the dirty water cold and kind of disgusting? Did he keep his mouth closed so as not to swallow any of the putrid swill? How steep was the bank as he scrambled up the muddy sides?

To avoid falling into the modifier trap, follow these bits of advice:

- Show, don't tell.

- Describe a situation or scene as fully as you can.

- Create two short sentences rather than one long one in the service of clarity—your reader will not mind.

- Return to the manuscript a couple of times and read it sentence by sentence. Employ a good line editor—someone who is skilled at seeing and deconstructing sentences.

- Search for sentences you've started with a participial phrase (look for *ing*—for example: Starting the car, the engine sputtered). Rewrite them without the participial (When Sarah turned the key in the ignition, the engine sputtered).

In Conclusion . . .

We've examined numerous culprits that weaken your prose. Take the time to look at each individual sentence in your story, then examine your word choices.

Weak construction sneaks in at the micro levels. Every superfluous or ineffectual word weakens your writing, so while you won't often stop to examine every single word as you write a first draft, seeking and destroying weak construction should be high on your list as you revise and self-edit subsequent drafts.

It can show up at the macro levels too, so be sure to step back and look at your scenes. Search for long passages (or entire scenes) in which characters aren't doing or saying much, or where what they are doing and saying doesn't move your story forward in a strong way.

Weak construction makes for weak scenes and weak stories overall. Take the time to ferret it out.

Fatal Flaw #3 Checklist

Go through your scenes and look for these types of weak construction:

- Too many sentences beginning with "be" verbs (*it was, there were, he was feeling*)

- Vague descriptions of people and places

- Excessive modifiers, such as *very, really, mostly*

- Excessive diminishers, such as *small, little, some*

- Use of generalities instead of specifics ("a car," instead of "a red Buick")

- Overuse of specifics

- Too many pronouns that make it unclear who is speaking or acting ("she thought she looked better than she did")

- Showing characters speaking but not doing anything else

- Stilted dialogue, monologuing, or lack of contractions in speech

- Characters who all sound the same in their speech and/or thoughts

- Redundancy and/or repetition of words or ideas in a passage

- Overuse of participial phrases to start sentences ("Turning the knob, he opened the door")

- Misused modifiers starting sentences ("Groaning and creaking, he watched the car sink")

Your Turn: Try to spot and fix all the instances of weak construction you can find in this passage. An example of a revision is on the next page (no peeking!). There isn't one correct way to rewrite a passage, so your final version may be different from the revision provided. The key is to test yourself to see if you've nailed Fatal Flaw #3.

She looked at the remote and started cleaning the buttons with a rag. She picked up a scarf that was lying on the arm of the couch. Betty wondered if Agatha had made it. It didn't seem Sally's style. She felt that not very much in the house did, now that she thought of it. Most of the furniture was old, and old-fashioned. She guessed it was the furniture she had grown up with. The TV was new, and the small stand that held the DVDs. The small microwave was new. The couch was new too, of course. That had shown up this morning—a couch with recliners on each end. That was new too. Those were the important things, she thought, suppressing a grin.

Walking through the house, she had seen some of the other rooms in the house just once, when she got here. Since then, she had primarily seen the living room, with occasional trips to the kitchen. The trip to the kitchen mostly led through the dining room. Once in the parlor, she'd had to stop there to catch her breath, and noticed there was a table was covered with dust. It seemed to be made from oak, and several place settings were also covered with dust. The kitchen was basic white, with white floors, blue trim, and white appliances. It was decorated with whales. It was odd. Thinking to herself, she had no idea what her bedroom was like. It was none of her business, she told herself.

"Sally?"

"Yeah?"

"You really miss Agatha, don't you?"

Silence.

She opened her eyes.

Sally was staring at the remote.

"Yeah," she finally said. "Why?"

"It just seems like everything in this house is really hers. You grew up here. I am not saying you should move or anything, but it just kind of seems like maybe you are living in the past a little."

"I love this house."

"It is a great house. Family houses are great. But do you see the stuff here as yours or as Agatha's?"

Sally sighed and stretched. "When did you get your psych degree, Dr. Johnson?" she asked lightly.

"Sorry."

She swung her head around to look at her. "No, I am sorry. I'm just . . . it does not seem like it has been that long since she died. Okay, it has been four months. The house feels like mine, but yes. Some of the stuff feels very much like it is Agatha's. I guess it will just take time to figure out what's what. I did replace the couch," she added.

Betty smiled.

Sally began to scrub at a little stain she saw on the counter. "I just don't want to go through and change everything all at once and then regret it later."

Betty wondered if she was still talking about the house.

"Okay," she said. There was nothing else to say. She closed her eyes. She felt bad for Sally.

Revision of the Previous Passage:

Sally picked up the remote and rubbed the buttons with a rag.

Betty studied a scarf that lay on the arm of the couch. Had Aunt Agatha made the scarf? It didn't seem Sally's style. Not much in the old house did, now that Betty thought of it. Most of the furniture was old, and old-fashioned. The TV was new, and the stand that held the DVDs, as well as the microwave and the couch. That piece of furniture had been delivered this morning—with recliners on each end. *The important things*, she thought, suppressing a grin.

Betty wandered through the house. She had seen the living room and kitched when she'd first got here. She stopped in the parlor to catch her breath, and noticed an oak table with several place settings covered with dust.

She continued to the kitchen and looked around. White floors, blue trim, and white appliances. Appliquéd whales had been affixed to the walls. Odd. *Wonder what the bedroom is like.* She smirked. *None of your business*, she told herself.

"Sally?" she said, wondering where her best friend had gone.

Sally walked into the kitchen, the cleaning rag in her hand. "Yeah?"

"You really miss Agatha, don't you?"

Silence. This must have been so hard for Sally. How much she must miss her aunt.

Sally stared at the remote.

"Yeah," Sally said. "Why?"

"It just seems like everything in this house is hers. I'm not saying you should move or anything, but maybe you're living in the past a little."

"I love this house."

Betty nodded. "It is a great house. But do you see the stuff here as yours or as Agatha's?"

Sally sighed and stretched. "When did you get your psych degree, Dr. Johnson?"

"Sorry."

Sally turned and looked at her. "No, I'm sorry. I'm just . . . it's been four months. The house feels like mine, but most was Agatha's. I guess it will just take time to figure out what's what." She smirked. "I did replace the couch."

"And it's a beauty."

Sally scrubbed at a stain on the counter. "I just don't want to change everything all at once and then regret it later."

Were they still talking about the house. "Okay," she said.

What else could Betty say? She closed her eyes and sighed, wishing she could find the right words to comfort her friend.

Fatal Flaw #4: Too Much Backstory

You've spent hours, maybe months, developing a rich background for each of your characters and the world they inhabit. As the creator of your story, you are omniscient. You know why your characters behave the way they do and how their past has fashioned them into who they are. And now your job is to somehow bring out those bits of history through your story.

The challenge is to learn ways to do this so the information comes out organically and doesn't feel as if a dump truck has just unloaded six tons of rock on a reader's head.

Sure, there may come moments in life when a friend sits you down and, in an hour-long monologue, tells you his life story. Or details how his planet was terraformed and attacked by an ancient race. Or explains his entire family tree back fourteen generations. But even in real life, chances are you will fall asleep mid-babble and wish you had stayed home under the covers.

Readers sometimes wish they could run on stage in a novel and tell the author to stop dumping information. "Just let me watch the story!" they scream. "Stop telling me all that boring stuff."

Boring? We authors think all that backstory is not only riveting but essential. Surely readers want—no, *need*—to hear it all. And the sooner they do, the better they will understand and enjoy the novel.

But honestly, that's far from the truth. Too much backstory is a fatal flaw in fiction, but *just the right amount* will enhance the story, engaging and informing the reader while not interrupting the present action.

In this chapter, we editors will show you ways to sprinkle in those key details you know are so crucial to understanding your story.

Editor:
Rachel Starr Thomson

Weaving It In

As the introduction indicated, backstory creates an interesting problem for writers. It's an absolute necessity in good fiction. Just as you and I have a backstory of our own, so do our characters, and it's often from that backstory that key plot points—or the whole plot—arise. Backstory lends richness and depth to our stories and the people who populate them.

Given all that, backstory can be problematic because it's not always easy to balance. You've likely heard the term "info dumping." When a writer dumps a pile of information on the reader, it usually interrupts the story and derails any real connection to the characters at the same time.

Really good writing creates a spell. It immerses the reader in another world. The trick is this: *We must write backstory, but we must write it in such a way that it does not feel artificial, forced, or so out of balance with the rest of the story that it breaks that spell.*

Avoiding Intrusion

In this chapter, we're exploring ways to relate backstory through dialogue, action, and internal monologue so that it stays balanced—a seamless part of the story rather than an interruption to it.

Ultimately, though, the key is to weave backstory so that it is always an underlying part of a scene, not a break from it.

Just as an individual has a history, so your characters will often have history together, and that will often have a major influence on the plot. Therefore, especially toward the beginning of a novel, you'll often find yourself needing to convey backstory when two characters come together.

The following passages are two versions of a scene from my novel *Abaddon's Eve*, when the shepherd boy Alack catches sight of Rechab, a childhood friend he has not seen in several months.

75

Keep in mind, as you read the passages below, that a lot of character backstory can be *implied*. Not everything has to be explained or stated outright.

Before:

He had not known she was back. He went to her quickly.

Alack and Rechab had been friends since childhood. She was the daughter of a wealthy merchant and he the son of a shepherd, but they had met one day in the town market when they were about five years old and interacted in their childish way. She remembered him after that, and when they would encounter each other at the town well or other locales, they would play. When they got older, they would talk. They became best friends over time, and in Alack's heart this friendship had turned to love. He had been in love with her for years now. He had not spoken about it to her, although he thought she knew how he felt. The problem was that with the economic difference between them, there was little hope they could ever act on their love.

"Rechab," he said.

She turned. "Alack!"

He thought she was beautiful. He had thought so ever since he turned about twelve years old and stopped thinking girls were icky.

"When did you return?" he asked. "As you know, you have been gone since late spring. Your father took you across the desert on his merchant journey like he always does. You know that I miss when you're gone—I always do."

"We only just returned . . . The journey has been long."

"But you are back now," he said. "Back for the autumn. That means we can spend time together like we've done since we were children."

Her face fell. "Alack, things are different now . . ."

Rechab too knew that they did not have much hope for a future. As she grew older—and more beautiful—her father had plans to cash in on her value by selling her off for a good dowry for some wealthy man. This had been going on for some time now. She always tried to avoid catching anyone's notice, but she had to go out with her father's caravans for long periods of time, and more and more often. She rarely had time to stay in the Holy City and see Alack anymore. It was only going to get worse as time went on.

She sighed. "You know I would stay if I could, Alack."

In a passage like this, both dialogue and narrative strike artificial notes. We get the sense that someone is intruding into the story— someone who nudges us with a pointy elbow and puts words in mouths that would never choose to speak them.

More effective writing will use other elements of the scene to fill in details like how Alack feels about Rechab, the threat to their relationship, and their history together. These elements include description, specific actions, thoughts and feelings, and great dialogue.

Working together, these elements make the backstory *part of the scene*—something that belongs to it, not something brought in from the outside.

After:

He had not known she was back, and his heart leaped at the sight of her. He pressed through the crowd, edging and elbowing his way to the well and her side.

"Rechab," he said, his voice catching.

She turned, light leaping up in her soft brown eyes. "Alack!"

He drank in the sight of her. Small and feminine, clothed in homespun, her dark hair tied back except for a few curls that had fought loose and hung around her face and neck. Rechab was startlingly beautiful by any standard, but it was her eyes that drew him most. Eyes that spoke of laughter and secrets and childhood, and at the same time of mystery and growing up—of love.

"When did you return?" he asked.

"Only just now . . . The journey has been long."

"But you are back for the autumn."

Her face fell. "Alack, things are different now . . ."

"You cannot be going out again so soon!"

"My father says trade is good. The nomads brought him riches; he wants to take them to the Holy City in just a few days."

"But . . . you do not have to go with him . . ."

She sighed. "You know I would stay if I could, Alack."

He swallowed hard. He knew the words she was not saying. That if he were less a boy and more a man, if he could put down the bride price, she would stay. Then they would not just be children playing at love; they would be betrothed, with a future.

A future that would never come.

The Past in the Present

As you can see, the second passage is shorter and relies far more heavily on implication than the first one did. It sacrifices certain *details* about the past—when they met, what exactly Rechab's father's plans are—*in favor of weaving the past into the present.* It shows us actions and reactions that demonstrate Alack's feelings about Rechab and the way she is pulling away from him.

Notice that the After passage

- never has one character informing another of something they both know except in a natural, confrontational context.

- implies tension and history rather than stating it outright.

- uses description and action to *show* attraction rather than telling us that "Alack had been in love with Rechab for years."

- uses one character's thoughts to unfold years of angst and regret rather than just saying "Alack had been trying to fix this for years."

Backstory is absolutely necessary for any rich, meaningful story. But it needs to behave as a seamless part of the story, not as something parachuting in from outside. You can avoid that sense of outsider artificiality by weaving the past into the present, making the backstory something that is accessible, meaningful, and pivotal to the scene at hand.

The 12 Fatal Flaws of Fiction Writing

How the Rule of Three Can Help Writers Avoid Flashback Trouble

When you use backstory to deepen characterization or add information about the plot, it's common to write it in flashbacks: specific memories that take the character somewhere in the past. They can be effective, but it's also easy for readers to become confused. If readers enter a flashback and wonder when or where they are supposed to be, confusion often turns to frustration, and they stop reading.

A flashback is any narrative passage or scene that occurred in time before the present-time story. Your POV character is in a scene when her "mind reels back." How can readers keep a firm understanding of when and where, in time and space, the story takes them?

Nobody Likes Cold Mashed Potatoes

A simple rule I call the Cold Mashed Potatoes Rule will help ensure that your readers are always oriented to time and place.

The Cold Mashed Potatoes rule goes like this: A character in a scene (maybe the Lady in the White Evening Gown) sits down at a banquet table and is served a plate of steaming hot, buttery mashed potatoes. Her mouth waters as she digs a forkful and raises it to her lips.

But then something happens. The mashed potatoes remind her of Grandma's mashed potatoes. She remembers that she looked forward to them every year at family dinners. Lady reminisces about how smooth those taters were, how her brothers fought over second helpings, how Grandma always surprised everyone by bringing a second heaping mound out of the kitchen. Grandma's potatoes impressed everyone so much that she learned to make a double batch.

While we are learning the reasons for Lady's love of mashed potatoes, we are transported to Grandma's kitchen. But what about the banquet table where we started? The forkful of mashed potatoes is still hovering in midair, paused as we travel back in time. *And the longer we remain in the backstory, the colder those potatoes get.*

I use this illustration to help writers remember that the longer readers are in the backstory, the more the real-time scene recedes from their awareness—which is a bad thing.

The Rule of Three

It makes sense, then, to limit the number of backstory sentences you write before at least touching back on the present-time scene. The Cold Mashed Potatoes Rule is easier to work with if you also use the Rule of Three: For every three sentences (or in some cases, paragraphs) of backstory, go back to the present scene at least briefly, to remind readers where the character actually is on stage.

A couple of other considerations will also help you know when and where to insert backstory, whether using flashbacks or another technique. My colleagues all agree that first-chapter backstory, if used at all, needs to be short and woven in and around the present action. For every detail but the most crucial, save the backstory for after readers are committed to your character.

And a word about flashbacks within flashbacks: don't do it. Readers are likely to feel hopelessly lost if we begin a flashback about Grandma and then move into Grandma's memory of who taught her to make delicious mashed potatoes. If the backstory about Grandma's youth is more interesting than Lady's memories, you may want to start the story in a different place.

Let's look at a Before and an After example:

Before:

Lady W sat down and smoothed her white silk gown. The butler helped push her chair closer to the table—laden with Sir Lumphrey's chipped bone china and tarnished silverware. "Evening." She smiled at her seat mates, Lord Havemuch and his corpulent wife.

Lorna Havemuch leaned across her husband. "I hear there will be mashed potatoes and roast duck," she said, licking her lips. "Sir Lumphrey always has the best mashed potatoes."

Lady W stared at the woman. "That so?"

"Why yes!" Lord Havemuch tied his napkin round his neck. "I can't wait!"

The servers emerged, bearing steaming tureens of Lord Lumphrey's famous potatoes, ladling fat globs upon every plate. Lady W picked up her fork, breathing in the delicious buttery smell. As she guided her forkful of potatoes to her mouth, her grandmother's legendary potatoes came to mind.

When Lady W had been a girl, she looked forward each November to Gran's luscious mashies. Lady would dream of those delicious potatoes and could scarcely wait until Gran called the family to the table. Then Gran would present the mashies—so good that Lady's brothers always fought over who got seconds. Gran refused to tell anyone her secret recipe, although Lady begged her grandma to share it.

When Gran was on her deathbed, she whispered to Lady, "Come closer, dearie. I'll tell you my secret for those mashies."

Lady listened closely. Gran had been just a girl herself when *her* gran had given out the secret recipe. Great-Gran took Gran out into the nearby wood, Gran's worn-out shoes slipping on the loose earth under a tree. She carried a small burlap bag for the secret ingredient, as Great-Gran called it.

Suddenly, Great-Gran dropped to her knees beneath the oak tree and began scratching at the ground. She bent forward and sniffed loudly. "Hand me the bag," Great-Gran ordered. Gran had obeyed, uncertain how what looked like dirt clods could be the reason the mashed potatoes tasted so heavenly.

Gran heaved a ragged sigh. Lady leaned in closer. "What was it, Gran?"

But Gran's eyes had closed for the last time, and Lady W had felt tears slide down her cheeks.

"Pass the potatoes, won't you?" Lord Havemuch's voice was much too loud and held a vague irritation.

Lady W startled, then stared at her fork, which still hovered in midair. She slid the bite into her mouth, laid down her fork, and passed the tureen. Ugh. The potatoes had not only grown stone cold, they'd never taste like Gran's. Sir Lumphrey was far too cheap to spring for shaved truffles in a bowl of potatoes. She pushed back from the table.

Okay, I admit to having a bit of fun here. The writer probably does need to know how Lady W found out what made Gran's potatoes so wonderful. But if the backstory is crammed all together as in the above example, it's difficult to keep track of when and where readers are supposed to be.

Now let's see how we can streamline the backstory, using the Cold Mashed Potatoes Rule and the Rule of Three.

After:

Lady W sat down and smoothed her white silk gown. The butler helped push her chair closer to the table—laden with Sir Lumphrey's chipped bone china and tarnished silverware. "Evening." She smiled at her seat mates, Lord Havemuch and his corpulent wife.

Lorna Havemuch leaned across her husband. "I hear there will be mashed potatoes and roast duck," she said, licking her lips. "Sir Lumphrey always has the best mashed potatoes."

Lady W stared at the woman. "That so?"

"Why yes!" Lord Havemuch tied his napkin round his neck. "I can't wait!"

The servers emerged, bearing steaming tureens of Lord Lumphrey's famous potatoes, ladling fat globs upon every plate. Lady W picked up her fork, breathing in the delicious buttery smell. As she guided her forkful of potatoes to her mouth, her grandmother's legendary potatoes came to mind.

When Lady W had been a girl, she'd looked forward each November to Gran's luscious mashies. Lady would dream of those delicious potatoes and could scarcely wait until Gran called the family to the table. Then Gran would present the mashies—so good that Lady's brothers had always fought over who got seconds.

Lord Havemuch elbowed Lady W. "Pass the butter please."

Lady W set down her fork and obliged. Lord Havemuch piled at least five butter pats upon his potatoes. Gran's potatoes had never needed that much butter—they were scrumptious all by themselves.

Gran had refused to tell anyone her secret recipe, although Lady had begged her grandma to share it. Then, when Gran was on her deathbed, she'd whispered to Lady. "Come closer, dearie. I'll tell you my secret for those mashies."

Now Lady tasted the potatoes in front of her. No, these were definitely not as good as Gran's.

Lady remembered that Gran had heaved a ragged sigh and leaned in closer. "What is it, Gran? What's the secret?"

But Gran's eyes had closed for the last time, and Lady W's tears had slipped down her cheeks.

"I *said*, pass the potatoes, won't you?" Lord Havemuch's voice was much too loud and held a vague irritation.

Lady W startled. She slid the next bite into her mouth, laid down her fork, and passed the tureen. Ugh. Sir Lumphrey's potatoes had not only grown stone cold—they'd never taste like Gran's. Sir Lumphrey was far too cheap to spring for shaved truffles in a bowl of potatoes. She pushed back from the table.

In the second example, we only go into one flashback. I used the Rule of Three in each bit of backstory, careful to insert the past perfect "had" at the beginning and ending of that bit. By bouncing back into the real time scene, readers are reminded of where Lady really is, and confusion is lessened.

So, yes, you do need bits of backstory. But if you abide by the Rule of Three, keeping those cold potatoes in mind, you won't lose your readers.

The Two-Edged Sword of Backstory in Dialogue

Like many things in life, backstory is all about how it's presented. Rachel and Linda talked about specific ways to integrate backstory so it enhances instead of detracts from the story. Now I'm going to discuss some aspects of how to use (and how not to use) dialogue to incorporate backstory.

Before:
"There has to be a better option than this." I dropped onto the bench outside Covington Hall's administration building and waited for Mother and Daddy to face me. "I don't know why I have to change schools. What happened wasn't my fault. I was just there."

Mother folded her arms across her chest. "Covington Hall will be a good change of scenery for you—and a change of peers."

I looked to Daddy. "But—"

"Cassandra. Need I remind you of what happened? You rode along with Emily Anderson after she took her father's Mercedes and went joyriding. Emily had no experience driving and crashed the car into our town Welcome sign." She sighed. "Yes, perhaps it wasn't your idea, but you were involved, and because Emily's father is one of our town's lawyers, everyone believed him when he insisted it had been your idea. The whole town blamed you."

"But I hardly even knew Emily. I didn't know she didn't have a license. It was about to rain, and I just wanted a ride home."

Daddy sat next to me and shifted to meet my gaze. "We know that, Cassie. We're not blaming you for what happened. But we do believe that you'll do well here. As you know, you're a smart girl with a 160 IQ. You could read before you were two, you were able to add and subtract at age three, and you'd

84

mastered multiplication by the time you were five. At age ten, you could play six different instruments, and you were writing high-school-level essays. Your old school was a good school, but Covington will be even better for you. You'll meet others like yourself here."

I dropped my head back and stared at the cloudless blue sky. "Great. So at Covington I'll be surrounded by geniuses whose extraordinary intelligence sometimes encompasses so much of their brain that there isn't much room left for common sense?"

Hmm. Now there was a thought. Attending Covington might turn out to be just as wild a ride as my escapade with Emily Anderson.

After:

"There has to be a better option than this." I dropped onto the bench outside Covington Hall's administration building and waited for Mother and Daddy to face me. "I don't know why I have to change schools. What happened wasn't my fault. I was just there."

Mother folded her arms across her chest. "Covington Hall will be a good change of scenery for you—and a change of peers."

I looked to Daddy. "But—"

"Covington Hall is a highly respected school," Mother said. "Here you'll be able to put what happened behind you and concentrate on the future. It'll be a second chance, which you desperately need."

Daddy sat next to me and shifted to meet my gaze. "We know you're hesitant about switching schools, but we've discussed this. Covington Hall is your best option to—"

"It's more than your best option," Mother added. "It's your *only* option."

"Try to see this as a blessing in disguise." Daddy placed his hand on my arm. "Covington Hall is tailored to meet the needs of young people like you. You'll thrive here."

I dropped my head back and stared at the cloudless blue sky. "Great. So I'll be surrounded by geniuses whose extraordinary intelligence sometimes encompasses so much of their brain that there isn't any room left for common sense?"

Hmm. Now there was a thought. Attending Covington might turn out to be just as wild a ride as my escapade with Emily Anderson.

Two things stand out to me about these passages. The Before passage shows how backstory can detract from dialogue, while the After shows how backstory can enhance it.

Let's look at the Before passage:

- First, we have Mother giving Cassie the blow-by-blow of what she did wrong. But Cassie's a teenager (not a small child), and she doesn't need her mother to explain it. She *knows* what she did, so obviously her mother's discourse isn't in the scene for her benefit. It's been written solely to give the reader backstory about what's happened.

- Then, we have Daddy providing Cassie with a long list of her personal achievements, starting with the dreaded "As you know . . ." In this example, her dad even admits that he's telling her what she already knows. Why? Because he's not really talking to her; he's informing the reader.

While dialogue is an excellent way to incorporate backstory, it needs to be in the right context. We never want to dump a ton of information that would be better received if it were presented so it sounded natural and didn't seem forced.

Now consider the After passage:

- Cassie's mother doesn't give the full story of what happens, but their dialogue makes it clear that Cassie's done something that's gotten her into big trouble. This passage sounds much more natural, and the reader's interest will be piqued by getting only a tidbit of information. *So what did Cassie do?* And how do they find out? They'll keep reading (and you, as the writer, will have the ability to convey what happened more cogently).

- Cassie's dad doesn't highlight each of her achievements; instead, he makes it obvious that she's different from most people her age—which she then explains with her next sentence. At this point, it's not necessary for the reader to know Cassie's timeline of accomplishments, and adding them here doesn't add to the scene. If anything, it takes away from it because it sounds forced and removes some suspense.

The bottom line is, backstory is incredibly important. But in dialogue, it can be a two-edged sword: there are good ways to convey it and bad ways to convey it. Dialogue can be an excellent means of showing "the story before the story," but it can also deluge the reader with information that would be best introduced sporadically or in another way.

Backstory in Action

When you start your story in the middle of the action as we've talked about doing, you need to give your reader a bit of information about who your characters are, how they got there, and why they're there. In other words, action scenes need backstory too. The key is to slip that information into the scene in a way that feels organic. When your scene has high action, sometimes that can be difficult—but it's not impossible.

Hold That thought—We've Got Some Backstory to Cover

Many writers give in to the temptation to tell readers everything they think they need to know up front. They figure the more readers know about a character, the more that character will resonate. But all that backstory just slows the action down. Tell the reader just enough for the scene to make sense. You can fill in the blanks later.

Before:
> I pulled my gun from its holster and disengaged the safety as I ran across the yard to the barn. Whoever was in there had left the door slightly open, and I could hear banging coming from inside. The prowler was in there right now.
> He wouldn't get away this time.
> I peeked through that narrow space. It was dark, but the scent of old furniture and stale hay reminded me of Reagan McAdams, the granddaughter of the woman who'd lived on this property since she'd inherited the house from her parents a couple of generations before. Reagan was my closest friend from the time we were in diapers. Our mothers were best friends, so we saw each other all the time. We went to elementary school together, then middle school and high school. When we were fifteen, I kissed her, and we were together until she left for college. After a misunderstanding

caused by our mutual friend Suzy, who'd told Reagan that she and I had kissed, Reagan left for college and never came back. I hadn't seen her since.

After I returned from my tour in Afghanistan, where I served as an MP, and then my years on the Boston Police Department, Reagan's grandmother, Dorothy McAdams, and I became close. Dorothy died two weeks ago, but before her death, she reported a few instances of prowlers. Peeking inside the barn, I thought the prowlers must be back. Dorothy had lived here alone, and Reagan was her only heir. And Reagan hadn't even come home for the funeral.

I stepped into the barn, my heart thumping. I had to be silent if I wanted to catch him. The barn was dark, the only light coming from a flashlight beam I saw bouncing around in the far corner. The space was filled with furniture and old junk. I stepped around a chest of drawers and nearly bumped into a long buffet table. It used to be in the dining room, but Reagan's mother had scratched it once when she'd been in one of her manic moods, before she'd kidnapped the baby and been sent to prison. Reagan still blamed herself for that, but what else could she do when her mother brought home a baby that wasn't hers? Reagan had only been eleven at the time. She couldn't have known her mother would die behind bars.

I wondered what the prowler was looking for. Dorothy had told me there was nothing valuable hidden on the property. Just all this old junk. The prowler hadn't stolen anything, as far as Dorothy could tell.

I rounded the corner and saw a woman standing behind a desk. I aimed my gun. "Put your hands where I can see them, and turn around slowly."

The main lights blinked on. Then she turned around.

It was Reagan.

Action at the Speed of Glaciers

That was supposed to be an action scene, but did you feel your heart pumping? Your adrenaline kicking in? Me neither. All that backstory slowed the action down.

No police officer is creeping into a dark barn in the middle of the night, gun at the ready, thinking about the historical details of an ex-girlfriend's life. He might think about that ex—it was her home, after all. But at that moment, he would be focused on two things—catching the prowlers and staying safe. Let's see what that would look like.

After:

> I inched my way inside the barn. I'd been in here enough over the years to know only a fool would rush through this place in the dark without a flashlight.
>
> Something banged. Nobody who had the nerve to break into Dorothy's place would get away with it on my watch. Dorothy had done too much for me over the years. The house would belong to Reagan now, not that she'd want it. She hadn't even made it home for the funeral. But for Dorothy, I'd take good care of this property.
>
> The sound of shuffling, muttering, and then a loud "Ouch." I felt my way past an old wardrobe and peeked around the last corner. One person. A slight form. A woman, from the voice. She was alone. I had her cornered.
>
> I lifted my pistol and pointed. "Police. Put your hands—"
>
> The person startled, and the overhead lights flickered on. I squinted and aimed my weapon. "Stop. Hands in the air."
>
> Her hands jolted away from what I thought was the barn's fuse box. The woman turned and zeroed in on me. Hands in the air, she tilted her head to the side. "Brady?"
>
> I blinked twice. The voice came straight out of the past. I hadn't seen that face in twelve years.
>
> "Are you going to shoot me," she said, "or can I put my hands down?"
>
> I pointed my pistol at the floor and engaged the safety without taking my eyes off of her.
>
> Reagan McAdams looked even better than she had in high school.

The second selection clues us in on just a few details about this police officer and the woman in the barn. They used to know each other, they went to high school together, and she's been gone a long time. We also know he cared about her grandmother, who has recently died, enough to enter a dark barn with his gun raised to catch a prowler. It's not all the information we had in the Before passage. It's just enough. We have an entire novel's worth of pages to fill in the rest of those blanks.

When you're writing your scenes and you need to add some backstory, don't try to fit in as much as you can. Instead, slide in as little as you can and still have the scene make sense. Try to make the backstory you do add organic—things this point of view character would think at this time and in this situation. Trust your readers to be patient and learn the rest in due time.

Editor:
C. S. Lakin

Too Little Backstory Can Be a Fatal Flaw

We've spent this chapter bringing to your attention the backstory dumps that writers often succumb to—the violations of good writing that cause passages to bog down or stop the present action of a scene. But too little backstory can also create problems. It's all about balance.

The best way to get the hang of sprinkling in backstory effectively is to grab your favorite novels (preferably cheap paperback editions from a used bookstore) and a yellow highlighter pen and mark up all the lines of backstory the author includes in her scenes. Great writers will have a nice little sprinkling throughout, with maybe an occasional larger passage (a paragraph or two) when it's needed and in just the right place (and usually not in the opening scenes).

Pay attention to these rules in particular as you study other works:

- *The backstory needs to be brought out in an organic or natural-seeming way through the POV character.* Instead of dumping in a few lines here or there at random from a list of key past details deemed necessary for the reader to know, an experienced author will slip in these points triggered by the present action or dialogue.

  For example, if I need the reader to know my character was injured in the war twenty years ago, I may show him reach up to a high shelf to grab something and get a stab of pain in his shoulder, which triggers his memory of how that bullet sliced through his muscle. As he rubs his shoulder, I'd have three or four lines, max, of him thinking of the past—in a way to get across all the info I need *at that moment*—then get right back into present action.

- *The information needs to be pertinent and important to the story.* You may have pages of information about each character's past (which is a very good thing before you start writing your novel). Of course, you aren't going to use all that backstory. In fact, you may use very little.

The purpose of developing rich, detailed pasts for all main characters is to make them real. But for the most part those details inform the character's mind-set, personality, attitudes, fears, dreams, and goals. The author needs to know all those little details, but the reader doesn't.

So when adept writers bring out bits of backstory, they make sure every bit counts, either to reveal something about the plot, build the world, or create empathy and understanding of the character—the last being extremely important.

- *Just enough information is given to provide what's needed in a particular scene, leaving much unexplained.* What can't be shown through a character's eyes during the action of a scene can be brought out in dialogue, direct thoughts, or narrative (which, in either first-person or third-person POV, is still essentially coming through a character's head).

Too Little May Just Be Too Little

But the answer to a good balance is definitely *not* "cut all the backstory and only include the bare minimum." Letting readers wonder, be curious for more information, is a good thing—to a point. Oftentimes, inexperienced novelists, in an attempt to leave out the backstory, do not include enough. Readers end up confused and frustrated if they don't get some backstory, especially in the first scene or two of a novel. This is not often discussed, but it's a big problem in first novels.

Some writers have had it so drilled into them that backstory is bad that they leave it out altogether. But lack of backstory is also a fatal flaw in fiction.

When you go through those ratty paperbacks and mark them up, pay particular attention to the amount and kind of backstory the authors introduce in the first three scenes. There may be later scenes in which a heavy bit of backstory is brought out—because the plot development at that moment requires it—but backstory in those opening scenes will likely be sparse. At the same time, *it will be there.*

Backstory is essential to opening scenes for a reason we'll identify right after the example passages.

Let's take a look at the first scene in which readers are introduced to my hero in my Western romance novel *Colorado Promise*. I'm going to give you two passages from one scene (separated by ellipses) to make my point. In the Before section, I took out all the bits of backstory. The After section shows them included. See what you notice.

Before:

"That's the Wilkersons' horse, ain't it?" Thomas asked. "How'd it get sick?"

Lucas looked back at the boys. "You recall how I told you about horses having sensitive stomachs?" The boys nodded. "Now, a horse that gets hot and thirsty will want to take a long drink, but if it drinks a lot of cold water, it can get colicky. Or even if it spends too much time in cold water, like wading across a deep stream. Now, some folks here, coming from the East, aren't aware how cold our Colorado rivers are. The water coming down Cache la Poudre is snowmelt—"

"And that's really cold," Thomas added with a twinkle in his eye showing he was pleased with his remark. . . .

"Well, boys, I need to be off. Things to tend to at the ranch." He tipped his hat and started walking toward the graveled path that led to the street.

Thomas tugged on Lucas's sleeve. "But when are you going to take us out to see the buffalo? You promised."

Lucas shook his head. "Now, Thomas—"

"Tex!"

"Now, Tex, I can't control when or where the buffalo roam. But if I catch a whiff of them anywhere around Greeley, I will come get you. So long as your folks say it's okay."

"They will! They will!" Thomas answered. "Hey, did you know that buffalo can jump six feet in the air? And they can run forty miles an hour!"

"Nope, didn't know that," Lucas said, amused at Thomas's beaming face. "All right. Now run along."

Lucas sighed and shook his head as the two boys ran out of the stables and down the road.

He hurried his pace over to the hitching rail outside the stables. His mustang opened its eyes, awaking from a lazy nap in the sun at his approach. He patted the gelding's neck, then tightened the cinch and looped the headstall over the horse's head.

After:

"That's the Wilkersons' horse, ain't it?" Thomas asked. "How'd it get sick?"

Lucas looked back at the boys. "You recall how I told you about horses having sensitive stomachs?" The boys nodded. "Now, a horse that gets hot and thirsty will want to take a long drink, but if it drinks a lot of cold water, it can get colicky. Or even if it spends too much time in cold water, like wading across a deep stream." He noticed the boys listening with their usual rapt attention, and a familiar pang of sadness rose up in his heart. *Push that thought away, Lucas Rawlings. It will do nothing but give you heartache.*

He cleared his throat, swallowing past the lump lodged there, and put on a serious face. "Now, some folks here, coming from the East, aren't aware how cold our Colorado rivers are. The water coming down Cache la Poudre is snowmelt—"

"And that's really cold," Thomas added with a twinkle in his eye showing he was pleased with his remark. . . .

"Well, boys, I need to be off. Things to tend to at the ranch." He tipped his hat and started walking toward the graveled path that led to the street.

Thomas tugged on Lucas's sleeve. "But when are you going to take us out to see the buffalo? You promised."

Lucas shook his head. "Now, Thomas—"

"Tex!"

"Now, Tex, I can't control when or where the buffalo roam. But if I catch a whiff of them anywhere around Greeley, I will come get you. So long as your folks say it's okay."

"They will! They will!" Thomas answered. "Hey, did you know that buffalo can jump six feet in the air? And they can run forty miles an hour!"

"Nope, didn't know that," Lucas said, amused at Thomas's beaming face. "All right. Now run along."

Lucas sighed and shook his head as the two boys ran out the stables and down the road. Ever since their father had taken them to Denver to see Bill Cody's Wild West Show, they wouldn't let up about wanting to see the buffalo. Well, it wouldn't be too hard. The plains were overrun with the beasts. And they were the cause of a lot of the Indian wars, Lucas reminded himself, thinking how not that long ago the Indians and white settlers had seemed to live peaceably together—until the disputes arose over the buffalo hunting grounds. Sarah had told him plenty of stories back when he'd come down from the mountains three years ago and began working for her. Her father had been a buffalo skin trader for two decades.

Three years. He'd pushed it out of his mind this morning when he woke, but the anniversary date of his arrival on the Front Range made him realize how quickly the time had passed. And how slowly the pain ebbed away. But he refused to indulge in the sadness that threatened to engulf him. He had to move forward, leave the past behind and find purpose and meaning in his life. Even though at times he wanted nothing more than to give up.

My son would have been three years old . . .

He steeled his resolve and pushed the image of Alice and the baby out of his mind. But every time he did so, a knife stabbed his heart. What hurt more than anything was how her face was fading more and more each day. All he had was the one daguerreotype they'd taken that weekend they'd gone down from Leadville to Denver. It had been Alice's idea to pose for a picture, as she wanted to frame it and put it on the mantle. Now it sat buried under a pile of clothes in his small cabin, where he lived alone and lonely.

Sarah had recently been hinting he should think about "getting out." Meaning, to start looking for a wife. But how could anyone ever replace Alice? No one could. He had loved her so much, and it had been his fault she'd died . . .

Stop thinking like that. You know it gets you nowhere. He'd hoped by now he'd have stopped blaming himself. He knew he'd done everything he could to save her and the baby. It was just a bad set of circumstances. The blizzard, her going into labor early, the doctor sick, not able to clear the snow and get any help. He'd tried everything. God knows he'd tried.

Lucas hurried his pace over to the hitching rail outside the stables. His mustang opened its eyes, awaking from a lazy nap in the sun at his approach. He patted the gelding's neck, then tightened the cinch and looped the headstall over the horse's head.

What did you notice about the second passage? All the backstory brought into that introductory scene is important to setting up just who Lucas Rawlings is and how his past pain has shaped him.

Get Readers to Care by Bringing in Backstory

The most critical thing a novelist needs to do when introducing a character is to hint at his core need, what past events have shaped and affected him, what his greatest fear is, and/or what his deepest desire is.

It's a writer's job to get readers to quickly care and empathize with the protagonist (and sometimes other main characters), and one of the best ways to do this is to bring in those bits of backstory in a natural way, right away, in the opening scene with that character (which may not be the first scene in your book).

So take some time to study the way great writers sprinkle in the backstory. Don't make the mistake of leaving it out altogether—that's just as much a fatal flaw of fiction writing as is too much. Then practice this technique in your own scenes until you get it down pat.

In Conclusion . . .

Backstory isn't evil. It's essential to any great story. The trick is to learn how to wield it proficiently. We've looked at ways to sprinkle in backstory organically, so the bits of information presented come across at appropriate moments.

Readers want mystery. They don't want to be told everything (and more), and especially not all at once, at the start of a story. A few hints of mood, a few lines of dialogue, or a brief direct thought can go a long way to revealing much about your plot and character motivation. Tension is built by curiosity—by readers wanting to know what is really going on, what might happen next. If you take all the mystery out of your scenes, you'll lose reader interest.

It's important that you, the writer, know everything about your characters and the world you put them in. But your reader doesn't need to know it all, even if you feel they should. Conversely, don't hold back too much of your character's background and motivation. You want readers to empathize and understand your characters' motivation. And a key to understanding anyone is to learn about their past. So work to find a balance with backstory. In doing so you'll conquer this fatal flaw.

Fatal Flaw #4 Checklist

Go through your scenes and look for these types of backstory violations:

- Having characters tell each other information they would already know, clearly written for the reader's benefit

- Explaining everything to the point that any mystery or curiosity about the story is destroyed

- Stopping to explain backstory in detail during a high-action moment, which the character would not naturally think about

- Telling how and why characters feel a certain way instead of showing it through dialogue and/or direct thought

- Detailing backstory in long passages instead of in short bits, such as two to three lines

- Putting backstory within backstory

- Not putting enough backstory in to help the reader understand and care about (or dislike) your character

- Not bringing backstory into your scene in an organic, natural way—triggered by something happening in the present action

- Inserting backstory that isn't pertinent or important to revealing key information about character or plot

Your Turn: Try to spot and fix all the instances of backstory violations you can find in this passage. An example of a revision is on the next page (no peeking!). There isn't one correct way to rewrite a passage, so your final version may be different from the revision provided. The key is to test yourself to see if you've nailed Fatal Flaw #4.

Allen picked up the lunch sack filled with food that Tracy had prepared for him, knowing that he would not be returning home anytime soon. He would have to disappoint Tracy again.

He pictured her long blond hair pulled back in a ponytail. It bounced as she performed her duties in his office twenty years ago. At the time, he was her supervisor. She had just received her degree in administration at age twenty-five. She had wanted to get a degree in education, but made a switch last minute. She decided teaching kids would eventually get tiresome, and it might be more fulfilling to become an administrator someday. Allen was glad she'd made that choice. He would never have met her otherwise.

He leaned back in his seat and pulled out a sandwich. "Things were so much simpler then, Ralph."

Ralph leaned back in his chair and answered, "Yeah, tell me about it."

"You were head of telecommunications for five years, when I started working at the company, and you used to dump your heavy workload on Sam. But that got you in trouble, so you hired me to help out. And now we both carry that load. But we have way more accounts now than we did then. When's the meeting?"

"About a half hour."

Allen closed his eyes as he chewed the stale bread and pictured Desiree, the rep he would visit next week. He had to admit, he was attracted to her. He felt guilty thinking of her, so he struggled with pushing thoughts of her out of his head. He knew she loved discussing innovative ways of solving software problems, so he would use this to his advantage, asking her to stay late after everyone had left the building. He would offer to take her out to coffee and ask her to tell him about her new products, just to hear her soothing voice. She could read a menu and he would be mesmerized. But then he thought about Tracy again, and he got nervous and anxious and tried to hide that fact from Ralph. But Ralph was busy typing on his laptop, not paying any attention to him. Ralph was like that. Once he dug into a project, you could drop a bomb on his head and he wouldn't notice.

He remembered back to one evening, when, to his surprise, Desiree had stepped into his office and shut the door behind her. She tossed her briefcase on his desk and just that action—that tinge of violence—had set his heart racing.

His heart now thumped like a fist in his chest. He wondered at that moment, *Will this be the week?* He could almost feel his hands tightening around her throat. It had been three months since he'd killed his last victim. She was nowhere near as pretty as Desiree.

About a year ago, Tracy became pregnant. They'd gotten married. They were both excited about the baby until Tracy got sick. The doctors told her to rest. Allen agreed with the physicians, but Tracy insisted she was fine. She always had to be busy doing something. And then, because she hadn't listened to the doctors, she lost the baby. Allen had been devastated, more than Tracy.

Tracy needed constant monitoring, but he wanted her home and out of that hospital, even if home was their tiny apartment. He hated leaving her side, but he had to work, or he would lose his job. He had already taken too many days off from work. He used all his vacation days, sick days, and family leave days. He got so upset and worried, that when that striking brunette came on him at the bar one night, he just couldn't resist. He supposed it was because of all his worry and agitation that things got out of hand. He hadn't meant to kill her, but once he let go of his hands around her neck and felt the exhilarating thrill of what he'd just done, he knew he was hooked.

"Looks like it's time," Ralph said, tapping the watch on his wrist.

"Oh," Allen said, wiping his mouth and stuffing the sandwich back into the sack. He hadn't even tasted the sandwich. He'd have to tell Tracy about the stale bread. Maybe she hadn't noticed. One time she made a sandwich for him and after he took a bite and cringed, he noticed the crusts were green with mold. He knew Tracy was just distracted, as always. She felt bad about the baby and wanted another one. But Allen didn't want to go through that again. Besides, a baby would mean more work hours and more time at home. And that would interfere with his new hobby.

Revision of the Previous Passage:

Allen picked up the lunch sack filled with food that Tracy had prepared for him, knowing that he would not be returning home anytime soon. He would have to disappoint Tracy again.

He looked at Ralph. "When's our meeting?"

Ralph opened his laptop on the table and started typing. "About a half hour. You ready?"

"Sure, sure," Allen said, but thoughts of Desiree distracted him. She was the SoftCom rep he'd met, and ever since that day she came into his office and threw her briefcase on his desk, he couldn't get his mind off her.

A twinge of guilt stabbed at him, and Tracy's face popped into his mind. Her cute nose and long ponytail. Her sad eyes. He let out a long breath and pulled out his sandwich. "Things were so much simpler then, Ralph. When we first started here."

Ralph leaned back in his chair and answered, "Yeah, tell me about it."

Allen closed his eyes as he chewed the stale bread and pictured Desiree. Again the guilt bubbled up, but the images came. And again the wheels spun in his head—how he would do it.

He would take her out for coffee, tell him about his software problems, late, after everyone had left the building. That would work. He took a few more bites of the tasteless sandwich, which made him think about Tracy again.

He looked down and noticed his hands trembling, then got busy stuffing the crusts into the sack, hoping Ralph hadn't noticed. But Ralph was busy typing on his laptop, not paying any attention to him.

His heart now thumped like a fist in his chest. *Will this be the week?* He could almost feel his hands tightening around her throat. It had been three months since the last time. Too long.

None of this would have happened if Tracy hadn't gotten sick and lost the baby. He wouldn't have been so upset that night and ended up in that bar, agreeing to leave with that brunette.

He supposed all his worry and agitation had just exploded. He hadn't meant to kill her, but once he let go of his hands around her neck and felt the exhilarating thrill of what he'd just done, he knew he was hooked.

"Looks like it's time," Ralph said, tapping the watch on his wrist.

"Oh," Allen said, wiping his mouth and crumpling the paper bag in his hand. He hadn't even tasted the sandwich.

"You're a lucky guy, you know?" Ralph said.

"Huh?" Allen frowned, confused. The way Ralph looked at him sent shivers up his neck. Did he know? How could he? He'd been careful—

Ralph nodded at the crushed bag in Allen's hand. "Tracy. She still fixes you a lunch every day. She's a gem, Allen. I wish I had a woman like her."

Allen gulped and got up from his chair. "Yeah," he said, relief washing through him. "Yeah, I'm a lucky guy."

Fatal Flaw # 5: POV Violations

Nailing proper use of POV (point of view) is a challenge for many fiction writers. It seems easy, right? Whoever has the point of view in a scene is telling and showing the events unfolding. You can only be in one head per scene, the current "rule" goes. Back in the day (some decades ago), head hopping wasn't tagged as a violation. But it is today.

However, it's not that easy. Pitfalls abound when it comes to POV, but with help, writers can spot them.

Seeing Life through a Toilet Paper Roll

One writing instructor handed out empty toilet paper rolls to his students in class and instructed them to look through the cardboard tube. He told them, "That's your character's POV—anything you can see through that tube." A clever way to get across the concept of POV.

But there is so much more to POV than what a character sees. Regardless of whether you are writing in first-person or third-person POV, deep or shallow or omniscient, the entire scene—including the narrative—falls under the purview of POV.

That means the character's voice, knowledge, background, and personality inform every word in a scene. Essentially, it's all in her head, spoken or not. And this fact is what often trips up writers. While keeping faithful to POV in action and direct thoughts, they fail to pay attention to the rest. And maybe some readers won't notice the slipups. But others will. And more importantly, the integrity of a scene breaks down when POV violations seep in.

So let's take a deep look at POV and how to spot those potential violations. You'll need more than a toilet paper roll!

Editor:
Rachel Starr Thomson

Whose Head? Point of View in Fiction

The commonly heard phrase "From my point of view" expresses something central to human existence: our whole experience of life is bounded by the fact that we are trapped in our own heads.

Life is all about point of view. Fiction, which emulates life, is too.

As mentioned in the intro to this chapter, how authors handle point of view has changed dramatically since the days of *Robinson Crusoe*. A hundred years ago the usual convention was to write omnisciently, from the point of view of an all-knowing, all-seeing narrator, who might be the author or possibly some kind of god.

Omniscient POV can be a joy to read, and some (few) authors still use it. But over time, the trend in fiction has been to limit point of view—to bring perspective down to one head at a time, the same way we experience it in our own lives. The usual rule is "one point-of-view character per scene." As a result, readers are immersed fully in the experience of the POV character(s), with all the greater opportunity for empathy, understanding, challenge, heartache, exhilaration, and growth that kind of close identification brings.

Head Hopping

One of the most central tenets of limited POV is that it limits us to one character at a time, and that means you can't write in the head of *more than one* character a time. Obvious, right? But it's surprisingly easy to get tripped up in practice. Jumping from one character to another within a scene is called "head hopping."

Head hopping is bad because it diffuses the most powerful thing about limited POV and the reason most authors switched over to using it in the first place: *staying in one person's head within a scene allows us to get far deeper into all the emotional and mental under-layers of a story and experience it all the way down, from the inside, the same way we experience real life.*

Let's take a look at this first POV violation.

Before:

Jackie tensed, staring at the frosted windowpane. Her heart raced as the footsteps outside stopped, where the man in the darkness stood thinking, weighing his next move.

The glass shattered.

She screamed. The temperature in the room dropped as cold air blew in and the stranger came in with it.

Peter straightened and brushed the glass from his coat and jeans with his free hand. With the other, he trained his gun on Jackie. This wouldn't be hard—all he had to do was take one hostage, and he could get home.

She stared into the barrel of the Springfield XD-S pistol. There were five, maybe six, feet between them. A bullet traveled at the speed of 2,500 feet per second. She could not possibly move fast enough to get away.

After:

Jackie tensed, staring at the frosted windowpane. Her heart raced as the footsteps outside stopped. Someone was out there. Something waiting in the dark . . .

This was so much like last time.

The glass shattered.

She screamed. The temperature in the room dropped as cold air blew in, and the stranger came in with it.

Tall, dressed in black, his eyes piercing, the man brushed the glass from his coat and jeans with his free hand. With the other, he trained his gun on Jackie.

She stared into the barrel of the handgun. There were five, maybe six, feet between them. She could not possibly move fast enough to get away.

Tears pricked her eyes. Would she ever be fast enough? Or was life going to end right here—too slow, too stupid to escape the doom she could always see coming?

In the Before example, we have POV violations from the first sentence:

- Jackie not only knows it's a man outside, she also knows what he's doing—thinking, weighing his next move.

106

- When he comes into the room, this "stranger" is suddenly identifiable by name—and she doesn't know his name.

- Not only that, Jackie knows way too much about guns and the laws of physics, not things her character would know, which makes the facts about them out of POV. (This is intrusion not of another character but of an omniscient narrator who knows more than the character does.)

The After passage keeps us inside Jackie's experience. It keeps us inside her fear, her perceptions, and her limited knowledge. That heightens the tension in the scene, as well as creates mystery the story can later unpack—who this stranger is, what he's doing here, and what events in Jackie's past inform the way she experiences this event in the present.

Your POV Character Can't Know Things She Doesn't Know

Keep in mind that limited POV means you can use perceived details to reveal your characters and their stories in intimate ways. If Jackie *knows* Peter, his name can be used—but her reaction to him will also be very different, and you can delve as deep as you want into the dynamics of their relationship and how she feels about seeing him here.

If for some reason she knows a lot about guns, the gun details can stay in—and her calculation of a bullet's speed would tell us a lot about her analytic personality. But this would necessitate setting up her expertise in this field earlier in the novel.

Your POV Character Can't Know What Others Are Thinking

In the Before example, the most egregious bit of head hopping is the line that tells us what Peter is thinking and what he's intending to do. There we've gone whole hog from one character's head into another's and then back again. This not only makes us dizzy, it also drains some of the tension from the scene and prevents us from closely identifying with one character.

When you self-edit, ask yourself whether your character knows the things you're conveying. Check to make sure that if you're in Jackie's head, and you're not relaying Peter's thoughts—or information that only an omniscient narrator is privy to.

Your POV Character *Does Know* What She's Thinking and Feeling

And *take advantage of the head you're in.* Let personality come through. Let your character's perception and history and hopes and fears color the way events are experienced. That's the reason for the lines added in the After paragraph. They fill in Jackie's feelings, her fears, and her past. The way she's experiencing this moment in the larger story of her life.

Ultimately, that's the power of fiction—to help us see stories in events. Someone else's story, and maybe even our own.

Editor:
Linda S. Clare

Smooth Switches: Multiple POV Tricks and Tips

As Rachel brought out, knowing whose skin we're in is key to keeping readers interested and pulling for a point-of-view character. She discussed the perils of head-hopping and used some terrific examples to set us straight. But unless you're writing in first person, there will be times when you'll want to change POV. So let's talk about how to make a smooth switch.

Who Will Tell the Story?

Many modern novels are told from more than one character's perspective. While the technique can add interest and richness to a story, you need to know why you're using it in order to use it well.

Your story can be told by multiple voices, but it's essential that one character be the one for whom the story matters most, who has the most to lose, or to whom the most important changes and challenges occur. No matter how many characters "take the microphone," writers still need to know whose story is being told.

Ask yourself, "Who has the most to lose?" and "Which character is most impacted by the events?" (The same questions can be asked when you determine the right POV character for a particular scene.)

Try writing a few scenes in different POVs if you aren't sure who should tell the story. Ideally, you'll come up with one main character at the center of the book. With that decided, you can then use multiple POV characters to tell the story at greater depth and make every scene matter more.

Get Her on Stage—Quickly

If you're writing a multiple-viewpoint novel, you already know to switch POVs at scene or chapter breaks. You can either leave a blank line (with a # in the middle) or start a new chapter to alert the reader that a new narrator is now telling the story.

109

One problem I see regularly is a writer will break the scene or chapter, following the rule, but then go into an omniscient description of the landscape or surroundings before letting the reader know whose head they're in. My mantra is this: *Readers should always know when, where, and who they are.* By putting us into the new POV character's head immediately after a break, readers don't have to worry about these three critical elements.

Go ahead and set up the scene, but do so in the head (and voice) of the narrating character. Don't wait until after a paragraph or two of description or exposition to let us know who we are. Little headings at the beginning of the scene (indicating that now we're Sarah, for instance) aren't always enough. Some readers will miss these tags completely.

Using Third-Person Omniscient POV

Point of view in fiction is usually limited to one character at a time. But as writers are urged to craft scenes in a cinematic way, how can they write scenes in which the main POV character is absent? This is a more advanced technique, but one that can be mastered.

For the bulk of scenes, you'll stick with *third-person limited*, meaning one character whose thoughts and emotions readers can know. It's similar to a camera following the character around. But what if important action occurs out of that character's experience, such as a murder or other important mystery? This is where *third-person omniscient* can be briefly blended into the story.

Readers would see the "other" character or characters, but not through the main POV character's eyes. Think of it kind of like a camera staying in place.

Using third-person omniscient effectively depends on some big ifs. Use it

- *if* readers aren't confused or lost or hesitant to identify whom they are following. Readers who get confused can quickly become nonreaders.

- *if* the writer has already established the third-person limited POV strongly. After readers are committed to following that character's journey, third-person omniscient may add rather than detract from the story. This means you

110

probably don't want to switch to third-person omniscient until your reader's a ways into the story and really cares what happens to the main POV character.

- *if* the switch from third-person limited to third-person omniscient is brief, contains crucial story information that cannot be deleted, and drives the story forward.

Confused? Let's take a look at a Before and an After example of third-person limited to third-person omniscient and back again.

Before:

The sun beat down on the mesas, rose-colored dust shimmering with heat. A dozen wild horses thundered through a dry *wadi*, alkali earth spraying from under their hooves, a high-pitched whinny here and there as the beasts rumbled across the desert. Hal and Owen were cousins in life but brothers in crime. Owen was ready to lasso any horses that tried to escape.

Hal stood at the narrow end of the wadi, where the horses would squeeze themselves into a corral. Hal used a cattle prod to spur the animals along. He said, "How much you think we'll get?"

Owen fingered his riata. "Plenty, I expect. The BLM pays top dollar, I hear."

Hal pulled his neckerchief over his mouth and nose. "What if them dumb injuns find out? Rumors are that Two Owl dude's onto us."

Owen spat. "You worry too much. Just do your job, and we'll both get rich."

Generations of Indians had witnessed these magnificent wild horses in their thousands. They'd tamed the horses and cared for them, only taking what was necessary. Now the horses fought for existence alongside parched sage and cacti, pushed ever back by the herds of grazing sheep. Soon the horses would be gone, and would the Indian follow? There was no chance for anyone in this ghostlike land.

Simon Two Owl stood at the entrance to his hogan, watching the last of the wild ponies disappear over the ridge.

111

His grandfather had told him of how white men would destroy the land, but that no one would listen. Simon wiped sweat from his brow and shook his head. These days the poachers stole the horses to sell in the marketplace.

Simon turned to Little Feather. "Another fence cut last night. Two more colts snatched from the mares."

His wife stopped weaving and looked to the horizon. "Who would do such a thing? Don't they know the wild horses are nearly gone?"

She was not even as tall as the upright loom where she worked, but that's what he loved about her. Her lips formed a thin hard line whenever she spoke of the beautiful horses she loved. He smiled at her passion for wild things.

After:

Simon Two Owl stood at the entrance to his hogan, watching the last of the wild ponies disappear over the ridge. Generations of Indians had witnessed these magnificent wild horses in their thousands. They'd tamed the horses and cared for them, only taking what was necessary. Now the horses fought for existence alongside parched sage and cacti, pushed ever back by the herds of grazing sheep.

Simon's grandfather had told him of how white men would destroy the land but that no one would listen. Simon wiped sweat from his brow and shook his head. These days the poachers stole the horses to sell in the marketplace.

Simon turned to Little Feather. "Another fence cut last night. Two more colts snatched from the mares."

His wife stopped weaving and looked to the horizon. "Who would do such a thing? Don't they know the wild horses are nearly gone?"

She was not even as tall as the upright loom where she worked, but that's what he loved about her. Her lips formed a thin hard line whenever she spoke of the beautiful horses she loved. He smiled at her passion for wild things. Soon the horses would be gone, and would the Indian follow? There was no chance for anyone in this ghostlike land.

#

Owen was ready to lasso any horses that tried to escape, and he worried that Hal wasn't up to the task. Hal and Owen were cousins in life but brothers in crime. Always the daydreamer, Hal stood at the narrow end of the *wadi*, where the horses would squeeze themselves into a corral. Hal used a cattle prod to spur the animals along. He was excited to catch his very first wild stallion.

He cupped his hand to his mouth and hollered at his cousin. "How much you think we'll get?"

Owen fingered his riata. "Plenty, I expect. The BLM pays top dollar, I hear."

Hal pulled his neckerchief over his mouth and nose. "What if them dumb injuns find out? Rumors are that Two Owl dude's onto us."

Owen spat. "You worry too much. Just do your job, and we'll both get rich."

In the Before passage, the setting is described but no one is narrating. We aren't sure if we're in Hal or Owen's skin or POV. Then we go deeper into Two Owl's POV and get the feeling he's the true narrator. The POV jumps around, and there is no scene break to indicate a switch in POV.

In the After passage, we begin in Two Owl's POV, and the reason for the scene becomes clear through his viewpoint. We see that the horses really matter to him and that poaching is a big problem. Owen is introduced as the second POV character, but only after we establish sympathy for Two Owl.

Getting the hang of this? There's more—read on.

Problematic POV—Characters' Names, Thoughts, and Senses

As Rachel said earlier, POV "rules" have changed quite a bit over time. In the past few years, I've worked with several beginning writers, and I can say without a doubt that POV is the fiction-writing tenet that I spend the most time explaining.

Writers tend to be voracious readers, with many having reading lists full of literary classics (who can blame us?). The classics authors wrote during an era when "omniscient" point of view was commonly used, so my writers follow suit and use an omniscient POV.

Gone Are the Days

But times change. Nowadays, omniscient POV is discouraged, and its use is often considered a telltale sign of amateur writing. Editors and publishers now prefer (and often insist) that each scene include the point of view of only one character.

Sticking to one character's POV encourages the reader to bond more strongly with that character, which is less likely if the reader is experiencing alternating multiple characters' points of view. In essence, POV's main purpose is now to get the reader to care deeply about the POV character and what's going to happen to him or her.

Let's take a look at two particular POV violations: using names in inappropriate ways and describing other characters' thoughts and senses.

Before:
I stared at my hands folded in my lap as I sat in the waiting room of Covington Hall's administrative offices with my parents, John and Marcia. Dark wood surrounded us—on the walls, the floors, and furniture—and the room reeked of old books. Marcia sat stiffly beside me, hoping our wait would be short.

The phone buzzed on the receptionist's desk, and Eleanor Doyle picked it up. "Yes ma'am," she said a few moments later, then replaced the receiver and looked over at us. "Mrs. Gray will see you now." She stood and walked around to a door, which she opened for us. "Right through there. It was a pleasure meeting you."

John smiled at her. "Thank you, Mrs. . . . ?" He stopped, realizing she'd never given us her name.

"Oh, of course. Doyle. Eleanor Doyle."

"Come in, come in." Susan Gray, a forty-something dress, appraised us from behind her desk. "Welcome. I'm Susan Gray, one of the school counselors."

We sat on upholstered chairs facing her, but I couldn't look away from my crossed feet, clad in black-sequined Converses despite Mother's protests.

"Thank you, Mrs. Gray." Marcia's overly friendly smile made me cringe. She leaned over John to tap my knee. "Cassandra, look at people when they're speaking to you."

But I didn't like making eye contact with people I didn't know. It seemed too much like a personal challenge. Even so, I met her gaze. "It's nice to meet you."

Susan smiled. "Welcome, Cassandra. We look forward to getting to know you."

I grinned back as politely as I could manage. Not that it mattered if I made a good first impression anyway. Little did any of us know, I'd only be at Covington Hall for a short time.

After:

I stared at my hands folded in my lap as Mother, Daddy, and I sat in the waiting room of Covington Hall's administrative offices. Dark wood surrounded us—on the walls, the floors, and furniture—and the room reeked of old books. While Mother wrinkled her nose just slightly, I breathed in what was one of my favorite smells.

The phone buzzed on the desk across the room, and the receptionist picked it up. "Yes ma'am," she said a few moments later, then replaced the receiver and looked over at us. "Mrs. Gray will see you now." She stood and walked around to a door, which she opened for us. "Right through there. It was a pleasure meeting you."

Daddy smiled at her. "Thank you, Mrs. . . . ?"

"Oh, of course. Doyle. Eleanor Doyle."

"Come in, come in." Mrs. Gray, a forty-something woman sporting chin-length blond hair and a navy-blue wrap dress, appraised us from behind her desk. "Welcome. I'm Susan Gray, one of the school counselors."

We sat on upholstered chairs facing her, but I couldn't look away from my crossed feet, clad in black-sequined Converses despite Mother's protests.

"Thank you, Mrs. Gray." Mother leaned over Daddy to tap my knee. "Cassandra, look at people when they're speaking to you."

I didn't like making eye contact with people I didn't know. It seemed too much like a personal challenge. Even so, I met her gaze. "It's nice to meet you."

Mrs. Gray smiled. "Welcome, Cassandra. We look forward to getting to know you." She glanced around the side of the desk. "And I just *love* those shoes."

I grinned back. Maybe I'd have an ally at Covington Hall after all.

So what POV violations did you see in the Before passage? Let's go through them:

- Cassie "introduces" her parents to the reader using their first names. Odd for a teenager. To stay in a character's POV, it's important to have the character refer to other people using the name he or she would naturally use for them. So a child or teenager (in most cases) would refer to parents as Mom and Dad, and teachers/adults as Mr. (Last name) or Mrs./Miss/Ms. (Last name). Conversely, adults would refer to children, and most likely to other adults, by first names, unless perhaps they were speaking with a superior, such as the boss of a large company. Bottom line for names: use the name your character would logically use when speaking to that person.

- She then states that her mother is hoping they'll have a short wait, so she's describing her mother's thoughts (something she can't know for certain).

116

- Cassie "introduces" the receptionist by her full name, even though it's soon clear that the receptionist never introduced herself to Cassie and her parents.

- She then continues referring to her mother as "Marcia" and also states that her mother's smile makes her cringe, although she can't see her mother's smile since she's looking at her own feet. And she "introduces" the guidance counselor by her full name instead of the name she'd use for her.

- Lastly, we have Cassie's ending declaration: "Little did any of us know, I'd only be at Covington Hall for a short time." While this kind of foreshadowing of something big to come was fairly common in stories written from an omniscient point of view, it's now considered a form of author intrusion (in this case, the author is injecting a statement about the future that Cassie can't know in this moment).

You may choose to write a novel in an omniscient POV, and there are certainly terrific novels that feature such a POV. But keep in mind that omniscient POV tends to distance the reader's involvement with the characters and leans toward excessive narrative summary. Most readers these days prefer getting deep into the characters, and the way to do that is to stick with one POV character per scene.

Staying in Character: The Convergence of POV and Voice

Jane Austen's books are all written in the same voice—hers. And many readers love them. But twenty-first century authors can't write the way Jane Austen did because modern readers have different expectations. Today's readers look for books written from deep point of view, and in deep point of view, not only are author voices different, character voices are too.

Did you ever watch the TV show *Frasier*? There's a scene where Frasier's new girlfriend invites him to go *antiquing* with her. Kelsey Grammer's character responds, "I'm not one of those people for whom *antique* is a verb." A funny line, but it tells us something— Frasier Crane's writers knew who he was. Do you know who your characters are?

Characters Putting On Airs

You create your character from scratch. Before you put pen to paper—or fingers to keyboard—your character is nothing but a figment of your imagination. You assign gender, age, physical characteristics, education, personality, fears, goals, etc.

You also have to give him a voice. And his voice has to make sense for his character. If it doesn't, you'll have a disconnect between the words and the character who's supposed to be thinking and speaking them. When a character thinks and says things in ways that character would never think or speak, it becomes a POV error.

Consider the speech patterns of a fifteen-year-old girl. Does she use the same vocabulary as her seventy-year-old grandfather? He sees fresh snowflakes and grunts. She sees them and thinks, "Little cotton balls from heaven." He's thinking about shoveling. She's thinking about a snow day. Take two forty-year-old New York City men. They could sound similar, perhaps. But what if one was a Wall Street mogul and the other an immigrant taxi driver? I guarantee they would have very different voices, and neither would describe snowflakes as little cotton balls from heaven.

In the example below, my character is a forty-something, barely literate convicted felon.

Before:

> The volunteer from the prison ministry had requested Clyde share his testimony with the other inmates taking part in their on-site program. They'd explained that they felt his story was quite implausible. He had conceded the point. What the Lord had done in his life was beyond anything he could ever have conjured up in his imagination. But like his mentor had said, nothing was impossible with God.
>
> In the prison library, he navigated to his favorite online dictionary, which had become his own personal fount of information. He'd learned more from the dictionary and other reference books than he had in all his years studying under his most learned teachers.
>
> He studied the various definitions until he found the one he assumed the ministry leaders had meant. *A public profession of a religious experience.* Indeed, he'd had quite a religious experience, and if his story could help others, then he'd be remiss if he didn't share it.

Did that scream uneducated, blue-collar convict from the rural Ozarks? Clyde doesn't know the meaning of the word *implausible*. The voice in that selection is so far off the mark, it's laughable. This is a serious POV error, because Clyde couldn't possible have thought the above paragraphs. He doesn't have the education or the vocabulary.

Let's read the same scene rewritten in Clyde's actual voice.

After:

> The ministry wanted him to share his story. It was unbelievable, they said. They was right. He wouldn't have believed it if anybody told him the story. But like his mentor always said, nothing is impossible with God.
>
> A testimony, they called it. Testimony was what people gave in court, after they done sworn to tell the truth, so Clyde was confused, 'cause he didn't have no court dates coming up.

119

He sat in front of the computer in the prison library, clicked to his favorite online dictionary, and typed in the word *testimony* with his index finger. He wished he could type like that fellow in charge of the library, but of course there weren't no computers where he went to school. No typewriters, neither. They was lucky they had books. He hated prison, but he loved looking at that dictionary. He learned more from it than he ever had in that little dump they called a school back in the woods.

Dictionary had all sorts of definitions for the word *testimony*. The rocks God inscribed the Ten Commandments on—that was a testimony. *A divine decree*, whatever that was. He skipped down a few and found the one he figured they meant. *A public profession of a religious experience.*

Is that what he'd had? A religious experience? To get to that, he was going to have to wade through a whole lot of swamp water, and did he really want to go there? He spent three years trying not to think of that terrible day. What good would it do to bring it up again?

But the ministry folks, they said it would help other guys to see there was a way out. And when he asked, his mentor had said, "You've discovered something beautiful, Clyde. Don't you want to share it?"

So he was gonna do it, gonna stand up in front of them inmates and tell them all the bad stuff he ever done. 'Cause if God could use somebody like him, well, weren't that somethin'?

I've used a bit of hyperbole in my examples. The first is way too highbrow, and the second might be a little exaggerated redneck-speak. But the principle remains. Your characters need to think and talk as they would think and talk in real life.

Find someone in the media or on a TV show who sounds like your character, then download an audio or video clip. When you're getting ready to write a scene from that character's point of view, listen to the clip first. That'll help you stay in character.

However you have to do it, be sure you stay in your character's head and voice when you're writing, because when you don't, you've slipped into a POV violation, and that can be a slippery slope.

Going Even Deeper into POV

One of the most important decisions a writer has to make is regarding what POV she will use for her story or novel—not what *character* to write in, necessarily, but whether to write in first or third person, and if the latter, what variant of third person to use.

Sometimes the reason writers fall into the POV pit is the wrong choice of POV in the first place. They may have chosen to write their novel in first person, but their plot and premise require showing a lot of action involving other characters at times when they are not with the protagonist. Genre may also influence this choice—for example, much YA today, especially dystopian, is in first person, present tense. This POV and tense provide the greatest intimacy with the main character, and that's what YA readers want.

Some stories are essentially one character's journey of deep insight and reaction to the world around her. Women's Fiction, for example, is often told in first-person POV, for a deeper sense of intimacy. Other stories need to show multiple characters' motivation, needs, and goals for the plot to work, and so usually the best option is multiple or shifting third-person POV. And yes—even despite all the warnings issued in this chapter thus far, you can use omniscient if you want to. It's your story, after all.

But more than genre should determine the choice of POV. The primary question is "Which POV choice will best tell this story?" Often that choice is third person.

Third-Person POV Pitfalls

Within third-person POV structure, choices need to be made for each scene. Linda already touched on this: Who is the best character to show, experience, process, and react to the events in a particular scene? If the wrong character is chosen, a writer may slip into POV violation. Why? Because the key points revealed in a scene may not be ones this character has access to. So the best way to avoid the POV pitfall is to *first think through the objective* and high point of your scene, then determine which character will be most impacted and impacting as the POV character.

Often that decision is a no-brainer. Your hero may need to find most of the clues in a murder mystery. And the killer in your story may be the only one witnessing the murder he commits. But other scenes may not be so obvious. Take the time to consider what various characters might bring to the situation if the scene was put in their POV. And note what things *they don't or can't know*, and how that might help or hinder your plot. Sometimes it's useful to have a character with limited knowledge witness events. That can provide for misunderstanding, misdirection, and plot complications. And those can be great developments for your story.

Variations on Omniscient POV

We've looked a bit at omniscient POV in this chapter. But let me take this a little deeper, because even here, there are possible variations.

Objective omniscient POV is a narrator without a "voice." Essentially the narrator is invisible; no personality comes through. Events are related as they happen, but the narrator doesn't share insights, reactions, or opinions. This POV is a silent camera, recording the scene.

Since an objective POV can only show actions and dialogue, what the characters feel can only be implied by their actions and speech. That means writers can't tell emotions: "She was angry (or sad or frustrated)." Take a look at this example:

Before:
Diane Chandler stood on the ledge of her eighth-floor office windowsill, afraid to look down at the heavy traffic below on Fifth Avenue. Her heart pounded as she inched out in her expensive Gucci high heels. Wind whipped at her, making her wobble. She clenched her hands tighter on the railing, her nails digging into the flesh of her palms.

But she ignored the slight pain in her hands, steeling herself for the greater pain she would soon feel when she tumbled to the street below.

She gulped, wishing there was some other way. But there wasn't. She had ruined everything. Her life was a disaster. Her

122

boss would fire her once he found out the truth. And John . . . that traitorous friend! Telling her he'd keep his mouth shut if she paid him off. She knew where that would lead—to a lifetime of blackmail.

Diane squeezed her eyes shut, trying to muster the courage to take that small, final step. She sucked in a breath, but then heard something behind her.

"Wait!"

Diane's heart sank to her feet. How had her boss found out so quickly? Traitor John must have run straight to Moore's office after watching her pull the money from the safe.

"Diane, please. We'll work this out. You don't have to do this."

Diane shook her head, not daring to turn to look at him. He didn't understand. Couldn't understand. He could sweet-talk her all he wanted. She'd still go to jail. And she'd never see her baby again. She couldn't bear the thought of her daughter seeing her behind bars. No, she couldn't bear it. Better for Angela to grow up never remembering her mother. *I'm sorry, sweetie. But Aunt Judy loves you. She'll take good care of you. Better than I ever could.*

Moore spoke again, and she heard the frantic urging in his voice. But it rolled over her like the wind. Tears spilled down her face. She loosened her grip on the railing and sucked in a breath.

Then stepped out into the welcoming sky.

I hope you can see this is truly deep third-person POV. I spent much time going into Diane's thoughts and feelings. And if that is my intent, I should stick with this POV. However, if I want to convey a detached objective take on this scene, wanting distance from emotion and a more insensitive camera feel, then the objective omniscient POV would be better.

Even if your novel is written in shifting third-person POV, it's common to see partial or even whole scenes in omniscient POV. Usually you'll see this at the start of a scene or in a novel's opening scene. The reason is the writer wants to keep distance, prevent the reader from seeing and knowing too much of what is going on. This can add mystery and grab the reader's interest right away, making her curious.

If I wanted that effect in my opening scene, for example, I would write it using the objective omniscient POV. Let's assume I'm the camera, and although positioned in the building across the way, I have a great telephoto lens and can get fairly close to the character. Take a look at the rewrite:

After:
A woman stood on the ledge of an eighth-floor office windowsill, her eyes closed and her hands gripping the wrought-iron railing that framed the window. She inched out on high heels. Wind whipped at her, and she wobbled.

Moments passed as the traffic below moved in fits and starts.

The woman stiffened.

"Wait!" A man's voice came from behind her, inside the office.

The woman kept her eyes closed, her head tipped back. She did not turn around.

"Diane, please. We'll work this out. You don't have to do this."

The woman shook her head.

The man spoke again. "Listen, just listen. Don't move. Just take my hand—"

She loosened her grip on the railing and sucked in a breath. Then stepped out into the air.

Of course the After passage is much shorter. Out went all the things Diane knows and thinks and feels. What's left is just what my camera records. The dialogue, the action. My camera doesn't know what brand of shoe she is wearing. Nor does it know it's the wind that's making her wobble (see the subtle difference in how I rewrote that phrase?). She could be wobbling because of her nerves. My camera doesn't know the characters' names or their relationships, so they can only be a man and a woman (until Moore says her name). That much I can tell from across the street. I decided I couldn't see her tears, but I could tell by her body language that she sucked in a breath.

Each passage has a very different style and creates a wholly different reader experience. So it's up to you, the writer, to decide what you want the reader to experience and to choose your POV accordingly.

Subjective Omniscient POV

Subjective omniscient POV features a narrator with a strong voice who can show the internal thoughts of the characters within the scene. An omniscient narrator can hop around into heads and go where he wants. And it can be very effective to have that narrator react to the thoughts and feelings of the other characters.

This is a fairly uncommon POV, but it can be done well and powerfully. Such a narrator has his or her own voice, and everything that is seen, felt, and experienced by the characters gets filtered through this narrator's mind and personality.

Sound confusing? It can be. That's one reason it's rarely used anymore. It is also a bit tricky to do well. Sure, it limits the POV violations—because when you're omniscient, you can know anything and everything. But that doesn't make it a great default POV for your story. Unless it serves your premise specifically to have an omniscient narrator with a unique storytelling voice, don't use this POV. It can be imposing and distracting to have this "main character" controlling the story. But again, when it's used well and to good purpose, it can be terrific.

Here's one way the above passage could convey a subjective omniscient POV:

> Diane Chandler stood on the ledge of an eighth-floor office windowsill, her eyes closed and her hands gripping the wrought-iron railing that framed the window. She inched out on high heels. Wind whipped at her, making her wobble.
>
> Her life was in shambles, and she knew it. But she saw no other option. Even though her death was going to destroy more lives, at this moment Diane Chandler only cared about one thing—ending her pain. She had extorted money from her company and gotten caught. It had been foolish for her to think her coworker John wouldn't have ratted to the boss. She'd always been kind of naïve that way. Quick to ignore the signs. Thinking everyone was honest and upstanding. Like she had been. Once upon a time. If only someone had pointed that out to her years ago.
>
> Moments passed as the traffic below moved in fits and starts.
>
> Diane stiffened.

"Wait!" A man's voice came from behind her, from inside the office. Moore, her boss.

Seeing Diane on the ledge came as a shock. But he had to stop her. He couldn't tell her how he really felt, how he didn't care about the money she took. He knew the trouble she was in, her dark and troubled past. Her criminal record she'd failed to disclose on her application. He didn't care about any of that. He loved her. He should have told her. That might have changed everything. Moore knew, though, it was too late. His heart ached.

Diane kept her eyes closed, her head tipped back. She did not turn around.

"Diane, please. We'll work this out. You don't have to do this."

Diane shook her head, not daring to turn to look at him. He didn't understand. Couldn't understand. He could sweet-talk her all he wanted. She'd still go to jail.

Sadly, leaving Angela with her sister, Judy, was not going to work, but Diane couldn't know that in this moment. In this moment, her sister was on the Interstate, talking on her cell phone to her boyfriend, and was about to get smashed by a truck veering across the divider due to the driver having a seizure. Angela was facing a life in the Child Welfare system. Would Diane have stepped off that ledge had she known? Who's to say?

Moore pleaded. "Listen, just listen. Don't move. Just take my hand—"

She loosened her grip on the railing and sucked in a breath. Then, to Moore's shock, she stepped out into the air.

Moore would suffer many years of nightmares of this moment—of reaching out and just missing her fingertips. But in time, he would get over her. Like all the others that had slipped through his hands . . .

There are lots of ways I could have written this, including more or less of Diane's subjective thoughts and feelings, adding more of Moore's, going into their past, explaining. Or I could have brought out the narrator's subjective voice more—more opinions, more personality. Again, it all depends on the premise and plot of your story.

Ask: Does my story need a narrator? If so, why and who? The narrator is palpably present in such a story, and so he needs to serve a purpose in being there. He may show up in the story at some point as a visible character, or he may stay invisible—heard, not seen.

Using omniscient POV can be a lot of fun, but watch out for those traps—especially the tendency to use excessive telling instead of showing.

Writers have the joy of being able to choose from a variety of POVs when telling a story. But with that choice comes the rules. We hope this in-depth look at Fatal Flaw #5 will prevent you from committing those heinous violations.

In Conclusion . . .

Mastering POV takes work. You need to pay close attention to who is experiencing a scene, and then be faithful to that character's purview. We've pointed out many subtle ways POV can be violated, along with some big offenders, such as head hopping.

Before you start to write a scene, think through your objective. Consider what key plot points you plan to reveal and how they would best be revealed and by whom. Then write your scene sticking faithfully to that character's POV.

If you're considering writing your novel in first person, be sure that's the best choice for your premise and plot. You'll be seriously limited in what you can show and tell when trapped in one character's head for an entire novel. If that's too limiting, you may choose to have your protagonist in first person and supplement with other scenes in third-person POV with other characters. Some novels have multiple first-person POV characters.

You may decide you want to try your hand at omniscient POV. It's your story, so you get to choose. But choose wisely, so you can tell the best story possible, and consider what's common for the genre you are writing in. Then follow the POV rules so you don't get ticketed for egregious violations!

Fatal Flaw #5 Checklist

Go through your scenes and look for these types of point-of-view violations:

- Head hopping

- Characters saying or thinking things they couldn't know

- Characters saying or thinking the names of characters they don't know (in narrative or speech)

- Showing a character knowing another's thoughts or intentions

- Not showing what a character knows at times when she would think about it

- Using omniscient POV for more than a few opening lines when in limited third-person POV

- Using a voice (narrative and/or spoken) for a character that isn't appropriate

- Having all characters sound the same in voice and/or narrative

- Choosing a poor POV for your story overall

- Using a POV character for a scene who doesn't really have a stake in what's happening

Your Turn: Try to spot and fix all the instances of point-of-view violations you can find in this passage. An example of a revision is on the next page (no peeking!). There isn't one correct way to rewrite a passage, so your final version may be different from the revision provided. The key is to test yourself to see if you've nailed Fatal Flaw #5.

The brawl took off in a roar of voices and flying fists. Everyone loved it. They were a large, obnoxious clan, and fighting came naturally to them. Although they couldn't have known it, every generation for hundreds of years back had looked just like this: violent, reckless, and happy about it. Kevin, a big, poetic soul in a kilt, swung his wooden sword and knocked over the man beside him, a stranger to him, named Clive, who was only visiting. Poor fellow—he would rather have been anywhere else at that moment!

Across the room, Lena frowned. Kevin was such a disappointment. This was just like when they were children, and she wanted him to fetch her flowers and he brought a weed instead. Now he was in that melee, trying from the bottom of his heart to impress her, but already aware that it would be futile.

He pulled himself up short as he caught sight of her expression, a skinny neck clenched in one massive fist and his wooden sword in the other. Lena was rejecting him again. When they were children she had secretly liked him, weeds and all, but she would never let him know that. His heart sank.

He dropped the owner of the neck and smashed his sword against the ground, shouting above the fray:

"Enough then!"

Revision of the Previous Passage:

With a roar, Kevin dove into the brawl. Fists flying, voices shouting, wooden swords thumping in gleeful cacophony. He relished every second, letting himself follow in the footsteps of his father, his brothers, his uncles and cousins.

Berserk.

He knocked over a stranger with his sword and laughed. And then, through the crushing mass of hysteria and shouts and cries of pain, as he let himself go like a cyclone across the face of water, whipping up whitecaps and crashing swells, Kevin spotted her watching.

She was frowning, like always. Like when they were children and she wanted him to fetch her flowers, and he brought a weed instead.

Like he was to know the difference between a flower and a weed. It was purple, wasn't it? It had petals, didn't it?

He'd thought the flower as beautiful as she, but she'd wrinkled her nose at his dirt and his weeds and rejected him.

Like she was doing now.

He pulled himself up short, a skinny neck clenched in one massive fist and his wooden sword in the other.

He dropped the owner of the neck and smashed his sword against the ground, shouting above the fray.

"Enough then!"

Fatal Flaw # 6: Telling instead of Showing

It's the golden rule of fiction: show, don't tell. To rephrase: immerse your readers in your story. Transport them. Involve them. Elicit emotion in them. Win their hearts.

But it's easier said than done. Show *too* much, and you'll bore even yourself. Show the wrong details, or show ineffectively, and you may find that your readers are mismanaged, indifferent, or asleep.

It's All about Balance

It turns out that "showing, not telling" is a matter of balance. Balance between scene and summary. Between thought, action, and emotion. Between narrative and dialogue (white space, anyone?). Between slowing down and cutting to the chase. Between adding vivid detail and deleting details that are irrelevant.

Effective showing means your readers don't just learn your story. They live it. They aren't just reading pages. They are immersed in a world, in a story, and in your characters' hearts.

The examples in this chapter will help you identify areas where you are "telling" and suggest ways to "show" with clarity and passion. They'll give you guidance as you rewrite and help you avoid the opposite error as well—showing when you really should just tell. We look at showing in the context of action, emotion, setting, and POV.

Mastery of showing makes us not just storytellers but storyshowers—able to bring readers into a full-fledged experience they will see, hear, feel, understand—and never forget.

Editor:
Rachel Starr Thomson

How Writers Can Be Storyshowers instead of Storytellers

Once upon a time, we were storytellers.
We wrote like Homer:

The men flew to arms; all the gates were opened, and the people thronged through them, horse and foot, with the tramp as of a great multitude.

Or whoever wrote *Beowulf*:

*Hwæt! wē Gār-Dena in geār-dagum
þēod-cyninga þrym gefrūnon . . .*

Okay, never mind about *Beowulf.* The point is, stories were *told,* and while that meant some especially poetic details were thrown in, for the most part stories got summarized, with huge swaths of action happening from a long-distance view, like in the *Iliad* above.

But then along came technology (hail, Gutenberg!) and changing literary conventions, and movie cameras, and somewhere along the way we became story*showers* instead.

We now have an axiom in fiction: "Show, don't tell." The rule works out in a number of ways, but in this section, I want to look at "show, don't tell" as it relates to *scene* vs. *summary.*

Essentially, we write in one of two ways: in real-time scenes—with specific action, dialogue, characters, a place, a time—and in summary. All novels use both to some degree, but the balance should always be *heavily on the side of scenes.* And even in summary, there are ways to *show* effectively.

In my novel *Taerith,* I needed to cover a period of time during which the hero is captive to a barbarian tribe. But I didn't want to just switch over to pure summary—I still wanted to write in a way readers could see and hear and feel. My goal was to open a window into the captivity and allow readers to feel as if they experienced it too, even though it's passed over relatively quickly in the book. So I wrote a scene instead of a summary, one that encapsulates multiple nights. You can judge how well I did.

Before:

The tribe kept Taerith captive for several weeks. They let him out of his bonds in the evening, so he would exercise to try to stay strong. The winter made it hard and painful, but he was glad to be alive.

After:

His arms were bound behind him most of the time, tightly pinioned with several thin cords. Each evening the barbarians cut loose the cords and watched him with a curiosity that was almost friendly, five or six standing guard at a time, while he swung his arms and rubbed them and set his teeth against the pain, allowing circulation to come back, making sure his arms stayed strong.

He dropped to the ground and pushed himself up a few times, even as his bare hands slipped and ached in the cold snow and the colder mud.

Aiden's lessons on survival thundered in the newly released blood flow through his arms and fingers. It hurt, but it was good. There were white and blue patches on his hands and feet where frostbite was setting in, and his face stung, but he was alive and still grateful for it.

The Before paragraph is pure summary—akin to the *Iliad* passage I quoted earlier. It shows us, from a distance and without any real detail, what happened. And it would be appropriate in some books, to help transition from one scene to the next.

The After paragraphs, on the other hand, show. What makes the difference?

- *First, detail*—especially *sensory* detail, the kind we can see, hear, taste, touch, or smell. Closely related is the need for time and place—so events don't just happen in white space but within a world that is present to the senses.

In the first paragraph, we read: "the tribe kept Taerith captive." In the second, we have thin cords, pinioned arms, and barbarians standing around to watch. He isn't just cold; he's got blue and white frostbite patches, and his bare hands ache. In the first paragraph, Taerith exercises to stay strong; in the second, he's slipping around in the snow and mud each cold evening. There's a strong sense of place and of time actually passing. We can see and feel the surroundings.

- *Second, action.* Specifics are the key here. He's not just "exercising"; he's doing push-ups, and blood thunders through his arms and fingers. Barbarians cut him loose and watch with friendly curiosity.

- Although there isn't any in this example, *dialogue* is a third key to *showing*—writing a scene rather than just summary. If you say, "He called out," you're summarizing. If you say, "Hey, you in the red coat!" we can *hear* what's being called out—specific words, and a tone and implied volume that go with them.

On occasion, a writer will send me a manuscript that is almost pure summary—one hundred pages of it or more. It's *told*, not shown. In a book like that, we do learn a story. But we don't enter it—we're never immersed. We never get into the skins of the characters or the world they inhabit.

Summary keeps readers at a distance. Showing invites them into an experience. We writers are storytellers, but if we want to immerse and engage our readers, we need to be more. We need to be story*showers*.

Where's the White Space?

There's a reason "show, don't tell" is one of the most common instructions given to fiction writers. Explanations tend to bore the reader, especially if the explanations are long and drawn out, and they make a story feel shallow and unbalanced. Sure, readers get what's going on in the book, but as Rachel pointed out, they don't *experience* it.

It's a Balancing Act

A great story has a balance of two components: dialogue and narrative. (Some editors add a third component—action—but I'm going to stick with dialogue and narrative right now because I think those two fiction components can individually provide "action.") Both of these elements play their own part in forging a reader's emotional connection with the characters and their story, and when one of them is missing, or when one seriously overshadows the other, the story often loses impact. The imbalance creates another form of "telling."

As a beginning writer, I loved my eleventh-grade English teacher. She gave excellent advice, and she presented it with such clarity that I never doubted her. *I need white space!* she once scrawled across the top of a short story I wrote.

I had no idea what white space was, so I asked her about it after class. "Look at your first page," she said. "How much white do you see? Very little, right? That's because you have five long paragraphs of black text. Try rewriting it, and I'll give you a hint—wherever you can, replace narrative with dialogue."

So I did, and lo and behold, two things happened: the white space appeared, and, more importantly, the story improved exponentially.

Let's take a look at a Before and After example of this.

Before:
> Mrs. Gray stood from her desk chair so she could take Mother, Daddy, and me on a tour of Covington Hall's grounds.

After she told me I'd be more comfortable after I was familiar with the school, we followed her out of the office into the waiting room, then down the hallway to the front doors. She opened the door, then took us outside and down the steps to the brick-cobbled walkway that wound through the campus's historic brick buildings and tall trees. There she informed us of the school's age and shared that many former students had gone on to accomplish great things. She said that she knew I would do the same.

She guided us toward the nearest building, which resembled a church with its white steeple and tall windows. Stopping at the pathway that led to it, she told us how it once had been Covington Hall's chapel but had been converted to a library ten years ago when the school built a new chapel. Daddy asked how often students attended chapel, and she answered that we were expected to attend on Sunday mornings as well as on Wednesday afternoons following lunch. Mother pointed out I'd still have a place for quiet time.

From there, we headed to the next building. Mrs. Gray explained that the large structure, which looked much newer than other buildings, contained the gymnasium, a pool, and locker rooms. I told her that I wasn't good at sports and asked if gym class was mandatory. She confirmed that gym class was required for all students and questioned if there were any sports that interested me. Completely serious, I told her that I'd be more than happy to participate in the Reading Olympics and would bring home a gold medal for Covington.

After:

Mrs. Gray stood from her desk chair. "Well, I'm sure you'd like to see Covington Hall's grounds, so why don't we take a tour? Students often feel more comfortable when they realize how easy the campus is to navigate."

Easy? I didn't need that. What I needed was familiar, and new schools only fell into that category . . . well, never. But seeing how I was now the only one sitting, I got to my feet.

She ushered us through the waiting room to the hallway, then walked us to the front doors and down the outside steps to the brick-cobbled walkway. "Covington Hall is celebrating its one-hundred-and-fiftieth year of educating exceptional students, and we're very proud of the accomplishments of our graduates." She smiled at me. "I have no doubt you'll go on to greatly impact the world as they have."

I pretended to be engrossed in the building's façade. "I hope so."

"This way." She led us toward what resembled a church with its white steeple and tall windows. Stopping where its path intersected the walkway, she turned back to us. "This was our chapel until ten years ago, when we built a new chapel. This is now the library."

Yay. "My favorite building, then."

Daddy placed his hand on my back. "How often do students attend chapel?"

"Twice a week, on Sunday mornings and Wednesdays after lunch. Its doors are open most of the time, though, and some students and faculty enjoy going in at other times as well."

Mother nodded at me. "See, Cassandra. You'll have a place when you want quiet time."

"Indeed." Mrs. Gray started toward the next building, a large, more modern-looking structure with darkened windows and a flat roof. "This is our sports building. It includes a gymnasium, indoor pool, and locker rooms."

So next to my favorite building would be my most dreaded building. "I'm not good at sports—at all," I said as we neared it. "Is gym class mandatory?"

She faced me, her brow pinched. "I never liked sports much either. But, yes, gym class is required for all students. Are there any sports that interest you?"

Well . . . maybe. "Do the Reading Olympics count? You let me do that in place of gym, and I guarantee I'll bring home a gold medal."

Granted, the Before passage probably seems extreme, but I've seen novels with similar use of narrative. So bear with me and consider the differences in the two passages. Even though both convey the same story bones, the After has so many improvements:

- It's much more interesting to read. After reading the Before example, I found it difficult to recount what had happened (and I wrote it!) because it was so dull. But with the After example, I knew exactly what was happening. The Before was "telling," using all narrative, while the After was "showing," using a balance of narrative and dialogue.

- In addition to clearly expressing the physical action in the scene, the After conveys essential emotive facets of the story: what's going on in Cassandra's head, insight into her sense of humor and who she is as a person, and insight into her parents' and Mrs. Gray's demeanors. In this case, the dialogue is what truly breathes life into the scene.

- Aesthetically, the After example is considerably more appealing—and this does matter. Take a look at both passages again. The Before example comprises large blocks of text, while the After has shorter paragraphs, which provide considerably more white space. Readers *like* white space. It helps them keep track of where they are when reading (and is less taxing on the eyes), it helps them process what's going on in the scene, and it makes the page more visually interesting and less daunting.

There's no doubt that narrative is necessary (and at times blocks of exposition are appropriate). But balancing dialogue with narrative provides a much more satisfying reader experience, both internally by "showing" the vital elements of the scene, and externally by providing a pleasant aesthetic.

Editor:
Robin Patchen

How Fiction Writers Can Effectively Show Emotions in Their Characters

If you've been writing for a while, no doubt you've heard it's not acceptable to name emotions. Don't tell us Mary is sad. Show us she's sad. It sounds good—yet emotion may be the most difficult thing to show in our novels.

Many writers lean on a clever trick to accomplish this—they describe a character's physical reactions to emotions. So characters are often crying, yelling, and slamming doors. Their stomachs are twisting, their hands are trembling, and their cheeks are burning. We hear exasperated breaths and soft sighs. Don't even get me started on heartbeats. Some characters' hearts are so erratic, I fear they're going into cardiac arrest.

So What's a Fluttering Heart to Do?

I'm poking fun, because I do it too. It's an easy way to show emotions. But I have a few problems with this old standby. First, these things are so overused, they've become cliché. (I know your stomach is twisting at the very thought.) Second, having a character clenching his fists might show us he's angry, but it doesn't show us the impetus for that anger. Is he feeling frustrated, slighted, or jealous?

All those—and a host of other primary emotions—can lead to anger. Finally—and to me, this is the most important—showing me your characters' physical responses provokes no emotional response from me. Your hero might clench his fists, but I promise, mine will remain perfectly relaxed. So you might have shown an emotion, but you haven't made your reader feel anything. And that, my friends, is the point of fiction—to elicit an emotional response.

Let's take a look at some effective and not-so-effective ways to show emotion.

Before:

Mary opened her eyes and looked at the clock. Her heart nearly leapt out of her chest. The baby had slept nearly eight hours. But little Jane never slept more than four hours at a time. Something must be wrong.

Not again. Her stomach rolled over when she remembered the last time a child of hers had slept too long.

Mary flipped the covers back and stood on weak knees, forcing herself to her feet despite the fear overwhelming her. She shoved her arms in her bathrobe, slipped into her warm slippers, and rushed for the door. Her hands were shaking so badly she could hardly turn the doorknob. Finally, she got the door open and ran down the hallway toward the nursery.

She threw open the door and lunged at the crib. She peered inside and saw the beautiful pink cheeks of her newborn daughter. She placed her trembling hand on Jane's back, felt the even breaths, and let out a long sigh. Tears of gratitude filled her eyes as she realized her baby was alive.

Our character is definitely feeling emotions. Do you think I can get the reader to experience a few of them? I'll give it a try.

After:

Mary opened her eyes and squinted in the sunshine streaming in through the open window. She stretched, feeling more relaxed than she had since . . .

She sat up and looked at the clock. It was after eight. Little Jane had slept through the night. For the first time.

Just like Billy.

Mary flipped the covers back and stood. She snatched her robe from the back of the chair and slipped it on. She wouldn't think about Billy. The doctor said it wouldn't happen again. The odds against it were astronomical.

Billy had been nearly six weeks old. Jane was almost two months. It was different this time. It had to be.

She shoved her feet into her fuzzy slippers, ticking off all the ways the situations were different. Billy had been sick. Jane had never even had a sniffle. Billy had been fussy. Jane was nearly the perfect baby, only crying when she was hungry or wet.

She must be both hungry and wet right now, but little Jane was silent.

Just like Billy.

No, God wouldn't do that to her again. She couldn't bury another child. She wouldn't.

She stepped toward her bedroom door, remembering Billy's skin, how gray and cold it had been. At first, she'd thought maybe someone was playing a mean trick on her. But then she'd lifted him. Seen his face. Those gray lips and lifeless eyes.

Maybe it would have been different if she hadn't been alone when she'd found his tiny body. Maybe if John had been there. But John had been gone on a business trip.

Mary turned and looked at the empty bed. Her side was a jumble of blankets. John's side was untouched. He was on a business trip. Again.

He'd rushed home that day two years earlier, assured her it wasn't her fault. How could she have known?

How indeed? How did a good mother sleep through her own child's death? How did she dream of beaches and butterflies while her son passed into eternity?

If Jane was dead, Mary would join her. Somehow. She couldn't live through this again.

She stepped into the hallway and took a first step. A good mother would run, but she could hardly force herself to walk. She inched her way down the hall.

She glanced at the stairs. What if she went to the kitchen, made some coffee? Never found out the truth?

She pushed the thought away and continued past the staircase, paused at the nursery door, and laid her hand on the cold metal doorknob. The clock ticked loudly in the hallway, like a steady heartbeat.

She stepped into the room and approached the crib. And there, sprawled on her back, lay the most beautiful sight she'd ever seen.

Jane's eyes opened at the sound of Mary's approach, and she smiled.

I hope you had at least a twinge of emotional reaction to that. I know I did. Please notice, there's not a single beating heart or trembling hand in that example. Her stomach doesn't clench, and her eyes don't fill with tears. Yet she felt a lot of emotions. Did you?

Counselors tell us that thoughts lead to emotions, and emotions lead to actions. As a writer, you can easily show your character's thoughts and actions. Readers are smart enough to deduce the emotions based on what the characters think and do. And if you write your scenes well, your readers will feel the emotions themselves and transfer their feelings to the characters. It's takes a little longer and requires a bit more thought, but what's the rush?

Slow Down Your Scene to Bring Out Emotion

When you have a very emotional scene, slow it down. Let us hear your character's every thought. Highlight a few details. Show the actions.

Why don't we write like this? For one thing, it takes a lot longer. My first example is fewer than two hundred words and took me about five minutes to write. The second is closer to five hundred and took nearly half an hour.

Writers have to dig a lot deeper to write selections like the second one. I had to remember what it was like to be a new mother, put myself in the shoes of a woman who'd already buried one child, and try to feel what she would feel. Not comfortable, let me tell you.

And you see a bit into my soul, don't you? What kind of mother would even consider going downstairs and making a pot of coffee? Yet as I put myself in that scene, I looked at the stairs, and I thought about it. Showing emotions means baring your soul.

Sure, it's fine to have some lines showing emotions by way of bodily response. But don't limit yourself to that technique. I hope this example helps you see ways you can elicit emotion in your reader through thoughts and actions.

Showing emotions can pull your reader in and get them to feel right along with your hero and heroine. And isn't that the goal?

The 12 Fatal Flaws of Fiction Writing

Editor:
C. S. Lakin

Showing through Your Characters' Senses

One of the reasons readers willingly immerse themselves in a story is to be transported. Whether it's to another planet, another era—past or future—or just into a character's daily life, readers want to be swept away from their world and into another—the world of the writer's imagination.

It's challenging for writers to know how much detail to put in scenes to effectively transport a reader. Too much can dump info, drag the pacing of the story, and bore or overwhelm. Conversely, too little detail can create confusion or fail to evoke a place enough to rivet the reader.

In addition to knowing how much detail to show, writers have to decide what kind of details to use. I often read scenes in the manuscripts I critique, for example, that have characters engaging in lots of gestures, such as rubbing a neck, bringing a hand to a cheek, pushing fingertips together, turning or moving toward something—all for no clear reason.

Showing body movement, gestures, and expressions can be an effective way to indicate a character's emotional state, but this needs thoughtful consideration so that the gesture or expression packs the punch desired.

We'll be taking an in-depth look at description deficiencies and excesses in Fatal Flaw #10, but since we're talking about showing instead of telling in this chapter, I'd like to speak to the importance of showing *setting*—and not just showing it in any old way. What is key to creating a powerful setting is to show it through your character's POV and in a way that feels significant.

Showing Significant Settings

When is setting significant to the reader? When it's significant to the character.

That's not to say every place you put your character has to evoke some strong emotion. A character who goes around gushing, crying, or jumping in excitement over every locale will appear to be missing some marbles.

But just as in real life, places affect us—some more than others. Each of us can think of numerous places in our past that bring a flood of emotionally charged memories. Showing setting colored by a character's emotions is not only effective and powerful, it also captures real life.

But let's talk about those *other* settings. The ones that aren't emotionally charged. The many places in which you set your characters to play out your scenes. Some of those places are merely backdrops, places your character traverses daily or on occasion. They're not important, right?

Let me just pose this possibility: even though you've thought a bit about the locales for your scenes, it may be that you aren't truly tapping into the power of setting. In the rest of this chapter, we'll look at ways to fix that.

Bring the Setting to Life

You may need to write a scene that shows a tense discussion between two characters. So you stick them in the coffee shop, since it doesn't matter where you put them. And, hey, a coffee shop makes sense. Everyone goes to them. It shows the characters doing ordinary things.

Sure, put your characters there (but please not twenty times in a novel). Or do something more interesting. I encourage writers to try to think up original, unique settings that bring a character's bigger world—town, city, region—alive. But even if a writer thinks up fresh and creative locales in which to place her characters, those settings might still come across in a boring, ineffectual way.

But it's the conversation that matters, the writer argues. That's what I want readers to pay attention to. The setting is just a backdrop.

In many scenes, that may be true. But if a writer wants to transport her reader, she'll think about bringing the setting to life via sensory details—which are observed by the POV character.

Let's take a look at a Before and After to see the difference between setting that is just "a backdrop" and setting brought to life by being shown through the character's senses.

Before:

On the fifth morning after the council meeting, about an hour after the late autumn sun had risen over the mountains to the east, the group of seven met at the base of the village. After the meeting, they had come to a consensus that they would travel together for as long as possible. Though some were still sick or wounded, they would delay no longer. They had been treated well and shown honor in Haknoor, but they were strangers and didn't fit into the routine of the closed community. Rhianna also realized that they were a burden to feed, for the resources of Haknoor were already stretched by the arrival of refugees. In any case, most of the companions were eager to return to their own homes, and to whatever family they still had. Even Grubb, who would not walk again for many weeks or months, was as eager as any to depart, though he did not speak much. "I feel trapped," he confided to Rhianna. "I do not want to be a burden on the journey, yet neither do I want to be a cause for delay."

Angor was the last to arrive. Rhianna had not seen him at all during those two days. She heard from the others that he had been in the mountains above the village helping mine the precious jewels the Haknoor people treasured.

As they loaded and double-checked their packs, they once again discussed their plans for travel. Three of their group were traveling north, returning to their own homes and villages. They had the shortest distances to go. The best route home for the other four also began in the same direction for the first few days, then veered more eastward along the trade road. The trade road passed the southern shore of Tule Lake and the easternmost of the Haknoor villages before beginning its descent alongside the Marsh River and down into Wildwood and the nearby desert. Eventually it led to Wildemere, the main city of Wildwood and the only large inland settlement in the region. Passing through Wildemere would take the travelers perhaps half a day out of their way farther west than they wanted to go, but they had agreed to the plan.

"We should float home on the Tule River," Valdon suggested, when he learned that it passed through the hills less than a day's journey away. Though his knee had recovered somewhat from the battle, he was still moving about with a

145

limp and did not feel fit for hard travel. "Save us all the walking through this blasted wilderness. The river would bring us almost to our doorstep."

Rhianna laughed, thinking Valdon was joking. When she realized the warrior had been serious, she explained why it was not a good idea. "That way cannot be traversed. The Tule Falls is but one of a dozen waterfalls in the canyon that would crush you, and even if we could build boats, there would be no way to portage them around the falls."

Valdon sulked but consented to the long walk home. He did not wish to wait until his knee was fully healed.

Rhianna hefted her pack and started along the wide rutted road, the other six following her lead.

So boring. There are a lot of details about the locale of this scene, geographically, and it seems to indicate Rhianna is the POV character, but her presence as the voice of this scene is minimal. Without connecting her to the setting, and without bringing out sensory detail, it's hard to get a feel for this place. And as a result, it's hard to care at all what these characters do—whether they head north or even fall to their deaths over Tule Falls.

So much more comes into play in a scene—the POV character's present needs, motivation, mind-set, physical and emotional condition, and goal or objective. But even if those things were brought out, if the setting were still just a backdrop, the scene would feel deficient.

Let's take a look at an After version, in which I attempt to show the setting through Rhianna's POV instead of tell about it in a dry, impersonal info dump.

After:

Rhianna stood on the jagged ridge of sharp lava rock and watched the late autumn sun peek above the horizon. The waft of warm air coming from the sun's rays did little to dispel the ache in her heart. Though the morning's amber glow seemed to set fire to the rolling hills that spread out before her, the chill in her bones sat heavy—a damp fog of pain full of the memories of her slain companions.

Already the others were gathering at the gates of the village. Even five days after the council meeting, where they'd come to a consensus that they would travel together for as long as possible, some were still sick or wounded, but they would delay no longer. Rhianna yearned for home.

The smoke from cook fires drifted to her, hinting of meats and sage and other savory herbs. How long had it been since she sat at her own hearth, stirring her gram's iron pot filled with lamb shanks and winter vegetables? She drew in a long breath, letting the aroma fill her mind with sweet memories as the crisp breeze tickled her ears and played with her hair. Even from where she stood, she could hear the children's happy banter, carefree laughter. What did they know of war? She hoped they would never have to face what she had. If only she could promise them they would stay safe. If only . . .

She and her remaining companions had been treated well and shown honor in Haknoor, but they were strangers and didn't fit into the routine of the closed community. Rhianna also realized that they were a burden to feed, for the resources of Haknoor were already stretched by the arrival of refugees. In any case, like her, most of her companions were eager to return to their own homes, and to whatever family they still had. Even Grubb, who would not walk again for many weeks or months, was as eager as any to depart, though he did not speak much. "I feel trapped," he had confided to Rhianna. "I do not want to be a burden on the journey, yet neither do I want to be a cause for delay."

She turned from the east and stepped carefully through the jumble of rock to join her friends. As they loaded and double-checked their packs, they once again discussed their plans for travel. Three of their group were traveling north, returning to their own homes and villages. They had the shortest distances to go. The best route home for Rhianna and the other three veered more eastward along the trade road.

"We should float home on the Tule River," Valdon had suggested, when he learned that it passed through the hills less than a day's journey away. Though his knee had recovered somewhat from the battle, he was still moving about with a limp and said he did not feel fit for hard travel. "Save us all the walking through this blasted wilderness. The river would bring us almost to our doorstep."

Rhianna laughed, thinking Valdon was joking. When she realized the warrior had been serious, she said, "That way cannot be traversed. The Tule Falls is but one of a dozen waterfalls in the canyon that would crush you, and even if we could build boats, there would be no way to portage them around the falls."

She pictured the thundering water, the roar that would fill her ears as she walked the river trail to and from her village to the distant lands. She loved the way the spray settled like mist on her arms, webbed her hair in water pearls, dispelled the heat of summer sun from her skin. How simple those pleasures were. How she had taken them for granted—the slow, peaceful days. She doubted they would ever return, with no end to this war in sight.

"We will just have to head north, on the trade road," she told him with finality.

Valdon sulked but consented to the long walk home. After all, he was the one who had urged the others to choose her as leader, now that Alden was no longer among them.

Rhianna wished she could make it easier for him—for them all. Walking would take weeks.

With a sigh, she hefted her pack and started along the wide rutted road, the other six following her lead.

Although I didn't add in all that much, those small bits of sound and smell and texture (water spray on her arms) make the setting more real to the r   eader. It doesn't take pages of description to bring out setting through the POV character's thoughts or feelings, but adds richness and interest to what might be a dry read, and it continues the ever-important task of connecting us deeply with that character.

If writers show setting—every setting, whether ordinary backdrop or essential locale—through the mind and heart of the POV character, they will avoid succumbing to this fatal flaw of fiction writing.

Editor:
Linda S. Clare

When It's Better to Tell than to Show

We've looked into ways to show instead of tell. But, consider this. In a fictional story, readers imagine that the characters have real lives, just as they themselves do. But the writer who tries to act out a character's every moment will find readers snoozing sooner rather than later. We're often told to "show, don't tell." But when is showing actually the *less* effective choice?

The Usual Routine

Most of the time, a character's routine is not crucial to the story. Habits such as hearing the alarm clock, shuffling into the kitchen for that first hot mug of coffee or tea, getting dressed, or other mundane activities may be commonplace for all of us but they rarely make for exciting prose. Readers will assume your character isn't running around naked or heading to work without brushing her teeth—unless being unclothed or unbrushed is important to the story.

And by important, I mean that readers won't understand the story or will be missing important information if any of these routines is not acted out. Most of the time, you can omit entirely any reference to the things we all do every day—from gargling to gassing up the SUV. If you must mention an action and it's *not* crucial, a simple summary will suffice (for example: she brushed her teeth.)

Remember, you are managing your reader. Whatever you dramatize will appear most important to your reader. If it's unimportant or assumed, use a quick summary—or better yet, leave it out.

Step by Step

As you manage readers, you'll be making decisions on not only which parts of the story you'll dramatize (that is, detail in scenes) but how you'll dramatize those parts.

I once had a writing student who wrote a scene about a man taking some girls to a Bob's Big Boy restaurant. Unfortunately, the scene was written in a blow-by-blow manner, as if we were actually living it. The waitress appeared to take their orders. Each of the three characters gave their individual orders, which the waitress dutifully wrote down. Then when the food arrived, readers suffered through each bite of the burgers, fries, and shakes. By the end of the scene, nothing much had happened (relevant to the story), but readers must surely have been starving and wanting to run for the nearest burger joint!

To grasp this concept, think about a good movie you've seen. Chances are, every moment was *not* acted out. Scenes in films and television often "cut away" to eliminate the mundane, the boring, or the irrelevant. As the late writing teacher and author Gary Provost taught: writers don't have to account for every moment in a story. If nothing happens, skip to the next important event.

Driving to the Story

Many first novels begin with a character traveling from one spot to another. This is usually not recommended. The character is usually alone or thinking about what she is plans to do; the writer usually inserts backstory; and the character rides, floats, or drives instead of being a part of solid action that plays out the story. (You may remember this as Fatal Flaw #2: Nothin' Happenin'.) In many novel drafts, these "driving to the story" episodes can be safely eliminated, and the spot where the action begins can move up to the opening.

Here is a fabricated Before passage of my historical novel *From Where the Sun Now Stands* to show you how writing about the mundane, writing too many blow-by-blow details, and driving to the story hobbles the reader and makes my job as a manager much more difficult.

Before:
    I was slow getting out of bed that April morning. I brushed my hair and poured water from the ewer into the basin. I splashed my face and wondered what the heathens would be like. I knew so little about the Nez Perce tribe and even less about the Idaho Territory. I pulled on my rose-madder-colored skirt and buttoned the bodice—those pearl

buttons were as tiny as hens' teeth. Would Sue or Kate McBeth even approve of my wardrobe?

I tried to be grateful for the coffee the riverboat's first mate offered. "Thanks," I said, curling my fingers around the tin mug. The sky's constant drizzle made for plenty of mud. I sipped the strong brew and asked a bearded deckhand, "How long until we reach the mission?"

He scratched his chin whiskers. "I reckon, miss, it's a three-hour trip at best. You might want to get some grub from the mess."

"What's on the menu?"

"Biscuits and gravy, I hear."

I took a last sip of the coffee, careful not to swallow the grounds. "I suppose I should eat something." I groaned, thinking of the lengthy boat ride. My back was already sore from the rough cot in the stateroom. But why was I in a rush to meet the two sisters from Ohio? I'd heard that at least one of them—the older, if I remembered correctly—was whip smart and most definitely in charge. But I'd also heard Sue McBeth was a humorless old maid, unlike her more jovial sister Kate. How two spinsters were able to tame the wild Indians was beyond me.

The deckhand grinned. "Just follow yer nose to the galley."

I shivered. Last night's gravy had been cold and lumpy. I only hoped this morning's breakfast was still hot.

And here's the actual passage from the novel . . .

After:

The heathens, as I called them then, pressed around the wagon that April day, their curious black eyes shiny despite the drizzle. Dogs and Indian children trotted beside many of the adults. The Nez Perce Indians did not frighten me in the least, but I doubt I could have climbed down without stepping on someone. I didn't have a chance to attempt it, for right then a petite, severe-looking woman dressed in black took charge.

The woman, who walked with a limp, waved her arms about, shooing the group away from where I sat in the wagon. "Stand back, all of you," she commanded, and most of the men and women obeyed, shrinking back like a gaggle of geese. One man, his black braids topped with a tall three-feathered hat, stood his ground, flanked by a large yellow dog. The woman's frown softened. "Desmond, see to it that Miss Clark's belongings are taken to her quarters."

Note that in the After version, the travel is eliminated, and the routine and the step-by-step of getting dressed are never mentioned. We get right into the story, and the character actually meets the other characters instead of hearing about them or planning to meet them.

In Conclusion . . .

Telling instead of showing is one of the most common flaws in manuscripts. It's tempting to explain and summarize a scene—because that's much easier than transforming it into a sensory-rich present-action enactment. But that's the difference between storytelling and storyshowing.

Don't rush through writing your scenes or try to pack in too many details or cover too much time. Focus on bringing each moment to life so your reader can be transported and experience the story through the characters' eyes and hearts. By doing so, you will win your readers' hearts.

Fatal Flaw #6 Checklist

**Go through your scenes and look for these indications of flawed"
telling" instead of showing:**

- Summarizing important moments instead of playing them out in real time

- Lack of sensory details to bring the scene alive: sights, smells, sounds, and textures, brought out through the POV character's senses

- Detailing insignificant actions that aren't important to the plot or don't reveal anything helpful about the characters (showing too much)

- Not starting in the middle of something happening in real time; instead, setting up a scene by explaining and filling in with information

- Showing characters moving (driving, walking, etc.) from one location to another when those actions are not useful to the story

- Including numerous paragraphs of narrative that summarize interaction between characters and lack actual dialogue, gestures, and/or body language

- Relying on excessive use of gestures, body language, and "body feelings" to show emotion instead of alternating or replacing with internal thoughts that imply the emotion

- Showing setting not presented through the POV character and void of sensory detail

Your Turn: Try to spot and fix all the instances of telling vs. showing that you can find in this passage. An example of a revision is on the next page (no peeking!). There isn't one correct way to rewrite a passage, so your final version may be different from the revision provided. The key is to test yourself to see if you've nailed Fatal Flaw #6.

Judy gasped for air as she watched another wave coming in. When the brine filled her mouth she started coughing. The water made her have to struggle with her wet clothes, and then she swam over the next wave and quickened her stroke. With a stretched-out hand, she touched an algae-covered boulder. A moment of relief escaped her as she lost her grip.

The next surge covered her. Darkness surrounded her. She knew it was useless to use her special powers of sight to figure out the direction. If she had wiped-out on a surfboard she would have floated up. The night changed perception so that she couldn't see which way was up. Unable to relax, her heart beat fast as she insisted on fighting the current. From the corner of her eye she saw a glimmer. Something serpentine snaked toward her. She didn't want to get friendly with it. In her mind she swam like an Olympian, but wet wool slowed her as she willed herself out of the breakwater. Pressure pushed against her boots moving her toward the jetty. She fumbled to grasp any crevice. The pressure under her boots continued until she steadied herself. She dared not rest as she clutched a boulder with both hands. Pulling herself out of the cold water, her feet hoisted up. *Splash!* A wheeze escaped her throat as she turned to spy what helped her out and made a splash. She put her weight on her hands, then pulled her legs under her. The sharp boulder cut into her knees as she coughed. She climbed up the side of the jetty. A prickly sensation went through her body warming her to the core. She was too young for a hot flash and it was too early for a fever. So it must have been her magical powers starting to appear.

On top of the jetty, she struggled to get out of the coat. The wet sleeves felt like suction cups of an octopus, holding onto a meal. She jumped, then pulled the collar with both hands, turning the coat inside out with the sleeves hanging from her wrists. Angrily, she yanked one sleeve off then the other, whipped the coat up only to hurl it on the ground as if to discipline it with a groan. It lay there in a heap with arms spread out. The octopus had lost the fight. Huffing with hands resting on her knees, she searched the estuary. Whatever it was had shimmery scales. And it appeared as big as a shark as it snaked toward her. She didn't see eyes just scales. Unable to see anything from land, she forcefully picked up the drenched coat then dragged it home by the sleeve.

The 12 Fatal Flaws of Fiction Writing

Revision of the Previous Passage:

Judy gasped for air as she watched another wave coming in. Brine filled her mouth. Salt burned her throat and she coughed. Struggling in her wet clothes, she swam over the next wave, then quickened her stroke. With an outstretched hand, she touched an algae-covered boulder. Her relief escaped her as she lost her grip.

Another surge drenched her. Darkness engulfed her. She couldn't see a thing in the black swirl of night and water. Her heart beat fast as she fought the current. Then, from the corner of her eye she saw a glimmer. Something serpentine snaked toward her. Her throat choked back a scream.

Swim! She pumped her arms, but wet wool slowed her. One hard-earned stroke after another, she cleared the breakwater. Surge pushed her toward the jetty as she flailed her arms, seeking to grasp anything within reach.

Finally she grabbed another boulder and steadied herself, sucking in short panicked breaths. Inch by inch, she crawled out of the cold water and hoisted her feet up onto the rock.

Splash! A wheeze escaped Judy's throat as she turned and glared into the darkness. Her pulse pounded in her ears as she strained to spot the shark fin she knew must be circling her. Nothing.

The sharp boulder cut into her knees as she coughed. As she climbed up the side of the jetty, a prickly sensation went through her body warming her to the core. Was this her power finally emerging? On top of the jetty, she struggled out of the coat. The wet sleeves felt like suction cups of an octopus. She yanked on the coat and turned it inside out with the sleeves hanging from her wrists. She huffed and swore under her breath, then whipped the coat off and hurled it onto the ground. It lay there in a heap. The octopus had lost the fight.

Breathing hard, with hands resting on her knees, she searched the estuary. Whatever had chased her had shimmery scales and seemed as big as a shark as it snaked toward her. She hadn't seen eyes, just scales.

She scanned the dark sea, but couldn't see anything but churning black water. Shaking, she picked up the drenched coat and dragged it home by the sleeve.

Fatal Flaw #7: Lack of Pacing and Tension

Strong pacing and tension are critical in a fictional story, but they're two of the hardest elements to understand and master. That's because there isn't one "right" way to pace a story, nor is there one definable factor that creates tension. And although pacing needs to vary depending on the purpose of a scene, the story still needs to be taut, keeping readers turning pages even in the "slow sections."

One thing readers will attest to, though: if a story's pacing drags for too long, they'll stop reading. And if they don't feel tension, they'll likely start falling asleep.

In this chapter, we'll tackle some of the secrets to improving these hard-to-master elements.

It may be surprising to you to learn that tension really has little to do with what action is being undertaken by the characters. In fact, tension can explode from scenes that have little to no action. In this chapter we'll look at the many facets of tension—in the story and in the reader—that writers need to pay attention to so as to avoid the pitfalls of this fatal flaw.

So how does pacing fit in? Pacing is the pulse rate of your story. At times you'll want a slow, thoughtful pace. Other times a racing one. And those elements that create tension impact the pacing of a story. No tension means a sluggish pace.

We've looked at how backstory and heavy information dumps cause a story to screech to a grinding halt. Overwriting also bogs down the pacing and kills tension. Telling instead of showing detaches readers' interest.

But there are many other offenders that contribute to poor tension and pacing, and we editors will cover them in this chapter. We hope that once you read through the passages presented, these nebulous elements will sharpen in your sights, and you'll be able to seek and destroy the culprits that are out to drag down your scenes.

157

The 12 Fatal Flaws of Fiction Writing

Tension and Pacing through Conflict and Emotional Narrative

Tension is what motivates your reader to keep turning the pages of the story. It grabs his attention and makes him want (or even better, *need*) to know what's going to happen next. Pacing is the rate at which a story is told, and it can vary from slow to fast depending on several factors—for example, the characters, the setting, or the scene's action (or lack of it). While pacing is always present and tension isn't necessarily, both require good storytelling if they're to work in a writer's favor.

Two great ways to keep up the tension and pacing of a story are the use of conflict and emotional narrative. Conflict, or a character's opposition with other characters or circumstances (or both), keeps a story interesting. Emotional narrative invokes readers' interest by allowing them to get to know a character and care about what happens to him. If a character's thoughts and motivations aren't shown, he seems more like a puppet just going through the motions.

Our Before and After passages illustrate how conflict and emotional narrative affect tension and pacing.

Before:
Mrs. Gray glanced back at Daddy and me as she led us across the narrow paved road toward another more modern one-story building. Like the gymnasium, this one also had plenty of large windows, and I could see students moving around inside.

"This is the cafeteria. Students are free to eat their meals here, which is more common on bad-weather days and school days, or in other areas on campus, such as outside or in the residence halls." She stopped at the glass double doors and opened one, then followed us inside.

The smell of food permeated the air, and I wrinkled my nose.

Mrs. Gray looked at me. "Is something wrong, Cassie?"

"Food smells and I just don't get along, especially if the food is cooked."

She cocked an eyebrow. "So you don't eat cooked food then?"

"Well . . . I prefer raw foods—fruit, vegetables, nuts."

Mother crossed her arms and sighed. "Perhaps there's no better time than now for you to resolve your food aversions, Cassandra."

"Maybe you're right."

Daddy placed his hand on my arm. "That would really work in your favor, honey."

"If you'd prefer to supply Cassie with much of her food, that's fine, and we have a good variety of fruits and vegetables available as well as yogurt and other uncooked foods." Mrs. Gray smiled at me. "Perhaps we can sit down and come up with a plan that will help you be more comfortable with that aspect."

"We'd appreciate that—to start anyway." Mother shifted her gaze to me. "But sooner or later, you're going to have to get over your food issues. Why not start now?"

Yeah. I could at least try.

After:

Mrs. Gray glanced back at Daddy and me as she led us across the narrow paved road toward another more modern one-story building. Like the gymnasium, this one also had plenty of large windows, and I could see students moving around inside.

"This is the cafeteria. Students are free to eat their meals here, which is more common on bad-weather days and school days, or in other areas on campus, such as outside or in the residence halls." She stopped at the glass double doors and opened one, then followed us inside.

The overbearing smell of food—ham and green beans among others—permeated the air. I raised my hand to my nose and held my breath.

Mrs. Gray cocked her head, her eyes widening. "Is something wrong, Cassie?"

Several students were seated at round tables throughout the large room while others stood in line getting their meals. I'd never understand how so many people could eat things without a second thought. "Food smells and I just don't get along, especially if the food is cooked."

She cocked an eyebrow. "So you don't eat cooked food then?"

"I eat raw foods—fruit, vegetables, nuts."

Mother crossed her arms and sighed. "Perhaps there's no better time than now for you to resolve your food aversions, Cassandra."

Seriously? Food odors killed my appetite, and I couldn't remember the last time I'd eaten something green. She expected me to not only get used to new surroundings, but also be around and ingest foods that almost made me gag? Not likely.

Daddy placed his hand on my arm. "I'm sure we can work out your meals with the administration, just like we did at your old school." He looked to Mrs. Gray. "Certainly you have other students with alternative eating habits?"

"Indeed we do," she said. "Most have allergies, but we're willing to work with families to ensure that students receive the nutrition they need. If you'd prefer to supply Cassie with much of her food, that's fine, and we have a good variety of fruits and vegetables available as well as yogurt and other uncooked foods." She smiled at me. "Perhaps we can sit down and come up with a plan that will help you be more comfortable with that aspect."

Oh, I loved this woman.

"We'd appreciate that—to start anyway." Mother shifted her gaze to me and lifted her chin. "But sooner or later, you're going to have to get over your food issues. Why not start now?"

Why not start now? Maybe because food odors were gross and, moreover, that anything the color of tomato hornworms and stink bugs shouldn't be anywhere near my mouth.

So what differences did you see in the two examples?

- *Conflict.* While there's *some* conflict in the Before passage, it's not enough to keep the scene interesting. Sure, Cassie reveals that she doesn't like certain types of foods, but when she's questioned it, she gives a rather neutral answer: she prefers certain foods. In the After passage, she tells it like it is: she flat-out doesn't eat certain foods.

  Her mother then states that she should work on resolving her food aversions. In the Before passage, Cassie simply agrees, while in the After passage, she gives the reader an explanation of why she can't.

  Her acquiescence in the Before passage continues at the end of the scene, when she again consents to her mother's suggestion. The lack of conflict significantly weakens the scene, making it boring and even questionably necessary to the story—hardly a page-turner and kind of blah-blah with pacing. The After passage, on the other hand, has plenty of tension, which increases the pacing.

- *Emotional narrative.* In the Before passage, Cassie describes very little of what's going on in her mind during the scene. She listens and answers, but we don't know the depths of what she's truly feeling.

  A reader's ability to identify with what a character is experiencing greatly influences whether that reader bonds with the character. The emotional aspect of Cassie's struggle with certain foods is something most people can relate to, at least to some extent (who doesn't have certain foods they don't like or can't stand?), and it also increases the tension and speeds up the pacing.

Pay attention to your use of conflict and emotional narrative. By working to infuse inner and outer conflict on every page, you'll find the tension and pacing of the story as a whole will ratchet up. And when your characters are experiencing and manifesting strong emotions, that will help evoke emotional responses in your readers. When readers care about what happens to your characters, they'll feel that tension, created by the need for a comfortable resolution to their problems.

Editor:
Linda S. Clare

Three Ways to Test Your Scenes

Pacing and tension play out in three major ways at the scene level. Your first draft may contain lots of unnecessary scenes. When you revise, test your draft against these three points when deciding if a scene should stay or be cut.

1. Five Easy Plot Points

Whether you're a plotter or a pantser, there will come a time when you need to be sure you maintain tension in the story by identifying the five most important scenes in the entire arc. These scenes contain what are known as plot points—moments that radically alter the course of the story.

If you aren't sure how to identify a plot point scene, you might try writing one summary sentence for each scene in your story. I counsel my students to use three-by-five cards or sticky notes, which enable you to string out the story in a timeline, then stand back to see the way it moves. When you see the forest instead of the trees, you get a better idea of the pacing and tension.

Identify the five pivotal scenes that cause your protagonist to either advance toward the goal, be thwarted in that movement, or take action to get around the obstacle. They are likely to be the inciting incident, the first time "things get worse," the "worse still" scene, a "no good awful even worse" situation, and of course the "do or die" scene called the climax.

There may be other tense scenes, but these five are the main ones that illustrate the struggle to gain the story's goal. Once you identify these points, ensure that every scene logically builds to them. This way, the story will always feel as though it's going somewhere—moving forward, not just meandering in circles.

2. But I Researched That!

As you write your summary sentence for each scene, you may notice that somehow you've written a scene or three that seems to march in place—a scene that doesn't add to the tension, releases too much tension, or has too many details or explanations.

Writers who love research often fall into this trap (I know I do!). You researched this really cool stuff, and you've got to get the info in there some way. If your character visits an exotic locale, or your setting is historical or maybe even futuristic, it's easy to allow the fun facts to quietly smother the tension. If your tension dies, your pacing goes on life support.

One of the most helpful tricks I know is to Resist the Urge to Explain, or RUE. You might know a lot of fascinating stuff, but to keep tension building, you'll need to be sure that *stuff* is a vital part of the character's struggle.

3. Skip the Boring Stuff

The late great writing teacher Gary Provost advised novelists that we don't have to account for every moment of our characters' lives. In terms of tension and pacing, this means only scenes that concern the story goal should be acted out. If nothing apropos to the story happens over a character's weekend, you don't write a scene that makes readers live through it.

Likewise, in scenes, you don't need to chronicle every motion. I think you can safely assume "She reached out her hand" if you write "She shook his hand." The same is true for nodding one's head (what else do you nod?), putting on one's hat on one's head (ditto), or turning to face someone (just write *he faced her*).

For our Before and After scenes, let's bring back Lady W and dear Lord Havemuch.

Before:

Lady W sat at her dressing table, combing her silken hair. Only a very few subjects in the Queen's realm received invitations to the royal Garden Party, the party which had been going on annually in England for 145 years since Queen Victoria's time. Queen Elizabeth *always* wore a matching dress, coat, hat and gloves. Lady W wondered if she should wear the peach-colored satin or the dowdy pin-tucked cotton. Lord Havemuch had spilled tea on her favorite gown, the ivory frock with matching hat and gloves, so Lady W was going to have Zelda the maid come in and alter both of her mistress's other choices. That Lord Havemuch! Lady W reached out a hand and picked up her silver-handled mirror. There was a bare spot on the mirror, a worn place that always reminded Lady W of her mother. That trip to the Grecian Isles last summer was the last excursion Mum had taken with her daughter. Lady W had snorted with laughter at how hard it had been to get her mother's corset laced up. Why, Lady W. had to use a well-placed boot to get the laces tightened. She chuckled. What a jolly holiday that had been and so much good food. She put the mirror back on the dressing table just as Zelda was coming in.

"Pardon me, missus," Zelda said, curtsying deeply. "Will you be taking your breakfast in your room again?"

Lady W sighed loudly and pointed with her forefinger. "Yes, Zelda, you may place my tray just over there." Right then and there she decided to send a cleaning bill to Lord Havemuch for the ivory gown. She really preferred it to the peach or the pin-tuck.

After:

Lady W sat at her dressing table, combing her silken hair. She wouldn't panic—not yet anyway. The royal Garden Party was tomorrow. But Lady W hadn't a thing to wear, thanks to Lord Havemuch, the boob who'd ruined her ivory ensemble. But Lady W only had two gowns left that she could still squeeze herself into—a very tight peach satin gown or a miserable pin-tucked cotton frock.

Zelda, the maid, knocked. "G'morning, missus." She curtsied, balancing a breakfast tray. "Will you be taking breakfast in your room again?"

Lady W sighed. "Yes, set it there. Oh Zelda, whatever will I do? The Garden Party is tomorrow and I've nothing to wear." She blinked back tears. "Since Lord Havemuch—that clumsy oaf—ruined my ivory frock, I've been tied up in knots." She stuffed an entire scone, bursting with orange zest, into her mouth. "You're my only hope. Can't you alter one of my other gowns?" Lady W tried to suck in her tummy but it was no use. A second scone would help her forget her bulk.

"Course I can, m'lady." Zelda picked up the silver-handled mirror and held it up for Lady W. "May I suggest I let out the peach satin? I can make it much, uh, roomier."

"Roomier?" Lady W. scowled at her reflection. The mirror's bald spot couldn't hide those puffy jowls, or how snug the peach gown had become. Why, she'd end up with a boot on her backside, just to get her corset laced. She whipped around, sending the mirror crashing to the floor. "Absolutely not the peach! I'd rather see Havemuch go bankrupt paying for my ivory ensemble!"

In the Before passage, I've allowed Lady W to think about her dress for the party without revealing the true conflict: that she's grown too pudgy to wear the peach gown. I inserted a couple of fascinating facts about the real monarchy to add "historical detail." There is no particular movement to the scene—Lady W is just living moment to moment. I explained the whole incident with Lord Havemuch and also included some backstory about Mum to explain the family tendency to be overweight. And I deliberately wrote "she reached out her hand" to show her picking up the mirror.

In the After passage, we understand that the tension is all about Lady W's inability to fit into her dress. I omit the facts about England's monarchy, which take us out of the story and do nothing to build tension. Instead, things build logically, from Lady W sheepishly thinking about what to wear all the way to her rage as Zelda the maid suggests the obvious. No history, backstory or explanations necessary.

So go through your scenes and find those sentences and phrases that show boring, mundane, or trivial actions, thoughts, or speech. Be sure you have all your scenes building to the important plot points with pertinent information that will engage your readers. Just cutting out those unnecessary bits will ramp up your tension and pacing overall.

Ramping It Up

You know how sometimes you can't put a book down—how the pages turn all by themselves as your heart rate speeds up and your eyes get wider and the book gets closer and closer to your nose?

Yeah, pacing does that. Books that use pacing *really* well—thriller novels and their kin—leave us feeling as if we need a nap. Or therapy.

No matter what genre you write in, it will serve you well to learn how to improve pacing. This happens on a macro level—in the way you build a plot and develop characters, as well as in the order of scenes and the way those scenes play out. And pacing can be fine-tuned on a sentence level, down in the verbs and the punctuation.

Our seventh fatal flaw is all about weak pacing and tension in fiction. I want to start right down in the details—in the words, rhythms, and techniques we can use to get our readers to the edges of their seats.

To illustrate these issues, I created a Before example from my book *Exile,* a supernatural thriller, and followed with the final After example.

Before:

"There's someone in the net," Chris said. He looked closer—yes, he was sure he could see someone in the fishing net they had cast over the side. He and Tyler were out fishing together, as they did most days. They had been best friends since childhood, and the ocean was their favorite place to go. They'd caught a lot of big fish over the years—but this was a human being.

"Tyler, haul the net in!" Chris commanded.

Dark clouds were gathering ahead. The boat was bobbing on the waves. Tyler heard Chris's command and looked incredulously over the side. Yes, he could see someone in there too—Chris was right. He could see an arm and maybe a shoe.

He wasn't sure because of the spray in his eyes. He pulled the
net up. Chris joined him, yelling, "Pull it up, Tyler! Pull it up!"

It was so windy that it made their job harder. Finally they
were able to get the net over the rail and dump it on the deck.
Fish and other things spilled out, along with the person they
had seen. It was a girl, a young woman, and they were pretty
sure she was still alive.

Tyler couldn't imagine where she had come from, but as he
thought about it, he realized she must have fallen from the
cliffs that were about half a mile away. It was noisy from the
wind, so he raised his voice and shouted, "Did you fall?"

She shook her head no. She hugged herself against the cold.
She gathered her feet under her. Her hair was long and dark,
and it clung to her face and neck.

"I jumped," she said.

He started to ask why she would do such a stupid thing, but
he looked at her eyes and realized she was suffering. Probably
in a lot of emotional pain. Why else would anyone do
something like that? She'd been trying to commit suicide.

After:

"There's someone in the net—Tyler, haul the net in!"

Dark clouds were billowing over a choppy sea, the boat
charging up and down the waves, when the words sank in.
Through the spray and the looming storm Tyler saw it too—an
arm, a flash of shoe. He braced himself and hauled, every
muscle in his arms and back straining, and Chris joined him,
still shouting:

"Pull!"

The wind gusted and pushed them like a thing alive.

They got the net over the rail and dumped it on the deck,
silver fish flapping, detritus, and the person—a girl—a woman,
young. Alive.

Tyler's eyes darted to the cliffs a mile off. "Did you fall?"
he screamed over the wind.

She shook her head, hugging herself, gathering her feet
beneath her. Long hair, water-dark, clung to her face and neck.

"I jumped," she said.

"Why the—" He started to swear, but one look at her hollow, tormented grey eyes shut his mouth.

Both examples tell the same story. But word choice and especially rhythm make them very different in impact.

Let's break down some of what's happening here. Chances are, you noticed the difference in terms of *speed*. The first rendition is slow. It actually makes an incredibly tense situation feel boring. The second rendition is rapid-fire; everything happens at once. Sight and sound and reaction all come at the reader quickly; we process like Tyler processes—in bits and pieces, through the senses, and with our hearts in our throats.

From a technical standpoint, what's making the difference?

Cerebral vs. Sensory

First, the Before passage is heavily cerebral.

It spends a lot of time in Tyler's thoughts, or telling us that he's "looking at" something. It breaks away from the opening declaration—"There's someone in the net"—to give ill-timed backstory on the characters. The momentum slows when the reader is told that Tyler and Chris are best friends who regularly fish together and love to be on the ocean. This is something that can become evident later; it shouldn't be brought up in a paragraph showing someone being unexpectedly dragged out of the sea in a fishing net. One major key to rhythm is making sure your content is appropriate to the scene.

In sharp contrast, *the After example is strongly sensory.* It throws impressions at us through sight, hearing, smell, and touch.

Beginning writers often make the mistake of spending too much time telling us what's in a character's emotions, rather than putting us in touch with the senses that are creating those emotions. Refer back to Robin's excellent section on "showing" emotion, in Fatal Flaw #6, for more on this.

In the first example, we get: "He looked at her eyes and realized she was suffering. Probably in a lot of emotional pain. Why else would anyone do something like that? She was trying to commit suicide."

In the second we see what he sees and are invited to react the same way.

There are times to camp out in a character's head. To process thoughts and feelings. But scenes in which you want to create a sense of urgency, fear, panic, or exhilaration are not those times.

The 12 Fatal Flaws of Fiction Writing

Flat vs. Vivid Language

Second, the language in the After paragraph is vivid and contributes to an overall atmosphere of tension. Compare the verbs in the two examples.

- In the first, the clouds gather and the boat bobs. In the second, the clouds billow and the boat charges. The whole effect is urgent, violent.

- In the first: "It was so windy it made their job harder." In the second: "The wind gusted and pushed them like a thing alive."

Every word should build the mood of the scene. Use active, strong, vivid verbs as well as specific nouns and adjectives that add to the atmosphere.

Feel the Rhythm

Third, pay attention to rhythm. Rhythm can be hard to define, but at its simplest level, it's created by sentence length. Short sentences or phrases are flashes of insight, hammering action, stark realization. They feel like a caught breath, or, in rapid succession, a pounding heart.

Look at the rhythm at the end of this description: "They got the net over the rail and dumped it on the deck, silver fish flapping, detritus, and the person—a girl—a woman, young. Alive."

On the other hand, long, complex sentences can create a feeling that everything is happening at once. They're helpful to overwhelm or to create a sense of things spinning out of control: "Dark clouds were billowing over a choppy sea, the boat charging up and down the waves, when the words sank in. Through the spray and the looming storm Tyler saw it too—an arm, a flash of shoe."

Personally, I like to alter them. The effect is conflict: the long and the short warring with each other. In a tense scene, that's exactly the result I want. The After paragraph uses this back-and-forth rhythm, with longer action sentences punctuated by short, tense pieces of dialogue.

Go for sentence wording and punctuation that mirror the flow of the action—staccato or flowing. Effective rhythm can also be created

169

through alliteration, assonance, and other tools from the poet's bag of tricks.

In conclusion: If you're writing scenes that feel as if they're slogging through molasses when you want them to move quickly, with a lot of tension and emotion, try this: scrap the scene as it stands now. Rewrite it entirely, focusing on the senses, using strong verbs, and playing with rhythm that mirrors the action. You might be amazed at what you can turn out.

The 12 Fatal Flaws of Fiction Writing

Editor:
Robin Patchen

Layering Tension in Happyland

There are a lot of ways to add tension to your novels. You can have characters who disagree, characters who want conflicting things, characters fighting battles against villains and weather and animals and, often, friends and siblings and parents.

But some segments of scenes have no inherent tension. You have to get your character into a position where the bad thing—whatever it is—can happen, but until the bad thing happens, everything seems fine. How do you bring tension into scenes like that?

By layering in subtle undertones of tension.

Take a look at these Before and After passages, and see if you notice the difference in tension:

Before:

> Reagan drove down Main Street and gaped at the town she'd grown up in. The hardware store had a fresh coat of yellow paint that matched the potted mums scattered near the front door. The dry cleaner's had been replaced with a jewelry repair shop. Next door, the lights in Lottie's Locks brightened the inside of the hair salon, and Reagan spied two women gabbing in the stylists' chairs.
>
> She slowed in front of McNeal's and admired the spiffy new sign over the diner. Used to be, McNeal's was nothing more than a greasy spoon by day and a local hangout by night, but everything about it looked new and clean. The lights inside spilled onto the sidewalk in cheerful yellow rectangles, and Reagan peered through the glass at the crowd inside.

Happy character in Happyland. If you write a lot of paragraphs like those, your readers' eyes will glaze over. They're reading your story for the tension. But what's an author to do?

If there's no inherent tension, you'll need to add some.

171

After:

> As she drove down Main Street, Reagan could picture the town as it used to be. It had changed in the years since she'd been here, but then so had she. The town, at least, had changed for the better.
>
> The hardware store had a new yellow paint job, though when she peered more closely, she could see where it was chipping away to reveal the decades-old brown beneath. Inside the beauty salon, frustrated women picked at each other's flaws like crows with roadkill.
>
> She slowed as she passed McNeal's. In contrast to the dark, dreary weather outside, the inside of the diner seemed a cheerful oasis. Customers filled the tables and booths, chatting and laughing, all privy to some inside joke Rae had never known.
>
> She turned her attention back to the road. The faster she could get this done and get out of town, the better.

Same situation, but by using the character's thoughts and focusing on different details, we've added a layer of tension. Instead of seeing the cheerful mums in front of the hardware store, Reagan notices the chipping paint. In the Before selection, old women gab. In the After passage, frustrated women picked at each other like scavengers. McNeal's is still cheerful, but I hope you picked up on the fact that Reagan doesn't feel cheered by it. No, she feels like an outsider and apparently always has.

By adding those little clues, we raise questions in the minds of our readers. Why does she figure the women are gossiping and "picking" at each other? What is it about her that makes her notice not the new paint, but the flaws? And how did she grow up in a town but never feel she belonged?

I don't answer those questions in this segment, and I don't want to. I don't even need the reader to realize she's asking them. I just want my reader to turn the pages. We're looking to create in the reader a compulsion to keep reading, and by inserting those small clues, I hope I've done that. Adding mystery adds tension, and creating an uncase or inner conflict in your character does too.

I also eliminated some details in the After passage. We don't need to know about the dry-cleaner-turned-jewelry-repair-shop. That adds nothing to the scene. Every detail must do double or triple duty. Through the details, we see the scene, we get a sense of how the character feels about what she sees, and we add some tension, so the reader wants to keep on reading.

Every scene needs tension, even a simple drive through town. By filtering every scene through your character's emotions and needs, you ramp up the inner conflict, and you'll have an easier time creating tension on each page. And strong tension equates to strong pacing.

4 Key Ways to Improve Tension and Pacing in Your Novel

Pacing and tension aren't always easy for writers to assess in their scenes. How can you tell if your scene is dragging and there is little tension? How do you know when to speed up or slow down pacing for best effect?

The four other editors have explored some great ways to ramp up tension and pacing in novel scenes. Here, let's bring it all together in four key points.

Don't Forget the Conflict . . .

1. Inner and outer conflict. First, overall, you want your pages full to the brim with conflict. Meaningful conflict. Showing a character fussing for a full page about her lousy manicure isn't all that meaningful.

Now, that situation could be the center of a really hilarious comedic moment, and if so, terrific. Humor—great humor—is so often overlooked, and it ramps up pacing and engages readers. But not all novels are full of funny moments.

Conflict is tension. Meaningful conflict creates strong tension. Hemingway said, "Don't mistake movement for action." Just because you have a lot of things happening, plot-wise, doesn't mean anything is really happening. You could have tons of exciting car chases and plane crashes and shoot-outs and the reader could be dozing off, nose planting into your book.

So be sure to provide meaningful inner and outer conflict everywhere you can. The more you can complicate your characters' lives, the more potential tension

. . . Or the Compelling Characters

2. Engaging characters. If I've said this once, I've said it a thousand times: if readers don't care about your characters, if they don't care what happens to them, they are not going to feel that tension. We want our readers tense. Worried, concerned, glued to the page, anxious to know what happens next. They aren't going to feel that tension unless you do the hard preliminary work of developing and then bringing to life from the get-go those empathetic, unique, compelling characters.

Yes, you may have a great plot. An exciting, riveting, original plot. But if your characters are boring, uninteresting, mundane, annoying, lacking passion or skills or interest in something, *anything*, all the great plot twists in the world won't create tension.

If you can take home one key bit of info about tension and pacing, make it this one.

Boring, Boring

3. Don't bog your scenes down with a lot of boring stuff. What's boring? Anything that isn't interesting. I shouldn't have to spell this out, right? When you read a novel and you find yourself drifting off, thinking about what to make for dinner, skimming over pages that you later realize you might have read but can't remember, you know you just hit a boring patch.

This can be applied to both macro and micro issues. You don't want boring scenes—characters sitting around in dull, uninteresting settings. That includes the overused scenes in Starbucks or restaurants, with characters just talking and drinking coffee.

Make Sure Every Scene Has a Point

As Linda pointed out, every scene needs to have a clear, important purpose in advancing and/or complicating your plot. Making it harder for your protagonist to reach her goal. Usually the reason so many scenes in first novels lack tension and pacing is there's nothing happening (and it's going nowhere). We explored all this when we looked at Fatal Flaw #2: Nothin' Happenin'.

Go through your WIP (work in progress). Ditch every scene in which nothing is happening. Or rework so that something significant is happening. I can't emphasize enough how important a scene outline is.

I can guarantee you: if you make sure every scene is important to your story and serves to advance the plot, you will find your pacing and tension ramping up.

Scrutinize Your Writing

On the micro level, look at your writing. Most of the novels I edit and critique are stuffed with extraneous words that drag. Pretend that each word has some intrinsic weight and that your readers are carrying your scenes up a steep hill. The heavier the sack of words they are carrying, the harder the struggle to make it to the peak.

If I were climbing that hill and the sack was too heavy, I'd stop, sit, and dump the contents out on the ground. Then I'd pick through all those words and toss out as many as I could that I really don't need. Often you can throw out four in exchange for one good word.

Make every word count. Your reader will climb to the climax of your story with a lighter, happier step.

Don't Write Like Everyone (or Anyone) Else

4) *Spend time developing a trademark writing style.* Maybe you hadn't considered that this could affect pacing and tension, but it does. This ties back in with "boring." If you use unimaginative words, phrases, descriptions, or narrative, you have to work all that much harder to keep your reader's interest. Your plot, characters, and other novel components will have to carry the entire weight of the tension and pacing.

In contrast, you can often have very little happening in the way of plot. And yes, I'll go so far as to say: you could even have that boring scene in that boring restaurant turn into a riveting, page-turning tense experience for your reader if your writing is spectacular. What I mean by that is your prose is beautiful; your word choice is fresh and surprising; your concepts and abstracts are imaginative and wholly new; your metaphors, motifs, symbolism, and similes are moving and thought-provoking.

No, it's not likely you are going to wow your reader with every line, but why not aim for every page to convey a firm grasp of the creative use of language? Make it your aim to be a fine wordsmith, to craft beautiful sentences the way a sculptor or painter handles marble or paint. The blank page is your canvas, and the words you write and subsequently publish showcase your talent and creativity to the world. Don't paint boring word pictures when you could do oh-so-much more than just slap words onto the page without careful thought.

Strong Pacing Does Not Mean Light Speed

One last comment about pacing. Having a strong pace throughout your book doesn't mean keeping everything moving at light speed. Don't confuse pacing with speed. You need to have slow, reflective moments with your characters. Novels are a cycle of action-reaction-action-reaction. Things happen, characters react, process, make decisions (act), then more things happen.

You might think that in those reflective moments the pace has slowed down. The car chase is over, and now the hero is sitting in a chair in the hospital looking at the woman he loves, who is in a coma. Sure, the action has slowed down. Remember Hemingway: movement doesn't mean action. Similarly, lack of movement doesn't mean lack of action. A poignant, heavy emotional scene in which there is little action can be as tense or even much tenser than that high-speed car chase. Why? Because you've gotten your readers emotionally invested in your characters. Make sense?

In Conclusion . . .

You probably didn't imagine there was so much to pacing and tension in fiction. We hope this chapter's exploration has helped you spot those flaws in your fiction (and in the novels and short stories you read) and remedy them so that your scenes sizzle with tension and your readers keep turning pages, eager to know what happens next.

Fatal Flaw #7 Checklist

Go through your scenes and look for these culprits that show a lack or pacing or tension:

- Events not unfolding quickly enough

- Lots of explaining, summarizing, or rehashing of information

- Inclusion of speech and narrative that aren't important to the scene

- Extraneous or weak words that make for boring and/or clunky reading

- Characters processing too long instead of reacting immediately to things that happen

- Lack of strong nouns and verbs

- Inclusion of mundane activities that clutter your scene

- Lack of conflict on every page (inner and/or outer)

- Lack of clear plot points and strong build to each of them

- Lack of high stakes for your characters

- Lack of a strong goal for your protagonist

Your Turn: Try to spot and fix all the areas that cause the tension and pacing to drag in this passage. An example of a revision is on the next page (no peeking!). There isn't one correct way to rewrite a passage, so your final version may be different from the revision provided. The key is to test yourself to see if you've nailed Fatal Flaw #7.

The stars spun and twirled and clogged up her vision. The back of her head pounded in a rhythm that hurt her head—*ba-boom, ba-boom*. Without any warning, her body grew weak and her limbs turned to Jell-O. She dropped fast and hard to the unlevel ground. As she spun full circle trying to regain her balance, a dark, blurry figure loomed above her, threatening her. He wore a black mask, revealing only his dark eyes and small mouth that smiled with vicious intent. Though the hunter's face was obscured, his smile gleamed in the dimly lit house that night. Amy could have sworn she heard him laugh aloud but wasn't sure. It was a bit higher pitched than she expected from someone his size.

Her attention moved to the man's right arm and down to his hand. He hunched over, wielding a baseball bat. She wondered how in the world he could have gotten into her house. Did he break in or find a way to pick the lock?

"What in the world do you think you're doing?" Amy's anger sped through her like a high-speed missile in a turbulent storm.

The invader pulled his arm back and raised it high above his head. The bat wobbled in the air, threatening. He paused, grinning.

Amy pushed up off the floor to face her attacker. The man twisted his body with precision and swung the bat down. Amy hesitated a beat too long, which was a big mistake. She chided herself for that tiny bit of delay, knowing it was due to her recent lack of exercise compounded with the cold she was trying to get over.

The bat smacked her cheekbone and it hurt like crazy. Amy careened backward in a burst of pain, grabbing her face. She slammed her back against the wall.

Teetering on the edge of the top stair, she lost her balance. She slid off the wall, then leapt high into the air. Her body tumbled and crashed on the steps of her staircase below. The fall seemed to take minutes, although it must have been only seconds. Before she could react, her head smashed onto the marble floor.

Her body twisted into a ball. Then everything at once faded to black and she went unconscious.

Revision of the Previous Passage:

Stars danced in Amy's vision. The back of her head pounded in time—*ba-boom, ba-boom.* Without warning, her body gave way. She dropped hard to the ground. As she spun around, trying to regain her balance, a blurry figure loomed above her. He wore a black mask, revealing only dark eyes and a small mouth set in a gleaming smile. Bill could have sworn she heard him laugh.

Her attention dropped to the invader's arm. He was hunched over, wielding a baseball bat.

Amy's anger exploded. "What do you think you're doing?"

The man raised the bat above his head. He paused, grinning.

Amy grunted and pushed up off the floor. The man swung the bat. Amy hesitated a beat too long.

The bat smacked her cheekbone. She careened backward in a burst of pain. Her back slammed against the wall, and she teetered on the edge of the top stair.

Her body tumbled and crashed down the staircase. With a loud *thwack*, her head smashed onto the marble floor.

Her body twisted in pain. Then all went black.

Fatal Flaw #8: Flawed Dialogue Construction

When are writing in complete sentences, being polite, and closely approximating real life in your fiction a bad thing?

When you're writing dialogue.

Dialogue is one of the most powerful, engaging, and memorable elements in fiction. Writing it well can mean the difference between a manuscript's being published and staying in a drawer collecting dust. But perhaps more than any other element of fiction, dialogue is dependent on good technique for it to really work—and it's the *only* element of fiction that is doomed if it too closely resembles reality.

Good dialogue never sounds realistic. It only fools us into thinking it does.

In this chapter, we editors examine the makeup of good dialogue. We look at the basic rules and tricks to achieve good rhythm, convincing tone, and engaging tension. We explore how to give your characters a unique voice and develop them *as* characters through the words they say (and don't say). We talk about adverbs and action beats, and when speech tags are a good idea and why.

Learning what your characters should talk about and what they shouldn't is not that easy. Most writers know that common conversations should be avoided ("How are you, Joan?" "Oh, I'm pretty good. How are you?" "Doing fine, doing fine."), but sometimes we need to show the ordinary in discourse. So we explore how to do that.

Good dialogue can heighten tension and create surprise. Through effective use of white space, THADs (Talking Heads Avoidance Devices), and beats, writers can avoid losing touch with the rest of the story while the characters are chatting—and even better, use these techniques to layer in meaning and metaphor.

The collected wisdom in this chapter can teach you how to revise your work so that your dialogue is stronger, giving your entire story new depth.

There is power in words. Nowhere is that more true than in dialogue—that fascinating place where the spoken word and the written word converge.

Let's explore!

Editor:
Rachel Starr Thomson

Dialogue Writing 101: Conversational Mechanics

Dialogue is special to me as a writer. Maybe it's because we live in a society saturated with sound. Maybe it's because I keep up a running conversation in my head at nearly all times of the day, discussing whatever I'm thinking about with invisible conversation partners (before you worry about me, I'm not any crazier than your average creative).

For whatever reason, when a story begins to come to me, I *hear* it first. To be more specific, I hear *dialogue* first. Before I picture settings, craft worlds, or brainstorm plots, I hear conversations.

The Technique of Conversation

Of all the discrete parts that make up fiction, dialogue might be the most dependent on good technique to make it really work. You can put fabulous dialogue in your characters' mouths, brilliant with personality, culture, and subtext—all topics my fellow editors will be discussing in this chapter—but if your technique is bad, the words will fall flat.

Thankfully, good dialogue technique is not hard to learn or to master. Much of it comes down to simple rules and tricks.

So let's dive into my Before and After passages, which are two versions of a scene from my novel *Renegade.*

Before:

Tyler was sitting out front, whittling a branch with a rusted knife he'd found in the desk inside the cabin.

"Reese, hey. Out for a hike?" he said welcomingly.

"Yeah, Tyler," she said.

"Can't be easy with your ankle," he nodded.

"It isn't easy, Tyler. But the ankle's healing. It's a workout, getting through the woods on crutches. I'm pretty tired after doing this for weeks, but I hope it will get better soon," she said.

"Y'know, Reese, if you want company, all you have to do is ask," Tyler said.

"Where's Jacob, Tyler?" she asked.

"Off somewhere like usual, Reese," Tyler shrugged.

Overhead, the sky was darkening. Reese looked up and frowned.

"Tyler, get inside," she said worriedly.

"What, Reese? What's going on?" he asked questioningly.

"Just get inside," she said commandingly.

"What's going on, Reese?" he asked persistently.

"Would you get inside, Tyler?" she shot back hotly.

"No, Reese. I'm going to help you," he insisted.

"Fine, Tyler. But whatever happens, it's not my fault," she said with annoyance.

Inwardly, she laughed with derision at her own words. Was *anything* not her fault?

The actual *dialogue* in the passage above isn't bad. But it has a few key (and common) problems:

- The characters constantly address each by name. (In real life, we almost never do this.)

- It uses a speech tag after every line of dialogue, which is wholly unnecessary and oftentimes annoying.

- The speech tags always come at the end of the dialogue, even when that's awkward.

- It uses adverbs to tell what the dialogue itself is perfectly capable of showing. (Yes, I had to stop myself from writing "he insisted insistently.")

- The passage doesn't use action or setting details, so all we have is talking heads in white space. This detaches readers from the scene. It's also lacking in any inner speech from the POV character, so there's an entire under-layer missing.

Here's the difference when the above problems are corrected:

After:

Tyler was sitting out front, whittling a branch with a rusted knife he'd found in the desk inside the cabin.

"Hey," he said, looking up as Reese approached. "Out for a hike?"

"Yeah."

"Can't be easy with your ankle."

Reese laid her crutches aside and lowered herself beside him, using the cabin wall to steady herself. "It isn't. But the ankle's healing."

Tyler nodded. "Good." Then he frowned. "You okay? You look like you just ran a marathon."

"It's a workout, getting through the woods on crutches."

"Okay." He seemed less than convinced. "Y'know, if you want company, all you have to do is ask."

She didn't say the answer that ran through her head. *No good. It's not safe to be with me right now. They're after me, and I'm not sure why. Better you don't get yourself killed being in my company.*

Tyler was a good kid with a good heart, but he had no battle training. She was happiest having him far away while she fought off the attacks.

"Where's Jacob?" she asked.

"Off somewhere. Like usual."

Overhead, the sky was darkening. Reese looked up and frowned. Clouds were blocking out the open spaces between the pines—clouds and something else.

"Tyler," she said, "get inside."

"What? What's going on?"

"Just get inside." She reached for the wall and got to her feet. Tyler jumped up but didn't make a move to go in. She turned to glare at him and saw a sword in his hand. He held it up.

"What's going on?" he asked.

"Would you get inside?"

"No. I'm going to help you."

"Fine," she said through gritted teeth. "But whatever happens, it's not my fault."

Was *anything* not her fault?

Breaking Down the Difference

As I said, much of good dialogue technique comes down to simple rules and tricks. I tackled five of them above.

1. Don't use direct address.

For some reason, it's really tempting to have characters address each other *by name* in dialogue. The more heated and intense the scene, the more writers will tend to do this. It's as if we think the dialogue sounds more serious if we keep repeating names: "Listen, *Rachel,* don't ever write dialogue like this, *Rachel,* do you get it, *Rachel?*"

In the Before passage, Reese and Tyler address each other by name a total of twelve times. *They do this despite the fact that there is no one else in the scene and they could not possibly be talking to anyone else.*

The rule for direct address is pretty simple: don't do it. You'll want to break that rule once in a while, of course; the trick for knowing when it will work is equally simple. Ask yourself whether you would address someone by name in this situation in real life. If you would, it will probably work in dialogue. If you wouldn't, cut it.

2. Use speech tags sparingly and alternate them with action beats.

Beginning writers often feel that they need to identify every speaker, every time, with a speech tag ("he said," "she replied," etc.). You don't. Structure will identify the speaker in most cases, especially when there are only two people in a conversation—just start a new paragraph when a new person speaks or acts.

Conversely, though, when you have three or more characters in a scene, you need to be sure it's clear who is speaking—every line.

You can also use action beats to identify the speaker. That's what I did in the following:

Reese laid her crutches aside and lowered herself beside him, using the cabin wall to steady herself. "It isn't. But the ankle's healing."

Using action beats (or narrative tags) this way has two more advantages: it defeats the "talking heads in white space" problem, and it can subtly advance the plot.

One more thing about speech tags: make sure that when you *do* use them, you primarily stick with "said." "Said" is invisible; most other tags aren't. And beware of speech tags that are not speech tags. Did you notice that in the Before passage, Tyler "nodded" and "shrugged" some of his dialog? Nodding and shrugging are not forms of speech, so they can't be used as dialogue tags. This is a surprisingly common gaffe.

3. Move your speech tags around.

The end of a line of dialogue can be the best place for a speech tag, but often it's better near the beginning, especially when the character has a lot to say. Tags should never come at the end of a long passage of dialogue. Remember this one from the Before passage?

> "It isn't easy, Tyler. But the ankle's healing. It's a workout, getting through the woods on crutches. I'm pretty tired after doing this for weeks, but I hope it will get better soon," she said.

That "she said" is like a flat note at the end of a bar of music. Also, with long paragraphs of speech, putting the speech tag at the end forces the reader to stop reading and skim to the end to figure out who's speaking, and that disrupts the flow and enjoyment of the read.

In the second passage, this whole paragraph is actually broken up into a more conversational flow, but it could be improved just by moving the speech tag. "It isn't easy," she said. "But the ankle's healing . . ."

4. Don't use adverbs.

I'm not an anti-adverb lobbyist, but I hope the Before passage demonstrates just how ridiculous they can be. Where dialogue technique is concerned, *let the words convey their own tone.* Don't use an adverb to *tell* what the words clearly *show*. If the words don't clearly show what they need to, consider rewriting them.

5. Use other elements.

Anytime dialogue takes off completely on its own, it creates a lot of white space full of sound—and only sound. We can't see; we can't feel; we don't know what the characters are thinking. We lose touch with the story world.

Intersperse dialogue with bits of action, description, and internal speech. Your readers will thank you for it—and more importantly, they'll stay immersed in the story.

Editor:
Linda S. Clare

How to Write Dialogue That Sounds like Real Speech

"Dialogue takes pains to appear totally realistic without being so at all, for it is very much the product of conscious craft."
—Oakley Hall

Writing realistic dialogue is a challenge for fiction writers. Seems like it shouldn't be. As Rachel mentioned, talking is a natural, daily activity in our lives, something we do without much forethought. So why is dialogue sometimes the hardest thing to construct well in our stories?

Seasoned writers know that in writing, dialogue sounds like real speech—but it isn't. While some writers have a natural ear for good dialogue, others must learn the principles of writing it. Here, let's look at three easy ways you can craft better dialogue.

Build Characters and Surprise

Ever hear feedback along the lines of "all the characters sound alike" or "they all sound like you"? One of the main ways readers imagine characters is through what the characters say and the way they say it.

When you create characters, pay attention to speech patterns, cadences, and slang use. A twelve-year-old doesn't speak like his grandpa. Men and women often have different and recognizable speech. Educated vs. uneducated, modern vs. historical, foreign vs. domestic—these particulars and more will influence how your character speaks.

As you craft lines of dialogue, you are also building character. If the character is dishonest, the dialogue might take on words of avoidance or embellishment. If your character is naïve, she'll speak differently than someone more experienced. What your character says and doesn't say will present readers with clues to personality, fears, desires, and motives.

189

Dialogue also helps build surprise. If readers aren't sure what your character will say next, tension increases. Rising tension is almost always critical to maintain readers' interest. If a character asks another a question, for instance, instead of having the other character simply answer yes or no, you can build tension by crafting an unexpected answer.

A classic example might be, "Who's there?" Instead of a simple, "It's me," your question might be followed by "Who wants to know?" The second response gives the character saying it an attitude, which is more interesting than the obvious answer. By crafting surprising dialogue, you build tension and character depth at the same time.

The Rule of Three for Dialogue

About ten years ago in my college writing classes, I started to see a lot of speeches, talking heads, and the like in student work. Three is always a good number, so I introduced The Rule of Three for dialogue.

When you are learning to write dialogue, this "rule" may help keep the speeches and talking heads to a minimum. This Rule of Three states that whenever a character speaks three lines (sentences) of dialogue, you then switch to 1) the other speaker, 2) a beat of action, emotion, or inner thought or 3) a brief narrative. Following this model, after every three exchanges of words (e.g.: Are so. Am not. Are so.), switch to action, inner thought/emotion, or narrative, which includes description or flashback.

Use Beats or Tags?

Rachel discussed the use of *said* and how it's "invisible." Savvy writers soon learn to avoid creative tags (he expostulated, he exclaimed, she observed) and "ly" emotions that tell instead of show ("she said anxiously"). But how can you get a more complete picture of *how* a line is spoken? Here too, beats, inner thoughts, and emotions placed next to the dialogue can be helpful.

Remember though: dialogue relies heavily on rhythm and pace. If you use the same placement and length of a beat again and again, it can turn singsong. It's up to you to choose an attribution or a beat, but variety tends to help any work of fiction. Just be sure to avoid those clunky tags that are formal or end in "ly."

Now let's look at Before and After examples:

190

Before:

Hannah pedaled faster. She had to reach Bob before the storm hit. As she neared the shop where her neighbor, Bob McGregor, tinkered on old cars, she braked and let her bike fall to the dirt. "Mr. McGregor, we must make haste! You will be engulfed by the rising floodwaters! Please, please, Bob, answer the door. I beg of you, we must be on our way. Now!" she exclaimed as she pounded on the shop's door.

"Get your automobile so that we may flee! Have you not heard of the impending flood? Why do you not heed the warnings?" Hannah exclaimed in urgency. "Mother informed me that the storm is almost upon us! It is only a matter of minutes before your shop will be completely underwater. The meteorologist forecast that the river will crest this hour."

Bob McGregor opened the door and shuffled out into bright sunshine. "All right, all right, I am answering the door. Who's out there? What is all this cacophony?" Bob said grouchily. "The meteorologist is the only occupation I am aware of where one gets compensated for being incorrect," he lectured. "Predicting the weather is not a science," he continued. "And I do not believe anyone can successfully predict where the winds and currents will rise up. Why, back in my day, we did not require a professional to tell us what my grandmother's rheumatic knees predicted. And she was ever correct," Bob orated.

Hannah pulled Bob's arm. "This time you are incorrect," she said breathlessly. "Mother stated that we need to travel upon the river road."

"Traverse the river road?" Bob asked in confusion and alarm. "How could it be? My knees are perfectly fine. Besides, I am in the midst of remodeling my workbench."

"It is expedient," she blurted out.

"You are an impertinent young girl," came Bob's dry answer.

"I only desire to remain a living, breathing female." Hannah's voice was strained.

After:

Hannah pedaled faster. She had to reach Bob before the storm hit. As she neared the shop where her neighbor, Bob McGregor, tinkered on old cars, she braked and let her bike fall to the dirt.

"Mr. McGregor, hurry!" She pounded on the shop's door. "Pull the car out!" Hannah's heart pounded in her ears. "Ma says the storm's coming!" She closed her eyes. Would old Bob put up a fight?

Bob McGregor opened the door and shuffled out into bright sunshine. "What's all this racket?" His scowl made Hannah's heart sink. "Dang weatherman's the only job I know where you get paid for being wrong." He waggled a finger under Hannah's nose.

Hannah pulled Bob's arm. "This time it's for real," she said. "Mother told me we need to take the river road."

Bob's eyes widened. "The river road?"

"It's fastest." She didn't add that Bob was possibly the slowest old dude on the planet.

Bob crossed his arms and didn't budge. "You're awful bossy for a young girl."

Hannah pulled him along. She couldn't waste another minute arguing with the old coot. "I just want to be a living girl," she said.

In the first example, Hannah's dialogue sounds like the minutes from a city council meeting. No young person would say these types of things. Even the adult, Bob, takes on a very formal tone. This lessens each character's distinction for readers.

There's no surprise here either. Both have the same tone—boring. Both characters ignore The Rule of Three, and there's a mix of ridiculous attributions as well as telling "ly" words.

In the After rewrite, each character says more age-appropriate things. I eliminated the silly attributions, substituting beats of action and/or inner thoughts or emotion. I used the Rule of Three to whittle deadwood from the conversation, thereby speeding up the pace.

Use these pointers to help you create dialogue that sounds like real speech but isn't. You'll find your dialogue will greatly improve.

Editor:
Christy Distler

Unnecessary Discourse, Talking Heads, and British Butler Syndrome

In this chapter we've been talking about common pitfalls in writing dialogue, and now I want to cover three more that I often see as an editor: unnecessary discourse, "talking heads," and what I call "British Butler Syndrome."

Let's look at a Before and an After example.

Before:

Mrs. Gray led us down the dormitory hallway, past several open doors on each side. "Cassie, you will be sharing a room with Ashley Jennings. You are in the same grade, so chances are you will have several classes together."

"What time does class start?" I asked.

"Students' classes begin at eight a.m. sharp. The cafeteria opens at seven a.m., and all students are expected to set appropriate alarms so that they can get up, have breakfast, and be to their first class at least five minutes before school begins."

"What about lights-out?" Mother asked. "Is there a particular time that students must be in bed?"

"Students are expected to turn their lights out and be in bed at ten p.m.," Mrs. Gray said. "This ensures an appropriate night of sleep so students are able to awaken early enough to eat a healthy breakfast and be prompt for class." She stopped at a doorway and knocked on it. "Ashley?"

"Come in," a voice said.

Mrs. Gray led us into the room. A blond, blue-eyed girl lay on the bed reading a book. She set it aside and stood up.

"Ashley, this is Cassandra Peterson and her parents. Cassandra is going to be your roommate. Cassandra, this is Ashley Jennings."

"Hello. How are you?" Ashley said to me.

"I'm well. How are you?"

Ashley looked at Mother and Daddy. "Hello, Mr. and Mrs. Peterson."

"Hello, Ashley," they both said.

She had been reading when we had walked in and had plenty of books in the room. At least we had one thing in common.

After:

Mrs. Gray led us down the dormitory hallway, past several open doors on each side. "Cassie, you'll be sharing a room with Ashley Jennings. You're in the same grade, so chances are you'll have several classes together."

I peeked into a room as we walked by it. Empty. Although the low din of voices carried into the hallway, I had yet to see anyone. "What time does class start?"

"Eight a.m. The cafeteria opens at seven, and you'll be expected to get up on your own, have breakfast, and be to class by five minutes to eight."

Impressive. With classes starting at eight—instead of seven twenty like at my last school—I'd be able to sleep forty minutes later.

Mother stepped into pace with Mrs. Gray. "What about lights-out? Is there a certain time students need to be in bed?"

Mrs. Gray glanced back at Daddy and me. "Lights-out is at ten p.m. That way you'll have a good night's sleep." She stopped at a doorway and knocked on it. "Ashley?"

"Come in," a quiet voice called.

She led us inside. The room held two single beds, two desks, and two dressers. Three doors lined the wall across from the beds—two closets and a private bathroom, I hoped. Books abounded on the occupied side of the room, filling a tall bookshelf and stacked against any open wall space.

A blond girl got up from where she lay on the bed reading. Her skinny jeans and T-shirt could've come right out of my closet.

"Ashley, this is Cassie Peterson and her parents. She's going to be your roommate. Cassie, this is Ashley Jennings."

Ashley grinned at me and then nodded at Mother and Daddy. "Hey."

I smiled back. Books everywhere, everything OCD neat, Converses under the bed, and a rolled-up towel—perfect for concealing late-night reading—behind the door. Awesome. I'd be rooming with myself, only blond.

So what differences did you see? Let's break it down:

- *Unnecessary discourse.* Near the end of the Before passage, there are four lines of useless greetings. Sure, people do engage in this type of speech (we'd be considered rude if we didn't greet each other appropriately), but it can—and often should—be worked around in fiction. Unless the greeting somehow advances the plot, leave it out or simplify it (e.g., with body language). Unnecessary discourse only bogs down writing.

- *Talking heads.* When writing is primarily dialogue with no other description, the characters tend to seem like nothing more than heads talking. The reader gets characters' speech reactions but has no idea what's going on in the POV character's head. The addition of Cassie's thoughts in the After passage gives a much clearer picture of her personality.

  Note: Many great writers focus on dialogue when writing the first draft of scene, then go back and add more description afterward. If this works for you, do it. Let the heads talk and then go back to enhance with narrative.

- *British Butler Syndrome.* This malady occurs when all characters speak similarly, using complete sentences and formal wording—like a British butler. In my years as an editor, I've worked with a few authors who, due to "rules" they learned in school, always wrote in complete sentences and never used contractions in their writing, not even in dialogue. The result was a monotony that didn't allow the characters their own voice.

Real people speak differently, and characters should too. For example, a twenty-five-year-old male character's voice will be different from his eighty-year-old grandfather's; a well-to-do character's voice will be different from the voice of a character who lives in poverty; and a twenty-six-year-old character in a contemporary novel will have a different voice than a twenty-six-year-old character in a colonial-era novel has.

The cure for this syndrome? Use contractions where appropriate, clip sentences when appropriate, and get to know your characters well so you can allow them their own unique voices.

Editor:
Robin Patchen

How Writers Can Seek and Destroy Banal and Obvious Dialogue

Earlier, Linda shared a bit on what it means to write realistic dialogue, and I want to elaborate on that and explore this extremely important aspect of dialogue at greater depth. As we've seen, the challenge for writers is to create dialogue that *sounds* realistic, but you don't want it to *be* realistic, for one very good reason—realistic dialogue is boring.

Here's an example of what I mean. In this passage, the heroine, Rae, is desperate to get some information from Walter.

Before:

Walter answered on the second ring. "Walter Boyle."

"Hi, Walter. It's Rae."

"Wow, Rae. How are you?"

"I'm okay, Walter. How about you?"

"Oh, it's been busy. I love my job, though. Working as a reporter for the *New York Times* was always my dream job, so I'm not going to complain. I haven't heard from you in months. I've been calling and calling, but you never call me back. Where have you been? What's been going on with you?"

"I'm glad you still love your job. I've been . . ." She thought of the infant sleeping upstairs. "Busy. Listen, I need a favor."

"Of course you need a favor. You always need a favor. You practically fall off the edge of the world, but as soon as you need something, then you call me. First, you need to tell me what you've been up to."

"I really don't have time to go into all of that right now. And it was awkward, you know, because we were together, and now I'm with someone else. I didn't know how you felt about that. But still, I really need a favor."

Realistic Dialogue Is Boring Dialogue

I could go on, but I'm boring myself to death. Remember what I said about this scene—Rae is desperate for information, and only Walter can get it for her. Did you get any sense of urgency from that exchange?

Lots of problems here. First, we have some telling. They both know he works for the *Times*. They both know he's been calling, and she's neglected to call him back. They both know they used to be together. So why is it in there? To tell the reader? Find a better way, please. Telling through dialogue doesn't work.

Second, we have the banal greetings. Hi. How are you? How long's it been? What's new . . . ? If the reader wants to hear all that stuff, she'll go have a conversation with the clerk at Walmart. Eliminate all the obvious stuff.

Finally, this dialogue is what we call "on the nose." One character says something, and then the next character responds directly to that, saying almost exactly what you'd expect. If the reader can guess what the characters are about to say, I guarantee, the dialogue will be boring.

Eliminate the Obvious and Surprise Your Reader

Here's the same scene the way I have it written in my current WIP. I hope you think it's better.

After:

Rae stood in the living room and dialed.
He answered on the third ring. "Walter Boyle."
"It's me."
"Rae? Where have you been? I've been trying to reach you for—"
"It's a long story," she said. "Listen, what can you tell me about the bombing in Tunisia yesterday?"
A long pause. "I don't hear from you in months. You don't return my calls. You fall off the face of the earth—"
"I didn't. I just—"
"You stop sending stories," he said. "You just disappear."
"Look—"

"Where have you been?"

"I've been . . ." She thought of the events of the previous few weeks, months. There was no time to explain. "Tied up."

"Literally? Because anything less than that, and you could've returned my calls."

She paced across the living room. "I don't have my phone."

"They sell phones on every street corner."

"Look, I'll tell you, but—"

"You married that guy, right?" Walter said. "Moreau?"

Rae froze. Swallowed. "How did you—?"

"It's not like it was a state secret."

"No. I know. I—"

"You could've told me."

She ran her fingers through her hair and paced again. "I should have. It was awkward."

"And this isn't? You disappear, then call for information like nothing happened."

"I'm sorry." Rae collapsed on the sofa. "You're right. I'm just . . . I need your help."

"Don't you always?"

"That's not fair."

"Is he . . . ?" His voice softened, and he started again. "Is he good to you?"

His concern nearly brought tears to her eyes. "You and I have been over for a long time. You ended it."

"Only because I was the only one really in it."

She imagined him then, not just as her conduit to information but as her friend. As more than her friend. She'd blown it with Walter like she'd blown it with everybody she ever loved. "I'm sorry, Walter. I don't know what else to say."

So what did I do? I deleted all the boring stuff. And because this is a tense scene, I made the paragraphs short. They're talking back and forth—not fighting, exactly, but certainly not friendly. There's enough subtext to keep the reader interested. But the main point of the scene remains the same—she needs information, and she has to deal with his questions before he's going to tell her anything.

You'll note that Walter has a different goal in mind. He wants to find out where she's been. So while she's trying to turn the conversation to her needs, he keeps shifting it back to his.

I hope the result is a segment of dialogue that intrigues the reader and moves the story forward.

Like any other component of your story, you want to eliminate "boring." That pertains to dialogue too. Sure, we want our characters to be realistic, but "on the nose" dialogue, however "real," is most often tedious or clunky. Read through your scenes and search for ways to tighten, reword, and trim to make that dialogue zing.

Editor:
C. S. Lakin

Talking Heads Avoidance Device

Christy touched briefly on the topic of "talking heads," but I want to take a longer look at this problem that contributes much to Fatal Flaw #8. Writers might get their dialogue mechanics down pat, using speech and narrative tags effectively and avoiding that "on the nose" dialogue that just doesn't come across as believable. But all the great dialogue in the world will still be problematic if it's floating in space, coming out of talking heads that don't seem to have bodies attached to them.

And there's not just a problem with missing bodies. Entire settings are missing. Yet, even if writers purposefully construct both bodies and setting, dialogue might still face a fatality. The real solution is deeper still.

So let's explore this talking heads syndrome a bit and look at ways to avoid succumbing to what might constitute the death of a potentially great scene.

I became acutely aware of this syndrome upon reading Elizabeth George's terrific book *Write Away*. She created what she calls a THAD: Talking Heads Avoidance Device, something that helps her, when writing dialogue-heavy scenes, to avoid having heads floating unattached in space. She defined this as "an activity going on in a scene that would otherwise consist of dialogue." In other words, she considers what she might have her characters doing *while they are talking*.

Surprising to me, many authors don't seem to consider giving their characters an activity while speaking. Oh, sure, they might have two characters sitting and drinking coffee, so on occasion the writer might throw in bits like "she lifted the cup to her mouth," "she sipped her coffee," "she set her cup down and frowned." Yes, those little actions, at times, are useful. A writer might also have one of the characters stand, pace, go to the sink, put her hands on her hips. But is that really what's needed to bring richness to a dialogue-heavy scene?

Here's what George says a THAD can do for a scene:

- Keep a scene from showing talking heads
- Reveal meaningful insights about characters via showing something interesting they are doing
- Reveal something key about the plot
- Bring depth by having the THAD be a metaphor or something symbolic in the story

Does writing "she sipped her coffee" really add anything to a scene? Maybe, but I'd like to challenge you to spend some time creating effective THADs instead of opting for the obvious. By considering the point of your scene (what key information you need to reveal to move the plot forward) and pondering its high moment (the climax or reveal at the end of it), you might come up with better activities for your characters to engage in while talking.

Of course, before even writing your scene, it will help to first consider the bigger picture—where you might set your characters for greatest impact. This is a whole other topic that I've spent many chapters on in many of my writing craft books. But let's say you've chosen a great setting for this scene, one that is significant to your POV character and serves a strong purpose in your story.

You have your characters in place, ready to talk, and you have planned some intense inner and/or outer conflict to take place, along with important plot reveals that add tension and move your story forward. It's time to come up with a THAD.

Make a List of Possible, Significant Activities

Make a list of things your characters could be doing as they talk. Can they be walking somewhere? Can one be busy working on some project that tells a bit about her passion, personality, abilities? Can you bring in humor by having something bizarre or hilarious going on?

Your choice is greatly determined by the purpose of the scene. If your characters are at a funeral, unless you are writing a dark comedy, they aren't going to be trying to dig out all the dirt as it's being tossed into the grave over the casket. Then again, if you're writing a serious relational drama and your character is completely losing it, that activity while conversing could be intensely poignant and even heartbreaking.

So think through, first, what your genre, tone, and scene purpose might dictate as to the THAD you choose.

I love to come up with symbolic THADs for my books. If you've developed powerful motifs that run through your story—an image or item, a phrase or word, or a concept—you can create appropriate THADs that use your motif and contribute to the "image system" for your novel. Here's what George writes:

> [In] *Deception on His Mind*: The THAD in a scene between Barbara Havers and her father-daughter Pakistani friends Taymullah Azhar and Hadiyyah deals with Hadiyyah presenting to Barbara a bee that she's captured and put in a jar. It becomes a metaphor for people being removed from their communities and consequently a metaphor for the Pakistani experience in Great Britain.

In some of her novels, the device George uses reveals clues in the murder investigation. In *Playing for the Ashes* (my favorite of all her novels), her character is an animal rights activist, so George has her characters engaging in conversations as they are rescuing animals. Showing your POV character in her "element," to show what she cares about or what she loathes, can be so much more useful to your story than having her sip coffee.

Here's a Before and After example from my novel *Conundrum*. This is the second scene in the novel, the first showing my protagonist, Lisa, at home in her ordinary life. The first scene ends with her arriving at her house after visiting her brother in the mental hospital, only to find her husband, Jeremy, packing up his truck with his belongings— moving out on the sly to avoid a confrontation with Lisa. There's a bit of dialogue at first, but just as they're about to go inside to continue their discussion, they hear a cry from the barn. One of Lisa's rescued goats is in labor.

In the Before passage, I substituted my meaningful THAD with mundane actions.

Before:

I stood in front of the house, staring at the truck full of Jeremy's belongings. I was speechless.

Jeremy said, "Let's go inside and talk. I'll make you some coffee." I nodded weakly and followed him into the house. I dropped down into a chair at the table while Jeremy put water in the coffeepot and got the coffee out of the freezer. He ground the beans and put five scoops into the pot, then turned it on.

"I got the document from the lawyer. The devise." Jeremy's tone was hard. Like he'd practiced saying that in the mirror.

When I didn't respond, he added, not masking his anger, "I'm going to insist she sign it. If she won't put the property in our name now, she's going to have to make good her promise that this house, this property, will be left for us in her will."

The coffeepot stopped gurgling. He poured me a cup and brought it to me, then leaned back against the counter, his arms crossed.

"Look, she already has it for us in her trust. You *know* this!"

"And she can remove it anytime she damn well pleases. This way she has to put her money where her mouth is. Sign something to prove she means it."

"Jer, she's my *mother,* for God's sake! Family means everything to her. Please, let's not do this. Not now." I sipped my coffee and then exhaled hard, wanting to be done with this argument already—the argument that had gone on for hours the night before.

"Fine!" I added. "Give her the paper and let her sign it. Then you'll see. All this fuss over nothing. You know it has something to do with her taxes—"

"A flimsy excuse. She owns your older brother too. Her name's on his deed. And Neal—she made him *sell* his house so she could have more ready cash. Dammit, Lisa, why can't you see this?"

I pinched my lips together in frustration. "She's my mother. Don't I know her better than you? You're just talking out of your paranoia." I gulped down more of my coffee, letting it burn my throat.

I thought about the adoption papers Jeremy had set on the cabinet yesterday. I choked up over all the years of frustration, heartache, and disappointment I had experienced. I kept my face turned, not wanting Jeremy to see my tears.

"Do you need me to stay here?" Jeremy asked.

"No. Just go." I just wanted to get in the bathtub and soak, lock the door, wallow in my misery.

One child. That's all I wanted. Was that too much to ask for?

After:

"First one's coming out," I said.

Jeremy hurried back and set down the basin and towels. He leaned close enough to see but didn't get in my way. I fished around with my finger until I felt the tip of a hoof in the canal. "Found a leg," I said.

We both grew quiet as I concentrated. Sassy's heavy panting sounded like a small tractor revving. Every once in a while she let out a little bleat of discomfort, but I talked softly and kept her calm. I managed to cup my hand over the small emerging head and loop a finger around the hoof. I tugged firmly and felt the small body move an inch. Then it hitched up. I muttered under my breath.

"What?" Jeremy asked. "Can I help?" I repositioned both my arm and the goat, which caused Sassy to wail again.

"Help me get her to standing."

My leg was cramping under me, and my stomach knotted up. The rancid smell of the barn and the amniotic fluids from the goat made bile rise to my throat. I fought another urge to throw up. Maybe the combination of stress, lack of sleep, Raff's urge to die, and the sting of my failing marriage was stewing inside me, merging into one sickening putrefying mass in my gut. I took deep breaths, caught Jeremy studying me in puzzlement. I avoided his eyes.

I hefted Sassy to all fours and tried with my left hand for better positioning in the birth canal. That proved to be a better stance. I withdrew my hand from the slippery space and yanked off my wedding ring. I handed the simple gold band covered in slime to Jeremy, who looked at it and flinched. The significance hit me, although I didn't have time to ponder it.

"I'll lose it in there. Please, just keep it for me—for a few minutes."

My words seemed to shake Jeremy out of his reverie. I never took off my wedding ring—ever.

"I got the document from the lawyer. The devise." Jeremy's tone was hard. Like he'd practiced saying that in the mirror.

When I didn't respond, he added, not masking his anger, "I'm going to insist she sign it. If she won't put the property in our name now, she's going to have to make good her promise that this house, this property, will be left for us in her will."

I spun to face him. "Look, she already has it for us in her trust. You *know* this!"

"And she can remove it anytime she damn well pleases. This way she has to put her money where her mouth is. Sign something to prove she means it."

"Jer, she's my *mother*, for God's sake! Family means everything to her. Please, let's not do this. Not now." I gestured at the distressed goat that stood panting hard and shaking from head to hoof. I exhaled hard, wanting to be done with this argument already—the argument that had gone on for hours the night before.

"Fine!" I added. "Give her the paper and let her sign it. Then you'll see. All this fuss over nothing. You know it has something to do with her taxes—"

"A flimsy excuse. She owns your older brother too. Her name's on his deed. And Neal—she made him *sell* his house so she could have more ready cash. Dammit, Lisa, why can't you see this?"

I pinched my lips together in frustration. "She's my mother. Don't I know her better than you? You're just talking out of your paranoia." I turned my back on Jeremy and concentrated on Sassy. I closed my ears to everything but her labored breathing.

Time moved slowly, and I hated seeing Sassy in such distress. Her groans and grunts tore at my heart, so I worked as quickly as I could, getting my hand around the head again.

"Why won't she push it out?" Jeremy asked.

"Because . . ." I grunted, "that leg goes to a different kid." I closed my eyes and with my mind followed my hand along as I traced the front hoof up to the stifle in that confining space, feeling the first bend forward, the second, backward at the hock. Hind leg, not front. I pushed that leg back into the uterus as far as I could and fished around for a front leg. I only needed one front leg that corresponded with the appropriate head and I would be in the clear.

Finally, I found one that connected to the neck of the goat sticking partway out of the birth canal.

"Got it!"

Sassy screamed as I pulled gently, foot and head, then waited until she got back to pushing. Along with her efforts, I cleared the shoulder over the cervix, the head and legs sliding out with the rest of the small wet body following. Jeremy handed me a towel, and I placed the small doe baby on it, under Sassy's nose, so she could sniff and lick it. I heard Jeremy chuckle, and a warm feeling rose to my heart, followed by a pang of despair that I hid in my attending to the next new arrival plopping out onto straw.

How simple it seemed to give birth to new life, and how very impossible. Something right here in my grasp was completely out of my grasp, denied me.

I choked up over all the years of frustration, heartache, and disappointment and dried off the next kid, a little gray buck with a white blaze on his forehead. Both kids were already standing on wobbly legs and baaing in cute warbly voices. Sassy spoke back to her babies between frantic licks. I always found it humorous watching does attend to their newborns. A third kid came with one more Sassy squawk—another buck, this one a runt. He fit in the palm of my hand. While Jeremy petted the other two, I rubbed that tiny guy with a towel, but got little response. Once I iodined the umbilical areas and made sure Sassy was done, had food and water, and passed her placenta, I stood. My legs shook from squatting so long, and my head spun hard until I got my balance.

I picked up the runt, still wrapped in a towel. "This one needs warming." I unlatched the gate, where Buster and Angel stood, alert, sniffing at my little bundle.

"Do you need me to stay here and keep an eye on these guys?" Jeremy asked.

"Only if you want to. But, they're doing fine." Better than I was. I just wanted to get in the bathtub and soak, lock the door, wallow in my misery. Instead of lifting my spirits, these three

new lives only sank me deeper. I gritted my teeth so hard my
jaw began to ache.
    One child. That's all I wanted. Was that too much to ask
for?

By using this THAD, I reveal a tremendous amount of important
information. We see the dynamics of Lisa and Jeremy's unraveling
relationship, and the dialogue makes clear what the issues are with her
mother and their house. The Before passage does reveal some of this,
but by having Lisa in this activity, it works as a painful trigger for her
about her infertility, which is also contributing toward her marriage
breakdown. We see her love for animals, we see her passion and
compassion, and we see something she's skilled at, which helps foment
empathy for her.
    I worked the scene from all these angles to accomplish the key
tasks: establishing that empathy for Lisa, creating tension between the
two characters and showing the value of their relationship and the love
between them. At the same time I created an interesting activity for the
characters to be engaged in that I hoped would make readers keep
reading. A whole lot more interesting (and unusual) than sitting and
drinking coffee, right? And in case you are wondering, yes, I've
delivered a lot of baby goats!

In Conclusion . . .

We hope this chapter helps you see the need to go further with
your dialogue scenes. By creating effective, powerful THADs, you can
avoid another pitfall of Fatal Flaw #8: Flawed Dialogue Construction.
And by applying all the points the other editors brought out through
their examples, you'll find your dialogue will come across more
realistic, engaging, and easy to follow.
    It's easy to write boring, "on the nose" dialogue. Great dialogue
takes work and thought. But if you spend time distilling that realistic
dialogue down into tight, concise, and often clever wording, your
scenes will pack a powerful punch. Remember, less is more. That
applies to dialogue too. So use some of what you learned in the earlier
chapters on overwriting and weak construction as you tackle your
dialogue. You'll see a huge improvement in your story as you conquer
this fatal flaw.

Fatal Flaw #8 Checklist

Go through your scenes and look for these culprits that show Flawed Dialogue Construction:

- Overuse of characters' names in direct address ("You know, Mary, that I'm right . . .")

- Using speech tags with every line

- Using flowery verbs for speech tags ("Go away," she cajoled . . . or extrapolated or interjected)

- Using inappropriate verbs for speech tags ("Go away," she sighed . . . or groaned or wished)

- Putting a speech or narrative tag at the end of a long passage of speech identifying who is speaking instead of placing it close to the beginning

- Using flowery adverbs to tell how the words are being spoken instead of showing the emotion ("Go away," she said angrily)

- Having all your characters sound alike, even though they have different personalities, backgrounds, and cultural influences

- Using "on the nose" dialogue, which means saying exactly what a character feels and which isn't very believable

- Padding scenes with a lot of unnecessary discourse such as boring greetings

- Lack of contractions in speech of characters that would use contractions in conversation (as well as in the narrative and internal dialogue in POV)

- Showing dialogue floating in space: talking heads that aren't attached to bodies engaged in activity and in real places in your scene

- Lack of an interesting, effective THAD for your scene

Your Turn: Try to spot and fix all the areas that flawed dialogue construction in this passage. An example of a revision is on the next page (no peeking!). There isn't one correct way to rewrite a passage, so your final version may be different from the revision provided. The key is to test yourself to see if you've nailed Fatal Flaw #8.

"I am so tired, Joe," she pleaded wearily. "I am really too tired to go on more night. I know this isn't a long conference and you aren't asking for much, but I do not think I can do it."

"It is just one more night, Sue," Joe said.

Sue shook her head. "I cannot take one more night, Joe. I need to sleep."

Joe tapped his foot impatiently. "Come eat your dinner," he said without feeling. "You will feel better after you eat."

"I don't think I will. It's sleep I need," Sue whined. "You should just go by yourself and let me get a rest."

He folded his arms. "I don't want to do that, Sue, as you know," he informed. "The conference is intended for ministerial couples, not just pastors. If you don't come with me, people will think something might be wrong between us," he argued.

"That's not very likely," Sue protested. "I have been there for two days of this three-day conference already."

He looked sternly back. "It would not be so bad if you came for the last day, then, would it? Surely you can find the energy to finish."

She looked at her feet. "I think maybe I'm sick."

"I think you're not."

Revision of the Previous Passage:

"I'm tired," she said, her eyes pleading with him. "Exhausted."
"It's just one more night."
She didn't get up—just stayed there, curled up on the couch with her feet up and her boots still on. "I can't take one more night. I need to sleep, Joe."
He scoffed and turned, flicking on the kitchen lights and rattling through the cutlery drawer. He set the table like it was a drill, every piece precise, slamming them down like gunshots.
He didn't look over his shoulder, just spoke. "Come eat your dinner. You'll feel better."
"I won't." Weariness made her voice sag. But a moment later, as he set the plates down, she shuffled across the living room floor toward the dining nook.
She lowered herself into the chair across from him. "You can just go on your own. Let me rest."
He shook out his napkin and laid it carefully in his lap. "I need you with me. The conference is intended for ministerial couples, not just pastors."
"For goodness' sake, Joe. It's not like I haven't already been there the last two days." Those pleading eyes again.
He looked sternly back. Her hair was disheveled; her mascara was smeared. She *did* look tired. Misgiving smote his heart for half a second, quickly put back in its place. All he was asking was that she come, sit beside him, make small talk, make them look good. She could come home and sleep for days after that if she wanted to.
He tried to soften his voice, without great success. "Listen to yourself—two days. I'm only asking you to come for *one* more day. Three days of small talk, Sue; it's not scaling a mountain."
"I think maybe I'm sick."
"I think you're not."

Fatal Flaw #9: "Underwriting"

By now it's been said a few times: fundamentally, when we write a story, we want to connect with readers' emotions. Engage emotion. Elicit it. Give readers a story they don't just learn but one they *feel* and will never forget.

Yet emotion is one of the story elements most commonly underwritten—and underwriting in general tends to harm emotional connection the most. Without question, underwriting is a fatal flaw. It can suck the life completely out of a story.

The dirty little secret, though?

Underwriting is sometimes (often) a direct result of following editorial advice like "show, don't tell," and "make sure your scenes are active and full of conflict" and "don't info dump or fill your scenes with backstory."

In this chapter, our editors eat humble pie and tackle the elephant in the room, looking at how editorial advice can go askew—as well as the newbie mistakes that commonly create underwriting "magic" where no magic should be. (Characters appearing and disappearing from a scene; motivation mysteriously lacking; actions that come out of nowhere—as editor Christy Distler would put it: "POOF!")

Words are the stuff of our worlds. Without words to translate into vivid images, actions, thought processes, emotions, settings, and more, none of those things can exist. So underwriting is actually as great a danger to a novelist as overwriting—perhaps even a greater one.

In the sections to come, we invite you to explore the fatal flaw of underwriting and, we hope, find room to breathe. With the help of great examples, in-depth explanations, and checklists, may you get a fuller, deeper appreciation for what it really takes to bring a story to life—without overwriting, yes, but also without missing a beat.

Editor:
Linda S. Clare

Don't Jump to Conclusions

Writers hear a lot about overwriting—tighten, tighten, tighten. We're advised: Show, don't tell. Act out scenes.

Yet, many writers "underwrite" in places where readers want to experience the steps characters make when they change. In this case, underwriting involves a "jumping to conclusions" mentality— something big happens in the story, but the protagonist simply responds without showing the process of decision.

Don't Skip Steps in the Process

For instance, your eight-year-old Main Character doesn't like broccoli. Hates broccoli. Would rather starve than eat broccoli. Then Mom says broccoli is good for you. MC suddenly gets excited and scarfs down that pile of green cruciferous veggies. What's wrong here?

If you guessed that no kid would change her mind about broccoli just because someone says it's good for her, you're right. Mom would probably need to work a little harder to see the plate cleaned.

To write this scene authentically, we need to show the stages of *yes*. That is, Mom is going to appeal to the kid by upping the ante on her. If Mom says broccoli's good for you, any self-respecting kid would still keep her mouth clamped shut.

But what if Mom ups the ante by saying unless kid eats broccoli, she won't get dessert? In my house, that kid will want to know what's for dessert before she agrees. Day-old vanilla pudding would not sway a broccoli-hating kid.

Okay, now Mom goes for the cherry on top. She asks, "What about a trip to Dairy Queen?" Yes! Kid might hold her nose (or cheat and feed the dog), but she agrees to eat broccoli.

The Rule of Three for Process

If you've ever had to talk someone into doing something, you know that it often happens in stages. In fiction, it often happens in threes.

You can use the Rule of Three to show the process your character goes through to reach a decision. *Caveat: In real life, we often must work much harder than three times, but we don't want the reader to get bored or give up. Three times gives the illusion that the character is wearing down gradually.* Illustrate three, but summarize if the process takes longer. For example: "Mom tried to get her daughter to eat broccoli night after night."

Applying the Rule of Three might look like this: The first request for a change of mind, emotion, or action gets instant rebuff—a knee-jerk *reaction*. The second time, a character weighs the possibilities *(dilemma)* but still clings to her first response. Third time shows not only the *decision* to say yes or no to the request but also the emotional, mental, or physical reason for the decision.

Let's see how this rule works in action.

Before:

> Jack hung his head. He'd never get Patty Ann Mason to go to the prom with someone like him. Without a job, he'd never afford all the fancy stuff a girl like Patty required. Limo service, dinner at some swanky restaurant, cool after-party—all that was beyond him. Jack sighed. He was a loser. He'd always be a loser.
>
> Just then, Katie Hudson, the ugliest girl in the whole school, sat down beside him. She peered through her Coke-bottle glasses. "Hi, Jack. Got a date for the prom yet?"
>
> Jack looked up. "No." Patty Ann was as good as gone.
>
> Katie, grinned, her braces gleaming in the noonday sun. "Why don't you take me?"
>
> Jack shrugged. "Okay. I hope you don't mind biking to the dance in your formal."
>
> Katie said, "And I hope you don't mind if my formal's made out of Saran Wrap."
>
> "I guess it's a date then?" He stood. "Walk you to class?" Losers had to stick together, after all.

After:

Jack hung his head. He'd never get Patty Ann Mason to go to the prom with someone like him. Without a job, he'd never afford all the fancy stuff a girl like Patty required. Limo service, dinner at some swanky restaurant, cool after-party—all that was beyond him. Jack sighed. He was a loser. He'd always be a loser.

Just then, Katie Hudson, the ugliest girl in the whole school, sat down beside him. She peered through her Coke-bottle glasses. "Hi, Jack. Got a date for the prom yet?"

Jack hid the urge to barf. "Maybe. Who wants to know?" Ugly Katie was probably an alien or something. And where'd she find such a hideous outfit?

"I don't believe you." Katie grinned, her braces gleaming in the noonday sun. "Why don't you take me?"

Jack glared. "Sure, if you don't mind biking to the dance in your formal."

"So that's a no?"

"Not only no but heck no."

Katie scooted closer. "Did you hear? Patty Ann Mason's going with Derek."

Jack groaned.

"Come, on. We'll have fun, you and I. What if I told you my formal's made out of Saran Wrap?" Katie's beady eyes shone behind her thick lenses. "It's strapless *and* see-through."

Jack studied her figure—not half bad. "I don't know." He shifted on the bench.

"Look." Katie's smile faded. "I know I'm no Patty Ann Mason. But I'll pay for everything—limo, dinner, after-party— the works. You don't even have to dance with me. What do you say?"

"Okay, okay." Jack would have to ask Katie to lay off the garlic on prom night. "It's a date then." He stood. "Walk you to class?" Losers had to stick together, after all.

The Before example doesn't show us how Jack came to the conclusion that going to prom with Katie was something he would do. In the After version, we see Katie putting more pressure on Jack, chiseling away at his defenses. When she offers the solution to the scene's main problem—Jack's lack of money to pay for the prom—it feels natural for him to agree, however reluctantly.

A good rule to follow: the more important the scene to the overall story, the more slowly the writer can show a change of heart. In scenes where the outcome isn't as critical, you can show a much faster transformation. But a decision arrived at with little or no transitional stages will likely be seen by readers as inconsequential.

A word about drafts: If you expand your scene to show these stages, it may end up too long or not long enough. Use subsequent drafts to refine this technique. I think it's easier to trim than to add, so with the first try at showing the transitions, don't hold back. You can fine-tune the scene later.

To avoid underwriting, the stages of yes or no must arise from a character's logical sequence of thoughts, emotions, or actions. These stages are similar to the sequence of a scene: reaction, dilemma, decision.

Weigh the scene's importance against the overall story goal, and use the Rule of Three to illustrate the stages by which a character decides on something. By avoiding underwriting in scenes, you'll increase readers' satisfaction and belief in the story.

Editor:
Rachel Starr Thomson

Telling the Whole Story

Modern writers have been heavily influenced by the movies. On the one hand this is good—the best of visual media will teach us pacing, plotting, great dialogue, and the mechanics of a good setting.

But books are not movies or TV shows, and getting our training from them can sometimes lead us to forget something: our stories are invisible.

A great deal is said about the dangers of overwriting. In fact, we've discussed many of those dangers in this series. Under the banner of "show, don't tell," we've demonstrated ways to cut back prose so the story comes leaping to life.

But the "don't tell" rule does not mean that essential elements of a story should be left out. Readers translate the words we write into images, feelings, voices, etc. If we don't actually put those words on the page, there's nothing to translate—nothing with which to bring our stories to life.

The Trouble with Underwriting

Because we already know exactly what's in our inner "movie," we can fail to realize that not everything is making it onto the screen. The constant refrain of "don't overwrite," while valid in itself, can cause writers to tighten back even further and actually leave things on the cutting floor that should have stayed in.

It's possible to underwrite setting, action, emotion, logic, and more. Linda gave us a great example of this in the process of decision making. The results can be so jarring that a reader is totally kicked out of the scene—or fails to enter it fully in the first place.

When a character starts talking and you didn't know they were in the scene? Underwriting. When a character at the start of a scene is in her bedroom but ends up in her office and you didn't know she had gone there? Underwriting. When someone makes a decision and you have absolutely no idea why?

Yeah, that's underwriting too.

To demonstrate, I want to share two versions of two passages from my whimsical fantasy *Lady Moon*. One majors on action, the other on dialogue. The Before passages are significantly underwritten. The After passages solve that problem.

Before (Dialogue):

Celine was still languishing when a wild head popped out. "Do me a good turn," it said with a friendly smile. "Marry me? It would get us out of here. You and I, as husband and wife. I say, what are you looking for?"

"Something heavy," she answered.

"What for?" it asked.

"To pitch it at you," she answered.

"You'd miss," the head said cheerily. "Now don't look angry. You want something—I can see it in your eyes."

"I do," said she. "An older brother. Or"—growing reflective—"a dog. You deserve to have *something* set on you." Her slender fingers ached for the lack of anything to throw.

A sudden racket of moving pebbles and shifting limbs was accompanied by a cloud of dust from above. The man dropped through the hole.

After (Dialogue):

Celine languished six and thirty days in a cavern on the moon, where her uncle had unceremoniously tossed her. She had been in the habit of throwing her scrub brushes at his head whenever he poked it through the door of the Great Hall, and the last time she'd done it, he'd taken a fit of temper.

She was still languishing when a wild head popped out of a smallish hole in the ceiling of the cavern. "Do me a good turn," it said with a friendly smile. "Marry me?"

Instinctively she looked for a scrub brush to pitch in the head's direction, but as nothing came to hand, she listened to it. It seemed determined to talk.

"It would get us out of here," the head told her. "You and I, as husband and wife. I say, what are you looking for?"

"Something heavy," she answered.

"What for?" it asked.

219

"To pitch it at you."

"You'd miss," the head said cheerily. "Now don't look angry. You want something—I can see it in your eyes."

"I do," said she. "An older brother. Or"—growing reflective—"a dog. You deserve to have *something* set on you." Her slender fingers ached for the lack of anything to throw.

A sudden racket of moving pebbles and shifting limbs was accompanied by a cloud of dust from above. The head was attached to a man—she had suspected so all along—and it proved as much by dropping through the hole, followed by the other necessary parts, into the cavern where she had up until now thought herself alone.

The Before passage is missing several key elements—elements that help us make sense of the entire scene. The setting is the most important. (A wild head popped out of where? Wait, now someone is dropping through the ceiling? Where did the pebbles come from—isn't she in a house or something? Why does it have a hole in it?)

Second in importance are the missing backstory details, which let us know both why Celine is "languishing" and also why her first reaction is to look for something to throw. The opening paragraph in the After version gives us keys to the situation and to Celine's personality. It also sets the genre—knowing how Celine got here moves this scene out of the real world and into whimsy.

Before (Action):

"Stand back," Sir Brian said. He swung his battle-axe. Tereska rushed forward.

"The axe rebounded," he said. "There's something else blocking the way."

She let out a noise that might have been a curse. "Umbria's spell," she said.

"We're trapped?"

"We're not going back," Tereska growled. She shoved Thomas's sword in farther and then tried to move the blade. It didn't want to budge. It felt as though she'd plunged it into a block of hardening molasses.

Tereska went right through with the rest of the sword. For a moment she thought it would squeeze the life out of her. She tried to gasp, but couldn't; where air had been, there was nothing now but a heavy, fuzzy pressure.

In the next moment she popped out the other side. Through her blurry eyes she saw the others pitch themselves from the wall and land in disarray around her.

"Ouch," she heard Sir Brian mutter. "That's going to leave a dent."

After (Action):

"Stand back," Sir Brian said. He swung his battle-axe and brought it into the door. The door shattered, and pieces of wood flew in every direction. Tereska rushed forward, but Sir Brian stopped her with his arm.

"The axe rebounded," he said. "There's something else blocking the way."

Gingerly, Tereska reached out. Her fingers touched something invisible, spongy, and warm. She let out a noise that might have been a curse. "Umbria's spell," she said.

"We're trapped?" came Aldon's voice from the rear.

"We're not going back," Tereska growled. She reached inside her cloak and pulled Tomas's golden sword out once again. It had sliced through a magical seal once. It could do it again.

Tereska thrust the sword straight forward. The tip went through the thick magic, half-burying the blade while the free end quivered. Tereska shoved it in farther and then tried to move the blade. It didn't want to budge. It felt as though she'd plunged it into a block of hardening molasses.

But when a woman is attempting to rescue herself, that woman does not allow magical molasses to stand in her way.

Tereska grabbed the hilt with both hands, let out a war scream that would have curdled milk, lowered her head, and charged.

The sword went the rest of the way through the magic, and Tereska went right through with it. For a moment she thought it would squeeze the life out of her. She tried to gasp, but couldn't; where air had been, there was nothing now but a heavy, fuzzy pressure.

In the next moment she popped out the other side, fell six feet to the ground, and lay gasping for breath on the greensward. Through her blurry eyes she saw the others pitch themselves from the wall and land in disarray around her.

"Ouch," she heard Sir Brian mutter. "That's going to leave a dent."

What was missing in the Before passage? It's unclear if Sir Brian and Tereska are on the same side, or if they're fighting in that opening line. Who asks about being trapped? Setting, motivation, and key actions are all absent.

A caveat here: certain actions don't need to be spelled out. I can write "I picked up the keys," and you'll get a clear picture of what I'm doing; I don't need to write "I reached out, uncurled my fingers, closed them around the keys, and lifted them." But where action *isn't* a natural one, the steps need to be there.

In a story like *Lady Moon*—where magic is involved and nothing is really what we expect—it's even more important to make sure enough details are given. But this is important in a "real world" story as well. Note that intangibles are also important: reasoning, logic, motivation, emotion. These connect the dots between actions, showing us why people are doing what they're doing.

When a story is underwritten, everything suffers. POV is weaker; personality and perception don't come through. Confusion reigns when it comes to action; settings are vague or even baffling.

In balanced writing—neither overwritten nor underwritten—the story becomes a true approximation of the human experience, even when it's a madcap fantasy romp in which people are banished to the moon. "A good book," wrote novelist William Styron, "should leave you slightly exhausted at the end. You live several lives while reading it."

Don't shortchange your writing. Connect the dots, fill out the setting, and even "tell" us the history. Give us the pieces we need to translate the invisible into a story we can truly live.

Avoiding Underwriting-Induced Magic

Magic has played a huge part in fiction over the years. In the past we had classics like C. S. Lewis's The Chronicles of Narnia series, J. R. R. Tolkien's *The Hobbit*, and a score of fairy tales. More recently, J. K. Rowling's Harry Potter books and Diana Galbaldon's Outlander series have garnered millions of readers. The truth is, magic sells. But it doesn't belong in *all* fiction—and sometimes it doesn't even belong in fantasy and speculative fiction.

Why? Because sometimes a character's "magical powers" result not from special abilities but from underwriting. Certain events or actions seem to occur out of thin air without proper setup, and this becomes a fatal flaw in fiction writing.

Have you ever been reading a story and found yourself completely confused by something that happens? Maybe a character does something that doesn't seem physically possible, or speaks but you never knew he or she was even part of the scene. That happened as a result of underwriting-induced magic—or telling the story without using enough information to make it logical and imaginable. (Needless to say, this type of magic does *not* result in best sellers.)

Let's see this "magic" in action.

Before:

> Once Mother, Daddy, and Mrs. Gray had left the room, Ashley sat on her bed. "So what grade are you in?"
>
> "Twelfth." I couldn't tear my attention from the books on her side of the room. The bookshelf nearly reached the ceiling. Some fiction and some nonfiction, the books were separated by category and then alphabetized.
>
> "Me too. A lot of people think I'm younger, but I'm just really short."
>
> Karli grinned. "Bet you never thought you'd be rooming in a library, eh?"

Ashley made a face at her. "You never seem to mind living across the hall from a library."

She laughed. "Nope. But I'm still waiting for you to get *Allegiant*."

Ashley grabbed a book off the top of the bookshelf. "Finished it last night. Just be sure to bring this one back when you're finished with it."

"Whatever." Karli pointed the book at me. "Have fun living in the library—and don't let the librarian shush you too much."

I looked to Ashley. "The librarian?"

She shrugged and dropped back onto the bed. "She calls me that all the time. But what do you expect from someone who's the queen of snark? Don't tell her I said that."

I grinned and moved closer to the bookcase. "I'll take books over snark any day."

After:

Once Mother, Daddy, and Mrs. Gray had left the room, Ashley sat on her bed and crossed her legs. "So what grade are you?"

"Twelfth." I couldn't tear my attention from the serious amount of books on her side of the room. The bookshelf nearly reached the ceiling and didn't have an inch of free space. Some fiction, some nonfiction, and all perfectly separated by category and then alphabetized by author name. This girl was awesome.

"Me too. A lot of people think I'm younger, but I'm just really short."

A knock on the door spun me around.

In the doorway stood a girl with a pixie face and long curly red hair that contrasted against her black T-shirt and leggings. "Hey. I'm Karli. I live across the hall."

"Cassie."

She grinned. "Bet you never thought you'd be rooming in a library, eh?"

Ashley scrunched her face at her. "You never seem to mind living across the hall from a library."

She laughed. "Nope. But I'm still waiting for you to get *Allegiant*."

Ashley got off the bed and stepped onto the stool in front of the bookshelf, then grabbed a book off the top of it. "Finished it last night." She hopped down and handed it to her. "Just be sure to bring this one back when you're finished with it."

"*What*-ever." Karli pointed the book at me and took a step toward the door. "Have fun living in the library—and don't let the librarian shush you too much." Heading back across the hallway, she called over her shoulder, "Later."

I looked to Ashley. "The librarian?"

She shrugged and dropped back onto the bed. "She calls me that all the time. But what do you expect from someone who's the queen of snark? Don't tell her I said that."

I grinned and moved closer to the bookcase to get a better look. "I'll take books over snark any day."

So what differences did you see in the two? Primarily, there's blatant underwriting in the Before passage. While much of the wording is the same in the two examples, the After passage provides much more information about the characters (physically and personality-wise) and what's happening. It also doesn't have the "magic" that's going on in the Before passage. Let's break it down.

- POOF. In the fourth paragraph of the Before passage, suddenly someone named Karli is speaking. But where'd she come from? She wasn't described earlier in the scene, so how did she just magically appear? If the character had the ability to materialize out of thin air, that would be one thing. Or it would work if the narrative described Karli talking and then the other characters realizing she'd just stopped in the doorway. In this case, however, Karli just starts talking as if she's been there all along.

- POOF. Three more lines down, we have Ashley grabbing a book off the top of her bookshelf. How'd she do that? She's sitting on her bed. Not only that, she's already told us she's short. So she not only has to get off the bed to get the book, she also needs help to reach the top of the bookshelf

225

(a stool)—unless, of course, she can elevate, but that's highly unlikely in this story.

- POOF. At the end, we have Cassie and Ashley talking about Karli. But is she still in the room or not? Going by what's said, it seems that she's not, but that hasn't been described. So technically she's either still in the room or she's transported herself to another place.

As an editor I've seen this type of unintended "magic" in plenty of manuscripts. Why is this so prevalent? Because writers *know* what's going on in their scenes; they know the character's quirks, and they know exactly what's happening. As a result, sometimes important information doesn't get conveyed through the writing. It happens, and not just to beginning writers.

Having a critique partner who reads your manuscript can greatly decrease the underwriting-induced magic. He'll see your story with fresh eyes and point out areas where something is confusing or more description is needed.

Another way to get better perspective on whether you're underwriting is to set your manuscript aside after you've finished it. After a few weeks, read it again. You may be surprised by how much needs to be added to make a good story great.

How Writers Can Avoid "Underwriting" Emotions

Great writers move from scene to scene quickly, including vivid details to help the reader imagine the settings, filling each moment with tension and conflict. But sometimes the emotions get lost along the way. And this can lead to underwriting—leaving out important pieces that are needed to engage your readers.

What's Missing When You "Tell" Emotions?

You certainly don't want to name emotions with fabulous writing like "She was sad." That's pure telling. So writers find a way to show it. "Her eyes filled with tears." Great, now we know she was sad. But there's always more to sadness than just tears.

The last time you cried, was your brain engaged? Mine was. In fact, what was happening in your brain is what caused the tears. Let me take it a step further. Every emotion we wear on our skin is an outward manifestation of something deeper.

You might be able to tell if your spouse is mad because of that little vein that throbs on his forehead, but can you tell what led to his anger? Was it frustration? Irritation? Jealousy? Was he feeling critical?

So if you just show readers the throbbing vein or the teary eyes, you're missing an opportunity to show us the character's emotions. You're underwriting.

The Bedroom Made Her Cry

In this snippet, my character Reagan is searching for something in the house she grew up in. Her grandmother, who'd lived there all Reagan's life, has just passed away, but her parents, who also lived there, died years before—her father eighteen years earlier, her mother fourteen. She's just stepping into her parents' old bedroom to continue her search.

227

Before:

> After breakfast, she carried the baby upstairs and laid him in the middle of what used to be her parents' bed.
>
> The room looked much like it had when her parents had shared it, though the knickknacks of daily life had been removed. Tears pricked her eyes, but she brushed them away to begin her search.

Why is she crying? We know she's sad about something, but what exactly leads to those tears? It probably isn't grief for her parents, who've been dead most of her life. And even if it is grief, it has to be triggered by something. The trigger isn't clear.

The reader may assume she's sad about her parents' death and move on, but they won't have an emotional reaction. There's nothing here to react to.

Mining for Feelings

I want Reagan to feel something in this scene. Sadness over her parents' death is easy—and a little obvious. What else might she be feeling? In her case, Reagan has always felt abandoned, but I cover that in other places in the book. And frankly, don't most kids who grew up without parents feel abandoned? The last thing I want is cliché or the obvious.

So what else might she be feeling here? Rather than go with sadness or the ache of abandonment, I dug deeper to a third, less obvious emotion.

After:

> After breakfast, she carried the baby upstairs and stood at the door of her parents' bedroom.
>
> The room looked much like it had when her parents had shared it, though the knickknacks of daily life had been removed. No half-finished novels lay on the nightstands. No jewelry casually lay on the bureau. Eighteen years had passed, and still Reagan could remember the scent her father's cologne. She'd always thought that the most comforting smell in the world. Deceiving, more like, because it had made her feel safe.

She cradled her newborn closer to her breast as her gaze scanned the space. She could still hear the echo of her father's laughter, imagine the slight smile he could coax from her mother, even when she was in one of her dark moods. Rae could feel his arms around her, protective, as though Daddy would never let anything happen to her. And she'd believed that, too, in her childish naiveté. Believed it until the night the car accident had ripped him from the world.

Turned out her father was flesh and blood, just like everybody else. The solid ground she'd thought her life was built on had been washed away like a sandcastle in the surf. First Dad, then Mom, now Gram.

She kissed little Johnny's head and remembered her parents' caskets at the bottom of those dark graves. If Julien found her, would it be her body next laid to rest? Or little Johnny's?

The image floated to her mind: the miniature casket, his tiny, perfect body sinking into a deep hole. She shook her head to throw the image off until just its shadow remained.

Not since the last time her father had stood in this room had she felt secure. Since then, her life felt built on shifting sand, and all Reagan could do was hang on and try to keep her balance. Before Johnny, all she'd had to lose was her own life, her own future.

But now, this child had become her sun and moon and breath and heartbeat. She'd lost everything to the tides of life. Would she lose him too?

Okay, so I never showed her tearing up. Truth is, sadness is just one of the many things she's feeling in that segment, and it's not even the most important. By digging down to the next layer of emotion, and then the next, I discovered something unexpected.

By skipping the obvious feelings, you can catch your reader off guard. My goal when I write is to connect emotionally with the reader. Can you write this much emotion into every scene? Perhaps not, but when your character has an emotional reaction, don't always just show us what happens on the outside. Instead, dig deep and show your reader what's beneath the surface, and maybe you'll find something lurking in your reader's heart too.

Check Your Underwriting—10 Key Questions to Ask of Your Story

We've been looking at the many ways writers tend to underwrite in their fiction. Choppy narrative that "magically" moves characters around. Dialogue that seems to be missing something. Action that has characters behaving in confusing ways. Characters lacking the natural process of emotional response to things that happen to them, or the logic that causes them to make decisions.

These issues are especially endemic to first novels, and when pointed out to authors, they seem so obvious. Writers will say, "Why didn't I notice these problems?"

I'll tell you what I think is the main reason most writers can't see the obvious flaws in their scenes:

Because of a lack of adequate writing experience, helpful critical feedback, and sufficient skill development and training, writers don't realize they aren't showing enough—especially in a scene's opening paragraphs—to help readers picture where a character is and when the scene is taking place in the story. As we noted in this chapter, writers themselves can imagine all the action taking place, the details of the setting, the sounds and smells their characters are experiencing. But they forget that readers aren't *mind readers*.

Like Rachel says, our stories are invisible unless we put the words on the page.

Yes, we want to leave much to a reader's imagination as she immerses herself in our story, but our job as authors is to create enough of our "world" for her to enjoy. *Immerse* means more than dipping a toe into a half inch of water. It means to be fully, wholly submerged.

The challenge is in determining how and how much to convey to readers what the writer is seeing in her own mind.

Here are ten questions to ask of your scenes—questions that cover the most common violations of underwriting. Keep your eye out for these flaws in your writing, and your readers will be able to immerse themselves fully in your story.

1) *Where is this scene taking place?* I shouldn't have to ask this, right? The writer is thinking, *Isn't it obvious? I know where this scene is taking place.*

2) *What does this place look and feel like?* What's usually missing is not just the locale but the smells and sounds, a sense of the time of day and year, the weather, and exactly where in the world it is.

3) *How much time has passed?* So many scenes dive into dialogue or action without clueing the reader in on how much time has passed from the last scene. Scenes needs to flow and string together in cohesive time. It's important to know if five minutes or five months has passed, and it only takes a few words to make that clear.

4) *What is your character feeling right now?* This is a biggie. It's probably the most important element needed at the start of a scene, but it's often left out.

5) *What is your character's reaction?* So many times I read bits of action or dialogue that should produce a reaction from the POV character, but the scene just zooms ahead without an indication of what the character is feeling or thinking.

6) *What is the natural, believable process of your character's reaction?* For every important moment, your character needs to react—but in a believable order. First viscerally, then emotionally, then physically, and finally intellectually. Oftentimes a writer will show a characters reacting with deep logical thought about a situation when their first natural reactions are missing.

   If you get hit by a car, you aren't going to first think logically about what happened and what you need to do next. First, you scream, or your body slams against the sidewalk and pain streaks through your back. *Keep this adage in mind: for every action, there should be an appropriate, immediate reaction.* That's how you reveal character.

7) *What is the point of this scene?* This is a scary question. Because if there's no point to a scene, it shouldn't be in your novel. Every scene has to have a point—to reveal character or plot. And it should have a "high moment" that the scene builds to.

8) *What is your protagonist's goal for the book?* If she doesn't have a goal, you don't really have a story. The reader wants to know your premise as soon as possible, and that involves your main character having a need to get something or somewhere, do something or find something. Or some variation of that.

9) *Where's the conflict?* Every scene should be bulging with inner or outer conflict or both. Conflict creates tension, which is a good thing. Conflict is story.

10) *Where's your opening hook and strong ending sentence?* Treat each scene as if it's a mini novel. Every scene should hook the reader with a strong opening line or two, and should end with a satisfying wrap-up or hanging ending that makes the reader want to dive right into the next scene.

I actually ask a whole lot more questions than these. And many are just as important to crafting a powerful novel. I've found when writing my own novels that if I just keep asking questions—the right ones—I'll find just the right answers for that story. And I'll avoid the fatal flaw of underwriting.

In Conclusion . . .

Underwriting, like overwriting, is sometimes hard to spot. But we hope, now that you've gone through this chapter, you've learned where underwriting might undermine your story.

Go through the checklist and find these areas and add what's needed to remedy the problem. Don't leave your reader scratching her head, wondering what you meant to say. Make her reading experience trouble-free by taking the time to ensure she can clearly follow your story.

Fatal Flaw #9 Checklist

Go through your scenes and look for these culprits that show underwriting:

- Important actions missing that show characters smoothly moving from one place to another or from one action to another

- Necessary speech or narrative tags missing that would make clear who is speaking

- Not showing all the characters on stage at the start of a scene, so that characters magically appear out of thin air

- Characters' reactions to things said and done missing, so the reader cannot tell how those characters feel about what is happening

- Lack of the characters' emotional responses to help the reader feel empathy for the characters or find them believable

- Lack of details of setting that ground the character in the scene from the start: weather, time of day, time of year, scenery

- Lack of clarity regarding how much time has passed for the characters since the last scene with them

- Showing characters using items that have not been shown earlier in the scene, such as picking up a gun and firing, when no mention was made of a gun on stage

Your Turn: Try to spot and fix all the areas that show underwriting in this passage. An example of a revision is on the next page (no peeking!). There isn't one correct way to rewrite a passage, so your final version may be different from the revision provided. The key is to test yourself to see if you've nailed Fatal Flaw #9.

Before long, the hansom cab pulled to a stop in front of the London townhouse.

"Listen to these floors," Agnes said as she walked through the foyer. "The creaking could wake the dead!"

"The rest of the house is probably just as noisy," Elena offered as she walked up the stairs.

Agnes frowned. "How disappointing."

"I'm sure it will take some getting used to, but—" Elena started to say.

"Oh, never mind," Agnes interrupted, opening her suitcase on the bed and rummaging through it. "I must change out of these clothes."

Elizabeth cleared her throat. "Dinner will be at six. And please dress for the occasion."

Agnes dismissed her aunt's behavior. She would just have to tolerate her rude manner.

"Don't you want to rest after our long journey?"

"But Elena is going to give me a tour of the town."

"Yes, we must learn our way around."

"Fine."

Elizabeth nodded. "But at least freshen up first. I'll have the servants draw a bath."

Agnes paced in the foyer waiting for Elena to come back downstairs. She sipped her cup of tea and glanced at the clock again. After waiting so long for this moment, she couldn't stand to be delayed.

"I need to speak with you."

Agnes walked out of the parlor.

"Of course," Elena said after a pause.

Agnes turned toward the door leading to the garden. A cold blast dazed her. She stepped into the sun and let the warming rays on her face remind her that for every problem, there was a solution.

Elena sat on the bench in the corner of the garden and looked at Agnes.

"I found this in a book." She handed the piece of paper to her. Her face paled. "It's Father's will. And . . . he's leaving the estate to Elizabeth!"

Revision of the Previous Passage:

Before long, the hansom cab pulled to a stop in front of the London townhouse.

Agnes stepped out of the cab and looked around. The gray stones of the building were water-stained, and the marble steps chipped. A gloomy mood hung heavy over the house, as dark as the thick fog dampening her hair on this cold winter afternoon. She'd hoped her aunt Elizabeth would have chosen a nicer place for them to stay during their weeklong visit to the city. But it would suffice. All that truly mattered was finding a solicitor to help her. Her heart sank from the hopelessness of the task.

With a sigh she walked up the steps and waited for her aunt and her best friend, Elena, to join her. The front door opened, and a glum servant gestured them inside with a polite but unintelligible mumble. The three women entered, and Aunt Elizabeth sniffed the air and wrinkled her face in disgust. The musty odor of unlit fireplaces permeated the room.

"Listen to these floors," Agnes said as she walked through the foyer. "The creaking could wake the dead!"

"The rest of the house is probably just as noisy," Elena offered as she walked past Agnes and up the stairs.

Agnes frowned. "How disappointing."

"I'm sure it will take some getting used to, but—" Elena started to say.

"Oh, never mind," Agnes interrupted. She followed Elena into the first room to their right, at the top of the stairs, and laid her suitcase on the bed. After they took a tour of the house, she'd decide which room she wanted for her own, but for now she wanted nothing more than to freshen up after the long ride from Bristol.

She opened her suitcase and rummaged through it. "I must change out of these clothes," she told Elena, who was studying the small photos on the dresser.

Elizabeth walked in and cleared her throat. "Dinner will be at six. And please dress for the occasion."

Agnes exchanged knowing glances with Elena. They'd both been suffering her aunt's matronly behavior. *But one week is tolerable*, Agnes thought. She'd had to get to London, and this had been the only way. It wouldn't do to upset her aunt. Agnes knew she must do all she could to keep her secret undetectable, even though she wanted to cry out in rage. How could her father have done such a horrible thing? She gulped down her anger and forced a smile.

Her aunt nodded perfunctorily and headed out the room. Then she turned back and said, "Don't you want to rest after our long journey?"

"But Elena is going to give me a tour of the town."

Elena nodded. "Yes, we must learn our way around."

Elizabeth grunted. "Fine." Then added, "But at least freshen up first. I'll have the servants draw a bath."

An hour later, washed and dressed in clean, pressed clothes suitable for a day in the city, Agnes paced in the foyer, clutching her reticule close to her side, waiting for Elena to come downstairs. She picked up the cup of tea the maid had brought her and glanced at the clock again. After waiting so long for this moment, she couldn't stand to be delayed.

Elena breezed down the staircase. "All ready." She smiled and made for the door.

Agnes stopped her with a hand and whispered, "I need to speak with you."

Elena's eyebrows rose in curiosity, but she merely nodded discreetly.

"Let's talk out here," Agnes said, gesturing to the door that led out to a side garden Agnes could see out the large picture window.

When she opened the door, a cold blast dazed her. Pulling her coat tightly around her, she stepped into the sun and let the warming rays on her face remind her that for every problem, there was a solution. But those usually comforting words her father had oft said only fomented pain in her heart. She doubted there would be any solution for her problem.

Elena sat on the bench in the corner of the garden and looked at Agnes with concern.

"What is it? What's wrong?" Elena asked.

"I found this in a book." She reached into her reticule and handed the piece of paper to her, trying to swallow past the rock in her throat.

Elena began reading, then stopped and lifted her head. Her face paled. "It's your father's will. And . . . he's leaving the estate to Elizabeth!"

Fatal Flaw #10: Description Deficiencies and Excesses

Have you ever read a scene in which the descriptions go on forever? Descriptions of clothing, hairstyles, furniture, buildings, and setting that make you start skimming pages to get to "the action"?

Back in the day, description was king. Novels were mostly description, and writers would devote whole chapters to just describing setting, to set the stage for the action to play out.

James Michener was famous for such a style. In *Alaska*, for example, the opening chapters are about the geological formation of the North American continent, and readers "watch" the gradual emergence of the Alaskan terrain—at just about the speed of those glaciers moving across the earth's surface. John Steinbeck, in *East of Eden*, covers the history of the central coast of California for numerous pages.

Maybe those novels mirrored the pace of life back then—thirty, forty, or more years ago. But in our current fast-paced world, readers have little time or patience for excessive description. Writers are told to be concise, to "write tight." And so the question plagues every modern writer: Just how much description should I put in a scene, and what kind?

Leaving all description out doesn't solve the problem. It's just as bad to leave your reader confused and unengaged.

So in this look at Fatal Flaw #10, we editors show you what excessive description looks like and how to trim it back. And we'll look at deficient passages and show you what's missing and why.

It takes a bit of practice and hard work to find the right balance for your story and your genre, but don't neglect this flaw. Writers who master description are in an elite class. Their novels are memorable for their powerful or exquisite descriptions. Read on to learn how you can join that group.

Writing "Personal" Description through Your POV Character

I love description. Yes, I know, lots of people quit reading in school because the books they were forced to choke down had too much, and I like a fast-moving plot as much as the next girl. But even so, there is nothing I like better than to be immersed in another place or time through words.

More than any other element of fiction writing, description creates immersion. Too little description leaves readers either confused or unengaged—or both. But too much irrelevant description bogs down pacing and kills tension. So how's a writer to know just how much is enough? And just what kind of description is best?

Description has grown sharper over time. The most important lessons we've learned since the days of Victor Hugo's chapters of architectural details and L. M. Montgomery's endless catalogs of flowers? Make it personal.

Making It Personal

Another way to say this might be "use description to reveal character." First and foremost, use it to reveal your *POV* character, whose eyes, mind, and heart we are looking through. But use it as well to reveal other characters, the character or mood of a *place,* and finally even the themes of the story.

Don't just look on the outward appearance, as the Bible might say; use description to open up the heart.

Make It Sensory

Before we dive into that, however, I want to say a few words about sensory detail. It's no secret that some writers write description that sounds like a laundry list (and is about that engaging), while others write description we can *feel;* the place lives, the atmosphere is almost tangible.

The difference is mostly in the details—specifically, sensory details. When you write description, you aren't primarily going after facts; you're going after sensory input. What can the character see, hear, feel, smell, taste?

Unless your character is blind, visual details (which I'm focusing on for the rest of this section) are the most common and important. But using all five senses makes the difference between an encyclopedia entry and a lived experience.

Quality vs. Quantity

A common pitfall in visual description is giving a laundry list of physical characteristics; ticking every box, so to speak. But it's hard to pick out *important* details from a multitude of unimportant ones—and readers will fill in a lot of gaps themselves, so much so that they can find it annoying to have every feature of someone's face spelled out for them.

The key with visual description, then, is to give just a few details—but make those details count by using them to reveal character.

Before:

April heard the sound of a window being pushed open as Richard climbed out of the second-story lookout. He made his way gingerly across the shining shingles and sat down next to April, handing her a warm travel mug.

They made an odd couple. Richard was a six-foot-two black man with a neatly trimmed beard that outlined a square jaw beneath intense brown eyes and fine eyebrows. His hair was close-shaved. He wore a well-tailored black suit, polished shoes, and a red tie. A ring on one finger was a gift from his father many years ago. His features were chiseled yet gentle. Beside him, April was a five-foot-two blonde, her hair light gold. She was slender, with pretty features, but had a toughness in her face that spoke of a past. Her hair was up in a ponytail, and a gray wool blanket was swathed around her shoulders.

The coffee warmed her quickly, and she shed the blanket, revealing black track pants, an orange tank top, and blue Nike sneakers. A rose-vine tattoo inked across her right shoulder made her look even tougher, yet with a feminine grace.

Warmed by the sun, April's shoulders and arms were well-muscled—she had the frame of a runner.

After:

April heard the sound of a window being pushed open and a grunt as Richard climbed out of the second-story lookout. He made his way gingerly across the shining shingles and sat down next to April, handing her a warm travel mug.

They made an odd couple, April thought—the six-foot-two black man with a neatly trimmed beard and close-shaved hair, wearing a suit, and the five-foot-two blonde with her hair in a ponytail and a blanket swathed around her shoulders.

The coffee warmed her quickly, and she shed the blanket. The sun warmed her neck and brightened the rose-vine tattoo inked across her right shoulder. She wore a tank top and track pants and sneakers. Ready to run.

The After example (from my novel *Exile*) gives far less detail about these characters. But it zooms in on important ones, heightening the contrast between them and hinting at aspects of their character: Richard's professional, self-controlled demeanor; April's mix of tough and vulnerable. Details like the color of their clothing, specific facial features, and muscles just distract us from seeing what's important in this scene.

When you're describing setting, things get even more interesting (borrowing from *Exile* as well):

Before:

Reese stood in the living room of a small cottage on a cliff, looking out over the ocean. The room was longer than it was wide, with low sloping ceilings. Windows covered three sides from a foot above the floor to just below the ceiling. The fourth side sported faded wallpaper patterned with fishing boats and nets. Cobwebs in the corners made it obvious the inhabitants didn't clean much. Stacks of books and old magazines sat on the shag carpet next to a worn-out plaid wool couch. They were dusty. The air in the room was warm and

241

smelled slightly burnt from the old electric space heater positioned behind the couch.

Outside, a storm raged over the water. Black tumultuous clouds. Forked lightning and thunder. Rain pelted across the water in sheets. Waves whipped up in a whitecapped frenzy. To the right she could see the town and the masts of boats in the harbor, bobbing in the storm. Far below, the headlights of a car winding its way along a cliff road streamed through the wet darkness.

After:

With windows on three sides that covered nearly the whole wall, Reese felt enveloped by the storm. Black tumultuous clouds. Forked lightning. Thunder that shook the walls. Pelting rain. It was a classic coastal storm, wind slamming the cliffs and churning the sea in a white frenzy she could just see from here, despite the darkness.

She stood by the window, placed a hand on the glass. Thunder cracked, and the glass strained against the wind howling up the cliff and battering the cottage.

Surrounded by the storm—except that she stood behind windows, in the warmth, smelling the faint burnt smell of an old heater, wrapped up and clean and dry except for her hair.

She sighed and leaned her head against the window as if it were too heavy to hold up on her own.

The Before passage is perfectly good description; I like the atmosphere it conjures up. But it focuses so much on various details of the room that it fails to use the setting effectively to reveal character and mood. Rather than revealing the story, it leaves it behind for a while.

The After passage, on the other hand, focuses on the storm, on the way Reese feels swallowed by it, and on the strong contrast between the turmoil outside and the warm atmosphere within . . . all of which mirror what's happening in Reese's own heart and in the plot of the novel.

In this example, yes, we're getting a setting. But we're also getting insight into a character and forward motion in the story itself.

(Most of those other setting details, by the way, do show up in the book—but in a different scene, where the focus is on revealing things about the characters who own the cottage.)

Enhancing Theme and Creating Mood

Well-written description doesn't just create a setting for your story, it can also contribute to theme, and of course, mood. If you've ever read a story that *felt* dark, or light, or gritty, or weird, or mythic, chances are that mood owed a lot to the author's use of descriptive detail.

Here too, quality is more important than quantity. The key isn't in tossing out every possible detail about a setting or character, or crafting clever similes or turns of phrase (there's nothing worse than a misplaced simile—"White hair like fluffy clouds" on a chillingly evil villain, for example). Instead, you want to use descriptive detail to create atmosphere and underscore thematic elements—the seen revealing the unseen.

Both the example passages above contribute to the themes and mood of the story: light clashing with darkness; the sun rising over the gloom; companionship in a place above the world; a storm brewing; the meeting of new world and old (represented by that old burnt smell from the space heater); turmoil and the search for a place of safety and peace.

One final word on the subject: While you're writing, try not to overthink description. Throw yourself into the scene and write what comes. The example passages in this section do strongly reflect the themes of the book, but I didn't think about that while I was writing them. In fact, it's *overthinking* that's more liable to get you writing laundry lists. Steep yourself into the mood of the story. Write. Then go back and make sure the details are doing what you need them to do.

Editor:
Linda S. Clare

Tricks to Writing Descriptions in First-Person POV

To avoid succumbing to Fatal Flaw #10, writers need to learn to balance description in fiction. As Rachel said, writers often struggle to find this balance—too much description bogs down pace and tension; too little will muffle the immersive experience readers crave. In a first-person story this is especially true.

Manage Camera Angles

A first-person point of view brings the camera as close as it gets. We know only what the character knows, and we feel what the character feels. In your own first-person viewpoint, you take in a wide range of objects, sounds, smells, tastes, and textures every moment. If you tried to write realistically to include all this, the reader wouldn't know what to pay attention to, what was important, and what was simply enriching the scene.

In fiction, it's important to manage the camera shots the first-person character experiences, including mostly *details that point to the story problem*—even if the character and the readers don't realize it yet.

Remember, describing something in detail says to readers, "Remember this! It's important!" Being less descriptive or leaving out a detail says, "This isn't vital to the story—move along."

Stay in Scene

Ideally, readers will perceive your "I" voice character moving through the story as if it were real life. Yet when description—or worse, exposition—intrudes into a scene, readers are stopped and forced to go in another direction. Often these kinds of descriptions slow the pace and ease tension as well, making it easier for readers to close the book.

Writers setting stories in earlier eras or strange places will often set a scene and then break away from the real-time action to educate readers about some historical event, scientific technique, or other information. If this happens, readers may wonder who is giving them this info. Does the "I" voice suddenly break into a recital of encyclopedic knowledge? This can yank the reader out of the character's head.

Instead of using description as information, let the character *experience* what you don't explain, bringing the camera ever closer.

Make Emotional Connections

All this camera and scenic management points to one goal: your character creating an emotional connection with readers. Writers hear a lot about emotions in fiction, and for good reason—emotions are what keep readers reading and caring about the story. If you can cause readers to invest in and identify with the character's emotions, you've probably hooked them. And in first-person fiction, these emotions are more important than ever.

First-person demands the closest possible camera shot because it is generated in the character's mind and heart. To make the most of this close relationship, filter all descriptions through the character's thoughts and, more importantly, through her feelings and attitudes. When those feelings and attitudes change, readers want to see that process.

We usually have reasons for changing our minds. As you describe the character's world, be sure to *show the makings of decisions* in a logical fashion that readers will identify with. Many fans of first-person fiction want to feel as though they become that character in the story.

Let's take a look at Before and After examples to illustrate these points:

Before:

> I sat at the far end of the long massive banquet table, across from Lord Havemuch, Sir Gotmore, and Lady Stickyfingers. Overhead hung colorful banners of Havemuch's heraldry. Lord Havemuch's family traced its ancestry to the War of Roses, a series of battles fought in medieval England from 1455 to 1485 between the House of Lancaster and the House of York. The name Wars of the Roses (sometimes mistakenly referred to as War of the Roses) is based on the badges used by the two sides,

the red rose for the Lancastrians and the white rose for the Yorkists. Major causes of the conflict include: 1) both houses were direct descendants of King Edward III; 2) the ruling Lancastrian king, Henry VI, surrounded himself with unpopular nobles; 3) the civil unrest of much of the population; 4) the availability of many powerful lords with their own private armies; and 5) the untimely episodes of mental illness by Henry VI. The wars ended when Richard III, the last Yorkist king, was defeated at the battle of Bosworth in 1485 by Henry Tudor, founder of the house of Tudor. I was served veal on a Wedgewood plate.

I shouted above a lively discussion going on between Gotmore and Stickyfingers. "Could someone please pass the salt?" They were talking about 1411, the year that Richard Plantagenet was born to Richard, fifth earl of Cambridge, and Anne Mortimer. His father was the son of Edmund, the first Duke of York, who was in turn the fourth son of Edward III. If Henry VI had died before 1453, the year of the birth of Edward, Prince of Wales, then Richard would have undoubtedly been crowned King of England, since there was no other noble (since the death of Henry VI's uncle and heir Humphrey, Duke of Gloucester, who had died in 1447) with such a strong claim to the throne at that time, other than Richard himself.

Lady S looked my way. "Pardon me, did you say something?"

I smiled. "Yes, I did." I pointed to the silver salt shaker, a replica of the same set used by Henry VI himself. "The salt. Please pass the salt." The silver was ornately carved with vines and tiny hearts.

She leaned across the table and shook her finger. "Why, I did no such thing!" Her enormous diamond brooch glittered in the candlelight.

I started to repeat my request, but then remembered: last week, my physician had warned me about the dangers of too much salt. I had to limit my daily intake to 1,500 milligrams per day lest I complicate my high-blood-pressure problem. "What a lovely brooch," I said.

After:

I sat at the far end of the long massive banquet table, across from Lord Havemuch, Sir Gotmore, and Lady Stickyfingers. Overhead hung colorful banners of Havemuch's heraldry. Lord Havemuch's family was rumored to trace its ancestry to the Wars of Roses, but I didn't believe a word Havemuch said.

What a pompous old fool. My stomach lurched when I saw the sickly-looking piece of overcooked veal lying helplessly on my Wedgewood plate. Why had I thought this dinner was a good idea?

I shouted above a lively discussion between Gotmore and Stickyfingers. "Could someone please pass the salt?" They were going on and on about 1411, the year that Richard Plantagenet was born to Richard and Anne Mortimer.

Lady S stared down her beaky nose. "Pardon me, did you say something?"

I forced a smile. "Yes, I did." I pointed to the salt shaker, a cheap replica of the type used by Henry VI. "The salt. Please pass the salt." My blood began to boil—Stickyfingers was such a snob.

She leaned across the table until her bosom was practically in the gravy and shook her finger at me. "Why I did no such thing!" Her gaudy diamond brooch—probably a cheap imitation—glittered in the candlelight. Havemuch and Gotmore stopped shouting and stared at me.

I started to repeat my request, but then remembered: last week, my physician had said I had to limit my daily intake. Darned high blood pressure. That did it. I was never coming to one of these awful dinners again.

"What a lovely brooch," I said through clenched teeth.

In the Before version, it's easy to understand why this exposition about the Wars of the Roses (lifted verbatim from Wikipedia) takes us away from the scene and tries to educate us. When the "I" character interacts with Lady Stickyfingers, readers don't see or hear anything more from Havemuch and Gotmore, risking the possibility that readers will forget they're on stage. And the POV "I" voice simply reports about what's happening, with little emotion.

The After version removes the exposition and instead adds the character's attitudes and feelings about the surroundings. We get what we need to know, but the info is filtered through the character's judgments. Note that Havemuch and Gotmore are mentioned again as a way to remind readers of who's on stage. The "I" voice reaches her decision not to attend another dinner in a gradual manner, as the little things pile up.

In first-person fiction, the camera is so close and tightly focused that managing camera angles becomes an important tool in describing a scene. If more than two players are on stage, it's often necessary to refocus the camera lest readers forget what they've been shown. Breaking away from action to insert expositional or descriptive information about the story is a pacing and tension killer that jerks readers away from the scene. Instead, try to filter vital info through your first-person character's thoughts, feelings, and attitudes, and don't forget to show readers the steps that character takes to reach decisions.

Body Parts Behaving Badly

No discussion of description deficiencies would be complete without talking about "floating body parts," or FBPs. If you've been writing fiction for some time, chances are you've seen editors and other authors discourage their use.

Now, I'm not talking about the severed leg that washes up on the coast in a murder mystery—that's a perfectly acceptable floating body part. There's another kind of FBP that's actually all too common in fiction: when a character's body parts start acting of their own volition. And while we're at it, we may as well look at a couple of confusing clichés that can have multiple meanings too.

Here are some examples, along with some parenthetical snark.

FBPs:

- *Her eyes flew across the room.* (So her eyes popped out of her head, grew wings, and took flight? Eww.)

- *His jaw dropped to the floor.* (Whoa. Now that is one huge mouth.)

- *Her face fell.* (Did it bounce when it hit the floor?)

- *His eyebrows hiked to his hairline.* (That would require some seriously stretchy skin.)

- *Her sad eyes held him in place.* (Strong grip they have.)

Confusing clichés:

- *He threw up his hands.* (Who wouldn't vomit? Hands are not meant to be snack food.)

- *She shot her arm out to catch him.* (Did she use a gun or a cannon?)

249

The list could go on and on—and I'm sure you could add plenty that you've come across. Even well-known authors use them. (Note: that doesn't mean that lesser-known writers will get away with such writing unscathed. In the fiction world, the big names sometimes can pull off things that other writers will get criticized for.) Which brings us to a couple of questions.

First, why do writers use FBPs and clichés?

- Other writers use them.

- Writers think FBPs/clichés are more "creative."

- Writers think FBPs/clichés give more variety to their sentence structure. Starting sentences with "his," "her," or "my" provides a break from so many sentences beginning with "he," "she," or "I." This is particularly true with first-person point of view, where it can be difficult not to use a beginning "I" a lot.

These explanations may seem pretty legit (the last one definitely is), so this brings us to our second question: What's wrong with FBPs and clichés?

- They tend to result in exaggeration or misread meaning, often to the point of absurdity. While ridiculousness may be quite entertaining in some forms of media (think Victor Borgia), it's going to turn off fiction readers unless they're hoping for some slapstick action.

- They convey weakness in writing. Great writers are known for fresh wording. FBPs and clichés imply that the writer couldn't (or chose not to) come up with a better way to describe something. In this case, taking a shortcut isn't going to work in anyone's favor.

- They remove the importance from the character and place it on an object. Downplaying the character usually doesn't benefit a story. The reader's bond with a character is a primary reason readers keep turning pages, so diminishing that relationship should be done with much care.

Ready to see some FBPs, confusing clichés, and their fixes? Here goes . . .

Before:

As we left the residence hall, two boys about my age approached us on the pathway. They stopped laughing as soon as our eyes met, and their feet scooted them to one side to give us room.

"Hey. You must be new here." The taller boy halted, facing us. He smiled as his hand combed back through his dark hair. "I'm Connor. He's Landon."

My face fell, an unfortunate consequence of my shyness with guys I didn't know, and I forced my eyes back to his. "Hey. I'm Cassie."

Landon's eyebrows jumped up in greeting. "Hey, Cassie. Morning, Mrs. Gray."

A smile leapt to her face. "Good morning, boys."

"Well, we'll see you around, Cassie." Connor shot his arms out from his sides. "Welcome to Covington Hall."

After:

As we left the residence hall, two boys about my age approached us on the pathway. They stopped laughing as soon as our gazes met and then moved to one side to give us room.

"Hey. You must be new here." The taller boy halted, facing us. He smiled as he combed his hand back through his dark hair. "I'm Connor. He's Landon."

I automatically looked to the ground, an unfortunate consequence of my shyness with guys I didn't know. Drawing a breath, I stared right at him. "Hey. I'm Cassie."

Landon raised his eyebrows in greeting. "Hey, Cassie. Morning, Mrs. Gray."

She grinned. "Good morning, boys."

"Well, we'll see you around, Cassie." Connor spread his arms wide. "Welcome to Covington Hall."

I don't need to point out the differences between to the two examples; they're pretty self-explanatory. The Before passage sounds silly, and the After passage tells the same story without the animate body parts.

I do want to answer one more question before concluding, though.

When are FBPs and clichés not discouraged?

- *If the body parts truly are acting on their own*—for example, "His hair stuck out in all directions." He's not making his hair stick out; bedhead is involuntary (most of the time). Here's another: "Her legs gave out." She's not making her legs give out; in this case, she has no control of them. Or "His hands shook." Again, it's a reflexive action, which is fine.

- *If, for some reason, the POV character can't see what's going on.* Perhaps a character has blacked out and is just coming around. She hasn't opened her eyes yet (or her vision hasn't returned), but she can feel a hand shaking her arm. The hand is what she's going to focus on, and she may not know who's shaking her arm. Maybe she was in a room full of people or walking along a busy street, and the shaker could be one of many people. She will feel the hand on her arm, though, so describe that.

- *If there's no other good way to say something*—for example, "He rolled his eyes." Some people consider this a confusing cliché (where did he roll them to?), but everyone knows what it means. Furthermore, how else do you describe it without it sounding awkward? "He shifted his eyes upward and to the side in annoyance" sounds absurd. Instead, stick with what's known.

- *If the body part (briefly) deserves more importance than the character's action*—for example, "His hand closed over mine, wonderfully warm on my near-frozen skin" has a much different sound than "He closed his warm hand over my nearly frozen one." In this case, temporarily giving the body part more emphasis can work in a writer's favor.

As always, keep in mind that breaking the "rules" isn't always unacceptable. Rules usually have good reasoning behind them, but there are writers who break rules well. And chances are, an FBP here or a confusing cliché there isn't going to get a story tossed aside. Just use them with care, because overuse will weaken the writing and may turn off readers.

Going beyond the Setting

After I finished my first novel, I paid for a critique of the first fifteen pages. It came back so riddled with red, I feared the editor had bled to death on my manuscript. One of her comments was, "Floating heads in a blank space." Apparently, writing description didn't come naturally to me. I remedied that, and my next critique partner highlighted paragraph after paragraph and added the comment, "You don't need this." I still didn't have it right.

Years have passed, and I find myself making similar comments to my clients. Yes, we need to describe our settings, but we don't want to bore our readers. There's a balance.

Emotion Makes All the Difference

Rachel and Linda have addressed the need to connect description with your character, making it personal, but I want to look at this specifically from the angle of *emotional* response.

You must infuse your descriptions with emotion. Put your characters in the scene, and don't just show us what they see—show us how they *feel* about what they see. Unless your character is Mr. Spock from *Star Trek*, he will have some emotional reaction. Two people can look at the same thing with very different opinions.

Think of George Bailey and Mary Hatch from *It's a Wonderful Life*. Remember the scene in which they are walking home from the party and stop in front of the old house? He sees a broken-down place worthy of nothing more than target practice. She sees a home. For each element in your scene, think about how your character would see it.

Before:

The covered bridge served as the gateway into Nutfield. Its weathered boards and planks dated back more than a century. I crossed the bridge to the sound of those creaking boards, then

254

passed the apple orchards. The scent of ripe fruit filtered through my open window. The post office was the first building in Nutfield's town square. It stood on my right. On the opposite side of the street, McCall's, the department store that had been there forever, advertised a sale on men's suits. Overhead, the sun shone and the birds flitted from branch to branch on the sugar maples that lined Main Street, singing their songs.

I followed the road and passed the old high school, a low-slung brick building with tall windows in each classroom. The flag waved on its pole in front of the school, signaling me that a slight wind blew. Beyond the high school stood the new police station, which was attached to the courthouse. Across the street, the park was filled with people enjoying the early fall day.

Bored yet?

Technically, there's nothing wrong with this passage. It describes a town that's very important to the novel, and I've even been careful to include a few of the senses—the sight of the town, the scent of the apples, the sound of the old boards, and the birds singing. I've included lots of details—the waving flag, the sugar maples, the brick on the high school. I even put people in the park. It's personal as well—we get a sense that the main character knows this town ("the department store that had been there forever").

So why is it so boring? Simple: the passage is missing emotion.

Whether you are writing in first person or third person, you can infuse description with emotion. So how might we fix the passage?

After:

The covered bridge had been old even when I was a kid. I inched my Honda across, waiting for those creaking planks to crumble and dump me into the river below. When my tires were back on solid ground, I looked in my rearview and hoped the bridge would stay standing long enough for me to cross one more time.

Beautiful downtown Nutfield, New Hampshire. It had hardly changed since I was a kid. The post office had a fresh coat of white paint. Across the street, McCall's was having a sale on men's suits. I peered in the window at those circular racks and remembered hiding inside them, the clothes hanging taller than I was, Dad sliding pants and sports coats aside to find me. His hand, warm and comforting, gripping my arm, his gruff "Gotcha" sending me into fits of giggles.

If only Daddy were here to welcome me home.

The police station had gotten a makeover. The courthouse, though, looked the same. My eyes were drawn across the street to the park. Bright green grass beneath a canopy of sugar maples just starting to turn red. On a clear day, I swore the New Hampshire sky was bluer than any in the world. I barely took it in. My memories brought me back all those years until I could see nothing but the horde of reporters shouting questions.

"Reagan, did you know what would happen?"

"Reagan, what would your father say?"

"Reagan, how do you feel . . . ?"

Stupidest question ever.

The park hadn't been beautiful to me in a long time. I'd hated reporters back then. Well, at least my brand of journalism never had me harassing eleven-year-old girls.

I hope you found that segment a little better. You'll notice there are elements from the Before passage that didn't make it into the After one. Rather than try to keep everything, I focused on the things that would bring an emotional response from my POV character. The covered bridge, for instance, signifies Reagan returning to her hometown. And you get the sense she's not thrilled to be there—that look in the rearview should show us that. The store brings back happy memories of her father, but the park across from the courthouse— what's that about?

And what didn't I mention? The singing birds, the waving flag, and the happy people. Those elements might be there, but we want the feelings in the scene to mirror hers, and she's feeling unsettled, not cheerful.

I left out the high school, because later in the story this character is going to visit it, and I can describe it then. And I left out the apple orchards, because they added nothing emotionally.

From the first segment, you got a nice view of an old New Hampshire town, but from the second, I hope you got a peek into a compelling story.

Imbue your descriptions with emotion, and they will be as compelling as the rest of your novel.

Editor:
C. S. Lakin

Description Errors That Result from POV Limitations

I'd like to close our discussion on description by veering off on a tangent: one that ties in with POV.

You may have noticed already how pivotal POV is to good description. The other editors have shown how important it is to convey the description of setting and characters through the POV character's eyes and even emotions. Just as we don't take notice of every single detail in a room or about a person we encounter (I think our brains would explode!), our characters are going to notice particular things, and that's determined by their personality and mood at the moment.

For example, if a beautiful woman wearing provocative clothing walks into a diner, a young man is going to notice different things about her than, say, a five-year-old child would. He's going to think different things as well, and it's likely that, if you put ten men in that diner, you could have each think very different thoughts about that woman because of who he is. An old priest will think different thoughts than a twenty-something bad boy. The priest might notice how tarnished and unhappy the woman seems. The young man may only be checking out her curves and the hemline of her dress.

By now, after going through this chapter *and* the fatal flaws on POV *and* showing instead of telling, you probably have this drilled into your head. Simply, scenes are going to feel deficient if description is dumped outside of POV.

But there are also other problems that can occur because of POV, and they stem from what happens when a writer forgets where his character is placed in his scene.

Characters and Their Sensory Limitations

Few writers pay much attention to character placement, but this is something of paramount concern to filmmakers, and a subject I cover in depth in *Shoot Your Novel*. A director has to lay out his camera shots, deciding when a close-up shot would be more effective than a long shot, for example. He may want the camera positioned far away from the action, to make details unclear and evoke curiosity or misinterpretation. Or he may have an extreme close-up to ensure viewers don't miss a tiny detail that is crucial to the plot.

Adept novelists mimic this technique in their books to good effect. But if writers don't think through where they are placing their characters, they may end up with description issues. Meaning, their character is reacting to and processing details that she really can't react to or process—due to where she is in the scene.

Here's what I mean.

Before:

Tracy stared out the windshield of her old VW bug at the red light. Would it never change?

Then she spotted a boy about seven or eight across the four-lane intersection, pounding on the Walk button over and over. He was humming something as he poked, straddling a too-large bike, with his new Nikes digging into the dirt. He looked at his feet, obviously unaware that all his button pressing was preventing the light from changing.

Tracy gritted her teeth, then swung the door open. The heat blasted in. She glanced around. No other cars on this Sunday morning in this tiny town she'd been driving through mindlessly.

She stepped out onto the sizzling pavement.

The boy looked up and saw her glowering at him. His face paled and he sucked in a breath, no doubt figuring how to make his escape. He hopped on his bike but didn't see the crack in the pavement. His front tire slipped in and wrenched the bike, which caused it to ricochet off the pavement. The boy slammed into the handlebars, which smacked him right in the nose, breaking it.

He quickly righted himself and looked up to see if she'd witnessed his mishap and flushed almost purple when he realized she had.

Mortified, and desperate to get away, he pulled with all his might and managed to lift the front wheel up above his head so he could pivot the bike around, but as he did so, the bike and its rider fell to the ground. He lay on the smoldering pavement like a fish out of water, wiggling and thrashing, his little legs tangled up in the metal spokes.

Then Tracy spotted something in the corner of her eye. She spun around. Behind her, the car lurched forward, almost knocking her down.

Oh no, I forgot to put the car in Park.

She ran over to her car door, hoping to jump inside, but smacked into it instead. Her right foot locked as the tire rolled over her shoelace and pinned her in place. She fell to her knees and watched helplessly as the unmanned car continued rolling across the street, heading straight for the little boy who was still flailing about beneath the giant bike, his face stricken with fear.

"Get up! Get out of the way!" She screeched as she struggled to her feet and scrambled to run after the car. Judging the distance between the car and boy, she knew she was never going to make it.

The boy wiggled and whimpered as Tracy ran, panting, trying to reach him.

Just in time, she caught up to the rolling car, threw open the door, lunged over the seat, and pulled up the emergency brake. She stared out the windshield, gasping for breath. The boy's bike was mangled under her tires. The handlebars were crushed.

Tracy turned around and saw the little boy sitting on the curb across from her, his head buried in his arms, trying not to cry. She ran over to him, relieved he was alive.

"Are you okay?" she asked him.

He nodded but wouldn't lift his head to look at her.

She let out a breath, her shoulders sagging. "I'm sorry about your bike. I'll buy you another one."

Did you spot all the problems with the description in this passage? At first glance it may seem as if it all works. But let's take a look at the After passage and then tear this apart.

After:

Tracy stared out the windshield of her old VW bug at the red light. Would it never change?

Then she spotted a boy about seven or eight across the four-lane intersection, pounding on what she guessed was the Walk button over and over. He was straddling a too-large bike, kicking one foot into the dirt. He looked down, obviously unaware that all his button pressing was preventing the light from changing.

Tracy gritted her teeth, then swung the door open. The heat blasted in. She glanced around. No other cars on this Sunday morning in this tiny town she'd been driving through mindlessly.

She stepped out onto the sizzling pavement.

The boy looked up and saw her glowering at him. He stiffened, then hopped on his bike. Suddenly the bike toppled sideways and ricocheted off the pavement. The boy slammed into the handlebars and smacked his face.

He quickly righted himself and looked over at her. Then he lifted the front wheel up above his head and pivoted the bike around, but as he did so, the bike and its rider fell to the ground. He lay on the pavement like a fish out of water, wiggling and thrashing, his little legs tangled up in the metal spokes.

Then Tracy heard something behind her. She spun around and saw the car lurching forward, almost knocking her down.

Oh no, I forgot to put the car in Park.

She ran over to her car door, hoping to jump inside, but smacked into it instead. Her right foot locked as the tire rolled over her shoelace and pinned her in place. She fell to her knees and watched helplessly as the unmanned car continued rolling across the street, no doubt heading straight for the little boy. Was he still tangled in his bike? She hoped he'd gotten out but knew it was unlikely.

"Get up! Get out of the way!" She screeched as she struggled to her feet and scrambled to run after the car. Judging the distance between the car and boy, she knew she was never going to make it. Across the intersection, she spotted the boy— still trapped. Tracy ran, panting, trying to reach him.

Just in time, she caught up to the rolling car, threw open the door, lunged over the seat, and pulled up the emergency brake. She stared out the windshield, gasping for breath. The boy's bike was nowhere to be seen. *Oh no, did I kill him?* She pictured the gruesome scene—the bike mangled under her wheels, the handlebars crushed. And the little boy . . .

Tracy turned around in the seat, craning to see out the side windows. *Oh, thank God!* The little boy was sitting on the curb across from her, his head buried in his arms. She ran over to him, relieved he was alive.

"Are you okay?" she asked him.

He nodded but wouldn't lift his head to look at her.

She let out a breath, her shoulders sagging. "I'm sorry about your bike. I'll buy you another one."

The details might be minor, but we want to be accurate in our descriptions, and the Before passage reveals a lot of problems as the scene is played out in Tracy's POV. Did you notice these things?

- She's too far away to hear the boy humming or know what brand of shoes he's wearing.

- She's too far away to see his face pale or hear him suck in a breath (and no doubt the sun is glaring on this hot morning, making visibility even worse).

- She can't see a crack in the pavement to know that's what caused the bike to fall.

- She's too far away to see that the bike hit him directly in the nose or that it may have broken it.

- She can't know he's mortified, or desperate to get away, or that he's pulling with all his might. From where she is, she might be able to tell he's struggling.

- She can't see something behind her from the corner of her eye. She has to completely spin around to notice the car is moving behind her.

- When she's on her knees next to the car and it starts to roll away, she isn't in position to see clearly that the boy is in the car's path and that he's still tangled in the spokes. She's too far away to see his face stricken with fear.

- She might be able to see the boy wiggle, but if the car is almost upon him, and she's coming up alongside the car, it's not likely. And she wouldn't hear him whimpering. Maybe shouting, yes.

- She can't see the mangled bike under her tires as she looks forward out the windshield.

- If she turns around, that implies she sees the boy behind her, through the back window. But he's sitting on the curb to her side.

- She can't really know he's trying not to cry. His head is buried in his arms.

It's so easy for writers to hurry through such descriptions without taking time to envision the scene's details and ensuring the POV character can actually see, hear, and do all the things written. By picturing a movie camera capturing the action, writers will catch these kinds of description errors.

Put yourself in your character's shoes and try to see what she can see and hear what she can hear. If you need your character to notice small details, get her closer. Conversely, if you want her to *miss* certain details, put her further away. It's all about distance when it comes to POV perspective. So keep this in mind to avoid this pitfall of Fatal Flaw #10.

In Conclusion . . .

Description is important. Without it, readers can't experience what your characters are experiencing, and they can't be transported to the world you imagine in your head. But too much description or ineffective details will bog down a story and put your readers to sleep.

Take the time to examine your scenes carefully for description of characters and settings. Make sure you include details that will bring your scene to life and that come through the senses and emotions of your POV character. Similar to backstory, a balance is desired. Study great novels in your genre to see how the authors wield description— what kind and how much, and told in what way. That's one good way to get a feel for proper balance. Think like Goldilocks: not too much, not too little, but just right.

Fatal Flaw #10 Checklist

Go through your scenes and look for these types of Description Deficiencies and Excesses:

- Description presented as an info dump and not coming through the POV character's senses

- Lack of sensory detail in the setting so that it's hard for readers to picture it

- Boring physical descriptions of characters and places that don't add interest to the scene

- Insignificant description details that are distracting rather than informative

- Body parts moving on their own

- Description that doesn't work in tandem with the character's mood or emotions (or works against it, such as cheerful details when the character is depressed)

- Details the POV character cannot see, hear, or know due to her positioning in the scene

Your Turn: Try to spot and fix all the areas that show description deficiencies and excesses in this passage. An example of a revision is on the next page (no peeking!). There isn't one correct way to rewrite a passage, so your final version may be different from the revision provided. The key is to test yourself to see if you've nailed Fatal Flaw #10.

As Rebecca was changing into casual clothing—some soft yoga pants, a white short-sleeved blouse, and flats—she heard her mobile phone ringing in the kitchen. She rushed out and put her hand out to answer the phone, out of breath.

"Rebecca, it's your dad."

Rebecca's heart skipped a beat. "What's wrong?" There was silence.

"It's your mother." Pausing, her father said, "She's been hurt. She's at the hospital. Can you meet me there?"

Rebecca's hand shook as she held firmly to her phone. Her legs turned to jelly, and she couldn't think straight. She stood wobbly, about to fall down, her feet glued to the floor in shock.

"What happened?"

"I'll tell you when you get here."

"I'll be right there." As she hung up, her hand grabbed her bag and rushed outside. Her black 2002 Prius with 200,000 miles on it and a bit dented was parked in the parking lot, at the far end, which would take her awhile to get to, so it would be quicker to take a taxi to the hospital.

Rebecca had lived in this apartment on Blake Street for six years. She had moved here after she graduated high school, and while she probably could afford something better, she liked saving money. It had been her dream all her life to travel to Europe. In tenth grade, she had loved history, and when she studied art history, she developed a yearning to see the Louvre Museum and go to Greece to see the ruins of the ancient Greek buildings. The apartment was one of many in a long row of "modern" apartments that had been built back in the 1990s to help with the large student population in town due to the nearby college. They hadn't been well kept up, although there was a groundskeeper, and the paint was peeling and there were cracks in many of the walls.

Rebecca wondered what happened while the taxi maneuvered through traffic. What happened to her mother? How serious was it?

Finally arriving at the hospital, Rebecca's legs rushed to the nurses' station and asked for her mother's room number. Her eyes flew to her father hovering over her mother's still body. With a nauseous feeling, Rebecca saw her mother's face and wondered who could do such a thing. Where were the police? Surely they would be investigating this incident.

"How are you feeling, Mother?"

"Oh, I'm fine—just a few scratches."

Rebecca sighed and shook her head, not bothering to reply. "What happened?"

Her mother looked away, so her father answered. "I had to work late tonight, so your mother was home alone. Someone broke in, and she was attacked from behind."

Revision of the Previous Passage:

As Rebecca was changing into casual clothing, her mobile phone rang in the kitchen. She hurried to answer it and hesitated when she saw her parents' number on the screen. She hadn't spoken to them in months. *What do they want now? To remind me yet again of the bad choice I'd made? Choices,* she added. She almost set the phone down, but guilt smothered her protestations.

"Rebecca, it's your dad."

She heard something in his voice—something off. "What's wrong?" She listened to the silence.

"It's your mother," he finally said, then paused. "She's been hurt. She's at the hospital. Can you meet me there?" His words were rough with emotion.

Rebecca's hand shook as she held firmly to her phone. Her legs wobbled. "What happened?"

"I'll tell you when you get here."

"I'll be right there."

She hung up and grabbed her shoulder bag and coat off the hook by the door. She stuffed her phone into the bag and pulled out her keys, then stepped out of her apartment and locked the door behind her.

Her mom—hurt? All the anger and hurt she'd been nursing since that big fight they'd had dissolved in a flare of worry. *Oh, please, let her be all right.*

Rebecca rushed outside and onto the crowded sidewalk and put on her coat. The cold December day hadn't gotten any warmer since she'd stepped out this morning to grab her usual coffee at the Human Bean. Snow still clung to the sidewalk in the shadows, and the gutters on the side of the street were a slushy mess, with tires spraying gritty black water as they plowed along.

Rebecca stared at the street packed with commuters heading home in the dying light, their cars' headlights like lidless eyes glaring mindlessly ahead. Traffic moved at a crawl. Horns honked—impatient drivers weary after a long day at work. She'd never have the patience to drive the two miles in this mess.

She hailed the first vacant taxi she spotted, and when the yellow cab inched up to the curb, forcing two cars to stop abruptly—one irate driver leaning on his horn—she threw open the back door and slid into the warmth of the old car that smelled of musty cigars and cheap perfume.

Finally, after a jerky trip across town, the cab moving slower than she probably could have walked, the male driver—whose only words to her were "Where going?" in some thick accent she couldn't identify—screeched into the circular drive that led to the entrance to the hospital. Rebecca paid the unsmiling driver, rushed inside to the nurses' station, and asked for her mom's room number. Every chair in the waiting area was filled. Parents with sick children, wiping noses and talking in low, stern voices. Old people hunched over, still bundled in coats although the room was stiflingly warm. One young man cradled a broken arm.

Rebecca looked down the hall, to the room she had been in three months ago. Her heart hurt with such a sharp pang, she sucked in a breath. *He made me do it*, she reminded herself—for the millionth time, swallowing back the tears.

She yanked her mind away from that day. From the pain and heartache. From the memory of Daniel dumping her on the curb outside as if she were a bag of trash. His words still ricocheted in her head. *Just get it done. Call me when it's over, and I'll pick you up*. He wouldn't stay with her. Coward.

Stop it, she told herself. Her mom needed her. None of that mattered now.

She strode with determination down the hall, past *that room*, and stopped at 108. The door was partly opened, and she stopped but heard nothing inside but the beeping of equipment. She sucked in a breath, pushed the door open, and stepped inside.

Her dad hovered over her mom's still body. Rebecca's gaze lit on the tubes running out of her mom's arm, the IV drip, the white crisp sheet covering her frail body. She swallowed. Her mom looked so weak—so vulnerable. And old. A TV mounted on the wall showed images of a pileup on the expressway, the sound muted.

Her dad turned and looked at her—a blank expression. No—one drained of emotion. As if he'd been crying and he'd run out of tears. Her mom's eyes were closed, and Rebecca couldn't see any signs of injury. No bones in casts. No bandages in sight. Was she bleeding internally? She turned back to look at her dad.

"Hey," she said quietly, unsure if she should speak aloud.

"Thanks for coming, Becs," her dad said. She was relieved to see his soft expression and hear the forgiving tone. None of the "I told you so" attitude he'd dumped on her when Daniel left her after the abortion.

The memory instantly nauseated her. She walked up to her mom and looked at her face. Now she could see bruising, and the trace of a swollen black eye. Had someone hit her in the face? Or knocked her down? She wanted to ask her dad so many questions, but knew this wasn't the right time.

And where were the police? Surely they would be investigating this incident.

Her mom opened her eyes and found Rebecca's. Rebecca gave her a warm smile, although she felt cold inside. This was just plain awkward.

"Hello, sweetie," her mom said, her voice papery thin, a forced smile on her face.

Rebecca took her hand. The skin was cool and dry. "How are you feeling, Mom?"

"Oh, I'm fine—just a few scratches." Spoken in her trademark style.

Rebecca sighed and shook her head, not bothering to reply. Her mom always acted the stoic victim. Somehow, everything circled back to her. Even when Rebecca had . . . done that terrible thing, and she'd bowed out of coming to dinner because of horrible cramping and bleeding, her mom made her feel like a disloyal daughter. She couldn't help it that she was too distraught and hurting to attend her parents' fancy anniversary party. Her mom hadn't wanted to hear how Rebecca's marriage was in the toilet. She had canapés to prepare.

Rebecca straightened and pulled her hand back. She calmed her racing heart and breathed deeply. She needed a drink. She needed to leave.

"What happened?" she asked her mom, hearing the sharp edge to her words. *Do I even want to know?*

Her mom looked away, so her dad answered. "I had to work late tonight, so your mother was home alone. Someone broke in, and she was attacked from behind."

Fatal Flaw #11: Pesky Adverbs and "Weasel Words"

If you've been writing fiction for a while, you've probably heard editors or other writers insist that adverbs and overused words (and actions) weaken writing. That advice may be followed by the famous writerly command "show, don't tell." That's because readers today want to "see" what's happening in a story, not have it told to them—and using adverbs and "weasel words" often leads to "telling." Before we start addressing this flaw, let's tackle a few definitions.

What's an Adverb?

Adverbs are words or phrases that modify a verb, adjective, other adverb, or group of words; they show a relation to manner, cause, degree, time, place, etc. The most picked-on adverbs tend to be words ending in *ly* (e.g., *quickly, softly, happily, sadly*), but others are also overused (e.g., *then, just, very, really*).

And What about a "Weasel Word"?

In fiction, "weasel words" are unnecessary words, phrases, and even actions that end up sucking the creative life out of writing. Some examples include using too many dialogue tags (e.g., "he asked" or "she said"), using the same bodily movements (e.g., "he shrugged" or "she smiled") repeatedly, and filling sentences with "to be" verbs and superfluous words.

So What's a Writer to Do?

Should writers omit all adverbs and weasel words from their manuscript? Of course not. As with most things in life, there's a time and a place for everything. Sometimes adverbs are necessary to provide the clearest meaning, and sometimes weasel words give a character color and voice. But the opposite is also true. Adverbs and weasel words often do mitigate good writing.

Fortunately, eliminating these flaws is a little easier than getting rid of some of the other writing flaws described in this book. Some adverbs and weasel words can be identified and removed using MS Word's Find and Replace feature, and others are blatant enough (once you recognize them) to be caught with self-editing. This chapter will help you see exactly what you're looking for in your manuscript when it comes to pesky adverbs and weasels.

Editor:
Rachel Starr Thomson

Actions Speak Louder than Dialogue Tags: Using Beats in Writing

Dialogue is an extremely common place for weasel words and adverbs to show up. But it takes more finesse than one might think to get rid of them. "Don't use weasel words," hears the overzealous self-editor. Well, the writer looks, and behold, there are instances of "he said" all over the place. Aha! Time to slash mercilessly.

But that's not always a good idea. *Said*, while boring, is invisible. Readers don't really notice it unless it's used *so* often that it becomes extreme. In almost every case, the words we would use to replace it are worse: "Shut up!" he implored. "No!" she protested. "Please stop!" they cajoled. These frequently awful constructions are weasel words at their worst.

But you don't just want to end every line of dialogue with "she said" either. And while paragraphing and conversational interplay will sometimes let us know who's speaking without any extra direction from the author, writing dialogue without any tags at all can get confusing (especially if you have more than two people in conversation).

The best call is to use dialogue tags—use *said*, in fact, and its equally invisible counterpart *asked*—but use them sparingly, not after every line of dialogue. And for the rest of the space? There are action beats.

Introducing the Action Beat

While it's fine and good to use *said* as long as you do so sparingly, in a longer conversation you can still end up with the problem of white space—the dialogue will lose contact with the setting, and your readers will get the sense that they're hanging in midair.

This is where the skilled use of action beats comes in. Used well, action beats not only do away with the need for a whole lot of speaker tags, they also keep us in touch with the setting, enhance characterization, and occasionally even help out the plot.

Here's a visual of what I'm talking about, borrowing from my novel *Comes the Dragon*.

Before:

"Of course we can't leave without helping them. What is happening here is wrong, and we can stop it. We must stop it."

"But how?" Rechab asked. "How, if they won't let us?"

"They are not free to trust while Azeda is still in power."

"What then?"

"We can take Azeda out of power."

"How?"

"Through seeing justice done," Aaron said. "You know the law. Eye for eye. Tooth for tooth. Blood for blood."

"But the people won't come and accuse him."

"Not while Azeda and the elders are the judges," Aaron said. "We should have known they would not. No, we would have to bring another court to bear."

"I don't know," she said again.

"Rechab! Remember the beggars! Remember the maimed women, the children who are slaves. Remember the greed in Azeda's eyes!"

"But you can't just kill him!" she yelled.

After:

"Of course we can't leave without helping them. What is happening here is wrong, and we can stop it. We must stop it."

"But how?" Rechab asked, her eyes pleading. "How, if they won't let us?"

A muscle in Aaron's face twitched. "They are not free to trust while Azeda is still in power."

"What then?" Rechab asked.

"We can take Azeda out of power."

She blanched. "How?"

"Through seeing justice done," Aaron said. "You know the law. Eye for eye. Tooth for tooth. Blood for blood."

Something in Rechab's core grew hard, and she swallowed. Her mouth went dry. "But the people won't come and accuse him."

"Not while Azeda and the elders are the judges," Aaron said. "We should have known they would not. No, we would have to bring another court to bear."

She put her hands to her temples. She felt like a fox that had chased something down a hole and discovered too late that the thing she had cornered was a poisonous snake.

"I don't know," she repeated.

"Rechab!" He stopped, every muscle quivering.

"Remember the beggars! Remember the maimed women, the children who are slaves. Remember the greed in Azeda's eyes!"

She shook her head. "But you can't just kill him!"

Those bits of action that intersperse the dialogue—a muscle twitching, swallowing, hands to temples, stopping—all give the dialogue a visual element. They keep the conversation inside the scene.

Description and internal monologue can be used this way as well. They identify the speaker, making the conversation easier to follow, but they also make the scene visual and reveal more about the characters through their actions as they're speaking.

In this example, most of the action beats are body language—expressions and minor actions. But you can also use beats to frame a whole conversation within a continuous action (those THADs Susanne talked about earlier), such as having your characters chat while sparring, driving, fishing, climbing a mountain, building something, whatever. Since that continuous action may be something integral to the story, beats then have the potential to reveal themes, character, and plot with far more power than "he said" could ever have.

By employing action beats, you not only toss out extra dialogue tags and the host of weasel words and adverbs that frequently come along with them, you strengthen every other element of the story as well.

Editor:
Linda S. Clare

The Cure for Prepositional Phrase-itis

Let's look at how prepositions are abused in fiction and how to fix them.

A prepositional phrase is often a directional or time place-keeper. Common prepositions include *in*, *to*, *of*, *from*, *on*, *over*, *under*, *through*, *above*, and *below*. Writers use them to help readers imagine scenes more completely. Instead of floating in space, a character stands *in* the room. She lays her keys *on* the table and opens a letter *from* a long-lost lover. When she slumps *to* the floor, readers are grounded.

It's difficult to write much of anything without using prepositions. Yet writers often overuse them—just in case readers didn't get the gist of a sentence the first time. In this case, prepositions become weasel words: they're unnecessary, distracting, and wordy. A case in point might be a paragraph with a POV character moving through it:

> Sarah went to the balcony and looked over the railing. On the ground below, Rick stood, spouting amorous poetry. Sarah stepped back from the balcony, away from the railing. "What are you doing spouting poetry on the ground?"
>
> Rick yelled from the ground below, "I love you, Sarah. I'll stand here on the ground until you come down from the balcony!"

Once readers are told where people or objects are in time and space, they don't need to be reminded in every sentence. It's annoying to read the same orientation over and over. Repeat the orientation (using a prepositional phrase) only when it changes (and if it's important) or if there are more than two characters in the scene.

Many times prepositional phrases can be eliminated by using a possessive with an apostrophe. Instead of writing "Sarah went to the balcony and looked over the railing," you could write, "Sarah looked over the balcony's railing."

Rabbit Holes

Another mistake writers make is trying to cram too many prepositional phrases into the same sentence:

Sarah went back into her bedroom, where she ran straight into the closet with all her love letters, tied with red ribbon, in a shoebox tucked safely on the top shelf of the musty old space, with cobwebs and mothballed clothing hanging from the racks.

The sentence has no less than nine prepositional phrases—enough directional changes to cause whiplash. When readers must follow multiple directions or actions, putting them all into a single sentence only adds to the confusion. It's better to break up these convoluted constructions than to challenge readers to stick with you through too many actions/directions.

Depicting Multiple Actions

When writers want to give readers the sense of several actions occurring at once, the adverbs *as* and *while* often come into play. Opening a sentence using adverbs can muddle the action and give the sense the character is doing multiple actions at once in an implausible way.

As he entered the room, he drew his pistol, hunkered down, spun around, let out a loud "hiyaa," and fired.

Did he also do the hokey pokey? It only takes an instant to enter a room, so it's hard to believe the character could do all these things in that moment. Moreover, readers will likely be forced to reread the sentence to be able to imagine the entire sequence, and any time you make readers go back over a sentence, it creates frustration.

Since readers process one action at a time anyway, it's better to separate them into smaller chunks. The perception of simultaneous action will be the same.

Before:

As she crouched in the corner of the dark closet, with the shoebox from the closet shelf in her lap, she carefully slid her finger under the red ribbon tying the letters in the shoebox, took a letter from the stack, unfolded the letter from the shoebox on her lap, and sighed. She refolded the letter, tucked it under the red ribbon, laid the letters in the shoebox, put down the shoebox, stood up, opened the closet door, left the closet, went to her bed, and sobbed.

After:

She crouched in the dark closet, the box of love letters in her lap. Sliding her finger under the red ribbon, she pulled out the stack and chose the latest missive. She sighed, hesitated. Maybe another day she'd be stronger. Blinking back tears, she put the letters away and stood. A sob rose in her throat, and she threw herself on her bed.

The second version is shorter and less tedious to read. Note the lack of repetition (we know she's in the closet), the shorter sentences, and the separation of multiple stage directions or actions. Prepositional phrases and adverbial clauses are vital, and when they're used correctly, they make the reader experience more enjoyable. But watch for those little words that can trip up your prose.

> ### Editor:
> ### Christy Distler

Common Weasels and How Writers Can Trap Them

Merriam-Webster defines a *weasel word* as "a word used in order to evade or retreat from a direct or forthright statement or position." That's different from how we're using it in general—but it does have some truth in fiction writing as well. In fiction, weasel words are not intended to purposely evade, but their use can certainly result in a less-than-concise sentence that lacks forthrightness.

Now that we've looked at the broader categories of prepositions and dialogue tags, it's time to dive into specific vocabulary. Let's review a handful of the most common fiction weasel words:

- Weak "to be" verbs: *is, are, was, were, had, had been,*

- Superfluous words: *that, very, just, really, rather, kind of/ sort of, nearly/ almost, quite, like, even, so, absolutely, usually, truly, totally, probably, actually, basically, extremely, mostly, naturally, often, particularly, started to/ began to*

- "Telling" words: *seemed, knew, thought, felt, wondered, mused*

Weak "To Be" Verbs

These words, in most cases, produce subpar writing. Consider these two sentences: "The dog was on the bed" and "The dog lay on the bed." The second sentence is not only more active, it's also more specific. "The dog was on the bed" could imply that the dog is sitting, standing, lying, etc. "The dog lay on the bed" gives a clear picture of the dog's action.

Superfluous Words

These words, in many cases, are unnecessary or can be exchanged with a word that paints a stronger picture. Consider these two sentences: "She told me that I could go with her" and "She told me I could go with her." Both sentences say the same thing; the only difference is the extra word (*that*) in the first one. Most editors agree that *that* should be omitted anytime a sentence sounds right without it. If a *that* is necessary for a sentence's clarity or because the sentence sounds awkward without it, keep it. (Note: "had" is acceptable when used to describe something that happened in the past.)

Now consider these two sentences: "He started to sing" and "He sang." In many cases, "started to" and "began to" are unnecessary and can be replaced with a description of what's happening. An exception would be if an action is interrupted, and it needs to be obvious that something was started and not finished. Then "started to" or "began to" is more accurate. Ultimately, use more active wording whenever it strengthens the writing.

Modifiers Can Suck the Life out of Your Sentences

Continuing through the list, you'll see that many of the other superfluous words are modifiers (adverbs and/or adjectives). A long-time editor once told me that modifiers are like leeches: they suck the lifeblood from the word they're attached to. These adverbs and adjectives can often be omitted or replaced, reducing the word count while not changing the meaning. Here's another comparison: "He quietly spoke to her" and "He whispered to her." Here, the verb (*spoke*) and its modifier (the adverb *quietly*) are replaced with a more vivid verb, *whispered*. To boot, the sentence becomes tighter. Win-win.

Back to the leech analogy. Like leeches, modifiers can provide benefit. Consider these two sentences: "I can't thank you enough" and "I truly can't thank you enough." Hear the difference in the emotion levels? The second sentence sounds more sincere. Here's another: "She occasionally brushes her teeth" and "She brushes her teeth." Big difference (especially if you're her dental hygienist). So, like many of the writing "rules," there are exceptions to the weasel word rule as well. Bottom line, these words are often extra and unnecessary. Other times, they're not. Learn to know the difference, and your writing skill will soar.

"Telling" Words

Like the first two groups, these words can often be omitted or replaced to strengthen writing. Consider these two sentences: "I pulled into the driveway and wondered if anyone would be home" and "I pulled into the driveway. Would anyone be home?" Omitting *wondered* not only tightens the sentence (it breaks it in two) and removes the "telling" aspect, it also provides a more "showing," in-depth character point of view.

Here's another example: "I felt sick" and "My head throbbed." In this case, searching for alternate wording that doesn't use "felt" results in a more active, descriptive sentence.

Of course, weasel words have their rightful place too. Consider these sentences: "Why had I done that? I knew better." Yes, "knew" is a weasel word, but it also provides a succinct, concrete meaning that would be difficult to retain with other wording. So, again, learn when the "telling" words should be used and when you'd be better off exchanging them or rewording.

Without further ado, here's our weasely Before and our weasel-free After.

Before:

I crossed my arms as we started walking toward the administration building. After seeing some of the campus and meeting some students, I felt that Covington Hall actually might not be so bad after all. Everyone seemed to be nice, my roommate-to-be really liked reading, and Mrs. Gray had even planned to work with me on my food issues. I knew I truly couldn't complain.

Mrs. Gray began to slow down so she could fall into pace with me. "What are your thoughts, Cassie? Do you think Covington Hall is a place where you can see yourself thriving, both academically and personally?"

I shrugged uncertainly. "I think I won't know for sure until I've been here a few weeks."

She patted my shoulder kindly. "That's perfectly understandable. And we do everything we can to help students transition."

Daddy, who had been walking ahead of us with Mother, turned around. "I know you're going to do so well here, honey. Change always has some uncertainties, but I think you're truly going to enjoy being here. Your mom and I will only be a forty minutes away if you need us—"

"And at the same time, you'll be far enough away from what got you in trouble in the first place," Mother added.

True. I doubted anyone in Covington knew one thing about Emily Anderson and her wrongfully accusing father.

Daddy smiled. "So you're going to give it fair chance?"

I glanced around at the surrounding campus. "Totally."

After:

I crossed my arms as we walked toward the administration building. Now that I had seen the campus and met some students, Covington Hall might not be so bad. Everyone treated me kindly, my roommate-to-be loved reading, and Mrs. Gray planned to work with me on my food issues. How could I complain?

Mrs. Gray slowed to fall into pace with me. "What are your thoughts, Cassie? Do you think Covington Hall is a place where you can see yourself thriving, both academically and personally?"

I shrugged. "I won't know for sure until I've been here a few weeks."

She patted my shoulder. "That's perfectly understandable. And we do everything we can to help students transition."

Daddy, who walked ahead of us with Mother, turned around. "You're going to do so well here, honey. Change always has some uncertainties, but I think you'll truly enjoy being here. Your mom and I will only be a forty minutes away if you need us—"

"And at the same time, you'll be far enough away from what got you in trouble in the first place," Mother added.

True. I doubted anyone in Covington knew one thing about Emily Anderson and her wrongfully accusing father.

Daddy smiled. "So you're going to give it fair chance?"

I glanced around at the surrounding campus. "Totally."

Okay, so I lied. The After passage isn't weasel-free (although it's considerably less weasely). As we discussed before, there are times when weasel words *should* be used—which brings me to my last points on when to leave weasel words alone . . .

Weasel words and dialogue. People use weasel words all the time when speaking. So be careful when removing them from spoken discourse. If a weasel word strengthens the dialogue (makes it sound more natural), leave it; if removing the word doesn't change the sound of the dialogue, take it out and enjoy less verbiage.

Weasel words and character voice. Take a character's voice into consideration before omitting or rewording weasel words. Consider Cassie's final response in the examples above: "Totally." While "totally" is a weasel word, replacing it with something like "Yes" would completely change her voice. If eliminating a weasel word compromises a character's voice, don't do it.

Ready to trap some sneaky weasels now? It's easy. Simply use MS Word's Find and Replace feature to search for each word, and then determine which weasels should go and which should stay.

Editor:
Robin Patchen

Writers, Wipe That Smile off Your Page

So much of our communication comes from body language, including facial expressions, hand gestures, and postures.

For instance, take the word *sure*. If it's delivered with a big smile, it means something very different than when it's delivered with a glare. One is agreement, the other sarcasm or distrust.

We authors know this—we're students of human interaction, after all. So it makes sense that we so often include facial expressions and body language in our stories.

But these nonverbal descriptions can quickly become weasel words and bulky phrases, shoved into our paragraphs to convey quickly—and perhaps lazily—our characters' feelings and reactions.

Let's jump right into an example.

Before:

"So." Brady leveled a glare at her. "Are you going to tell me about him?"

Rae's heartbeat kicked into high gear as she imagined her son upstairs. "Him who?"

He frowned. "The man who put that ring on your finger."

She sighed in relief and tried to smile. "What do you want to know?"

"Where is he?" Brady's face took on a quizzical look.

"Paris."

Brady's eyebrows lifted. "Why isn't he with you?"

She made her face impassive. "Work."

Brady closed his lips in a tight line.

"What?" she asked.

He took a deep breath and blew it out. "You don't offer much, huh?"

She shrugged, and he continued. "So—Paris. Is that where you've been living?" He ran a hand through his hair. "Dorothy told me you were in Africa somewhere."

"He has an apartment in Paris." She wrung her hands beneath the table. "He's there now."

Brady's eyebrows lifted again, then fell, and he nodded. "When are you going back?"

"Soon as I can." She blinked a few times. "You want something else?"

He nodded to the bag. "You pick first."

She chose the blueberry scone. "That okay?"

He chuckled. "I knew you'd pick that one. You always were a sucker for blueberries."

She giggled, remembering the time they'd picked enough blueberries from the bushes out back for a couple of pies, then eaten so many Gram had scolded them. By the look on Brady's face, he remembered it too.

She shrugged. "Not a lot of blueberries in Tunis."

Emotional Placeholders

A moment of transparency here. The above segment—that's often what my first drafts look like. When I'm getting the plot on the page, focusing on building deep, multifaceted characters, I dump lots of that stuff into my prose. They're sort of like emotional placeholders.

But I try not to keep them, because as you saw in that last segment, they can get overused very quickly. Yes, people smile and shrug and nod. And in real life, we do all those things all the time. But real life is boring. Don't believe me? Turn on C-Span.

Figure out what your weasel words and bulky phrases are with regard to facial expressions and bodily motions. For some reason, my characters are often shown breathing—she sighs, he heaves a breath, she takes a deep breath, he blows out a breath. It's as though if I don't write that they breathe, they might just suffocate on the page.

Figure out what yours are and delete them—or replace them with something better.

After:

"So." Brady finished his sandwich and wiped his fingers on a napkin. "Are you going to tell me about him?"

Rae pictured Johnny sleeping soundly upstairs. How did Brady know? "Him who?"

"The man who put that ring on your finger."

Right. Him. "What about him?"

"Where is he?"

"Paris."

"Why isn't he with you?"

"Work."

Brady closed his lips in a tight line, and she recognized the look of frustration. "What?"

He took a deep breath and blew it out. "You don't offer much, huh?"

She took another bite of her sandwich but barely tasted it. She had to tread carefully.

"So, Paris," he said. "Is that where you've been living? Dorothy told me you were in Africa somewhere."

She set the sandwich down. "He has an apartment in Paris."

Brady seemed to be waiting for her to say something more, but she'd probably already said too much. After a moment, he continued. "When are you going back?"

"Soon as I can." She grabbed the basket of scones off the counter. No reason to panic. All she had to do was convince Brady that all was well with her and Julien.

Rae'd perfected the art of lying in college. The stories that rolled off her tongue back then had surprised her. But lying to Brady? That was something she'd never even attempted He knew her too well. Unfortunately, she didn't have a choice. She glanced at him now, saw him studying her, and pasted on a smile. "You want something else?"

"You pick first."

She pulled the cloth off the scones and took the blueberry one. "That okay?"

"I knew you'd pick that one." His lips twitched—nearly a smile. "You always were a sucker for blueberries."

She remembered the time they'd picked enough blueberries from the bushes out back for a couple of pies, then eaten so many Gram had scolded them. By the look on Brady's face, he remembered it too.

"Not a lot of blueberries in Tunis," she said.

You'll note I didn't eliminate all the facial expressions and other reactions, because they are important. People do laugh and sigh and smile and glare, and sometimes those are great ways to show us what your characters are feeling. But you can also use thoughts—as I did above, where she tells herself not to panic. And you can assume your reader will figure out some things without being told. Find key moments to use those smiles on the page, but use them sparingly, or they'll become weasel words.

Editor:
C. S. Lakin

Oh, Those Lovely Adverbs

One of my editing clients just this week asked me, "What's the problem with adverbs? Are they really bad to use? Why does everyone say I should take them out of my book?"

Adverbs do have a bad rep. Stephen King was endlessly requoted for saying that fantasy author J. K. Rowling "never met an adverb she didn't like" (and that wasn't a compliment). Out of curiosity, I read some comments on one of the Harry Potter forums to see if "normal" readers are bothered by them as well—or if it's just us authors who have a bug up our broomstick. Here's one comment:

> Does anyone else get sick of reading *calmly, serenely, cheerfully, smilingly* after everything Dumbledore says? By the sixth book I keep thinking, "Alright! I get it! . . . I don't need to be reminded with *calmly* stamped after every sentence. J. K. Rowling's adverb affair is the only thing I find tedious when reading the HP books. Gems like *unconcernedly, disconcertedly, disconcertingly, reprovingly*. AGH! But the Dumbledore adverbs by far outstrip the rest when it comes to pointless repetition.
>
> That nerd rant aside, I understand the books are for a wide audience that includes children, and those kinds of dialogue tack-ons are there to reduce the chance of the reader misunderstanding what the author intends in the character's dialogue. But still.
>
> "What are those things?" Harry asked, terrifiedly-ly.
>
> "They are adverbs, Harry," Dumbledore replied serenely, "There is nothing to be feared from an adverb, Harry. It is only fear of not being understood that we see when we find an adverb," he added calmly.
>
> "But still," said Harry unargumentatively but still worryingly. "They're pretty annoying after the 500th reading," he added, trying to sound as calmly and serenely and cheerfully and smilingly as Dumbledore.

"Yes, I think that once we try to use them after every sentence, we will find them less useful. We shall then call to our aid long sentences that basically denote the same thing," he said as if they weren't floating through a sea of obnoxious adverbs but discussing the matter over drinks.

I just had to share that. I don't even need to come up with my Before and After passage now, right? You can take that wonderfully creative example "Zevi" wrote at the www.PotterForums.com, delete all the adverbs, and you'll have an After passage.

However, Zevi makes another good point, noting that in lieu of an abundance of adverbs, Rowling will often use a long sentence to achieve a similar effect.

Try this:

Jane ate her food slurpily and happily as she kicked her feet swingingly and smiled hugely at her friends.

Now this:

Jane ate her food with a slurping delight and with great happiness as she kicked her feet back and forth in a swinging motion and gave her friends a big wide smile.

I've dispensed with all those adverbs, but ended up with just as awful a sentence. Do I really need all those descriptive details? I think not.

Jane slurped her drink, kicking her legs as she sat on the swing. She grinned, glad the school year was finally over.

Here's what "rinnyface" says in answer to "Zevi":

Why [does Rowling use so many adverbs]? I think when someone is trying to get a scene down, they want to articulate how each character is feeling/being characterized without stopping and going into an in-depth tangent. At the same time, you can argue that she could totally just have cut a lot of it out. Then it's just, "Harry said." "Ginny replied."

I guess she doesn't cut back on her adverbs simply because it shows the reader how her characters are affected without having to molest the reader with description. Who knows!

Some other great comments about adverbs. Kevin Spacey's character in the movie *Outbreak*: "It's a lazy tool of a weak mind."
Getting back to Stephen King, though, here's a short bit from *The Stand*:

"Huh!" Harold said, squeaked actually.
"Go away!" he yelled tearfully.
He looked up at her finally, his face tear streaked and still wanting to blubber. "I want my mother," he said simply.
"You're already getting one," she added critically, looking at his shoulders.

Notice any adverbs? Granted, *The Stand* was written in 1978, possibly pre-adverb-bashing. Extra Brownie points go to authors who learn and grow and improve in their writing, right?
Here's something a poster said on another forum:

I don't mind [adverbs] after dialogue if they make sense and it would weigh down a story to try and show it another way.
"That's lovely," Bob said dryly.
As opposed to "That's lovely," Bob said with a hint of sarcasm that wasn't really sarcasm, but more that special tone he used when he was trying to sound sarcastic, but not really.
Sometimes, you can be more efficient with an adverb.
Maybe that's a bad example above, but I think they're okay here and there. I do watch them myself and try to find other ways to get the moment/emotion across. But, it doesn't always work out.
Sharon Sheehe Stark uses adverbs spectacularly. "The jeep lurched stupidly." I'll never forget that one.

I agree with "CrastersBabies" above. There is a time and place for an occasional adverb. Maybe think of it like this. You get ten "adverb" chips per novel (similar to what Elmore Leonard said about using exclamation points: no more than two or three per 100,000 words of prose). So if you have limited use of an adverb, make it a good one, and in just the right place.

Leonard also said this about description and the use of adverbs:

> In Ernest Hemingway's "Hills like White Elephants," what do the "American and the girl with him" look like? "'She had taken off her hat and put it on the table." That's the only reference to a physical description in the story, and yet we see the couple and know them by their tones of voice, with not one adverb in sight.

He also said using an adverb to modify the word *said* is "a mortal sin." It's pretty evident that Leonard sides with King on the adverb issue.

I hope this look at "pesky" adverbs as part of our Fatal Flaw #11 exploration has been insightful and fun (she said happily).

In Conclusion . . .

Not all adverbs are pests and should be eliminated, but it's safe to say many writers overuse adverbs and rely on them too much to tell what their characters are feeling and doing. Adverbs packed into sentences to help speed up action ("He ran quickly as he hurriedly pulled his phone out of his pocket") actually do the opposite—they drag the pace. Imagine each extraneous adverb as a heavy rock in your character's pocket. The more rocks, the slower the narrative moves. Toss those rocks out and watch your scenes pick up speed.

And ditch those other weasels too, for they are also rocks in disguise. By lightening your load, you'll best Fatal Flaw #11 and be glad your manuscript is pest-free.

Fatal Flaw #11 Checklist

Go through your scenes and look for these culprits that might indicate pesky adverbs and weasel words:

- Excessive use of speech tags instead of interspersing with action beats

- Overuse of adverbs overall

- Overuse of prepositional phrases ("He went into the house, picked up the dog, opened the cupboard, took out a beer, and sat down on the couch.")

- Overuse of "to be" verbs ("I was going," "he is feeling bad," etc.)

- Overuse of superfluous words and phrases ("just, very, started to, began to," etc.)

- Overuse of "telling words" ("he knew, he felt, he thought, he wondered," etc.)

- Overuse of bodily movements that can feel tedious and repetitive

Your Turn: Try to spot and fix all the areas that show pesky adverbs and weasel words in this passage. An example of a revision is on the next page (no peeking!). There isn't one correct way to rewrite a passage, so your final version may be different from the revision provided. The key is to test yourself to see if you've nailed Fatal Flaw #11.

John quickly checked the clock on the wall. 6:35. Kara still wasn't home yet, even though she never ever pulled into the driveway any later than 6:15. She always answered her phone too, but his call had gone right into voicemail. He wondered where she could be. Something just had to be wrong.

He stood up and started walking to the front window. A few moments later, headlights rounded the curve and then slowed down as they approached. He began heading for the door as soon as the turn signal started blinking. Finally.

Kara already had the car door wide open when he hastily stepped out onto the porch.

"Hey, babe," she called. She carefully slid out, her purse on her shoulder and a bag in her hand.

He sighed in relief. "What happened?" he asked. "I was worried."

"There was an accident on the way," she said. "Then I didn't feel like cooking, so I stopped to pick up dinner. Got your favorite." She held up the white bag, and in the light from the car he could see *Chick-fil-A* scrawled in red across it. "The drive-thru was almost as backed up as the accident."

"But you didn't answer your phone either," he said.

"I guess I didn't hear it," she explained. "What's wrong?"

He sighed again. "Nothing. I just thought something had happened to you."

"Nope. I'm fine." She grinned and handed the bag to him. "Here."

Going by the weight and shape, it contained two sandwiches and a side of waffle fries. "What? No shake?" he asked.

"How could I forget?" She leaned over into the car, kneeling right on the driver's seat. When she emerged out, she held two really tall white Styrofoam cups, one with whipped cream and a cherry peeking through the clear plastic dome lid and one without. "Sorry I worried you."

He quickly took the whipped-cream-topped shake and grabbed the cherry with his teeth, then started chewing it and swallowed. "You're forgiven."

Revision of the Previous Passage:

John checked the clock on the wall. 6:35. Kara still wasn't home yet, even though she never pulled into the driveway later than 6:15. She always answered her phone too, but his call had gone right to voicemail. Where could she be? Something had to be wrong.

He stood and walked to the front window. Moments later, headlights rounded the curve and slowed as they approached. As soon as the turn signal started blinking, he headed for the door. Finally.

Kara already had the car door open when he stepped onto the porch.

"Hey, babe." She slid out, her purse on her shoulder and a bag in her hand.

He sighed in relief. "What happened? I was worried."

"There was an accident on the way. Then I didn't feel like cooking, so I stopped to pick up dinner. Got your favorite." She held up the white bag, and in the light from the car he could see *Chick-fil-A* scrawled in red across it. "The drive-thru was almost as backed up as the accident."

"But you didn't answer your phone either."

"I guess I didn't hear it." Her brow pinched as she looked up at him. "What's wrong?"

He needed to chill. "Nothing. I just thought something happened to you."

"Nope. I'm fine." She grinned and handed him the bag. "Here."

Going by the weight and shape, it contained two sandwiches and a side of waffle fries. "What? No shake?"

"How could I forget?" She leaned into the car, kneeling on the driver's seat. When she emerged, she held two tall white Styrofoam cups, one with whipped cream and a cherry peeking through the clear plastic dome lid, and one without. "Sorry I worried you."

He took the whipped-cream-topped shake and grabbed the cherry with his teeth, then chewed it and swallowed. "You're forgiven."

Fatal Flaw #12: Flawed Writing Mechanics

If you're a fiction writer, chances are you're also a fiction reader. Most writers agree that to write well, you need to read often. And if you're an avid reader, I'm willing to bet you've read some incredible books that have sent you running to all your reader friends, proclaiming, "I just finished this *awesome* book. You've got to read it." Beautiful writing inspires, and we all can use some inspiration—both in our lives and in our writing. One way to help ensure your writing shines is to use proper writing mechanics.

Genres Vary, but Good Writing Mechanics Are Universal

Genres and their particular "rules" vary greatly—women's fiction versus edge-of-your-seat suspense, cozy mysteries versus historical romance, horror versus fantasy—but whichever genre you pen, good writing mechanics are crucial. No matter how good your characterization and how spot-on your dialogue, poor writing mechanics will flatten a story. Though it takes time and effort to learn to write well (and then to do it), I know few writers who would settle for fair when they know their story could be great.

A Wide Spectrum

As you'll see in this chapter, writing mechanics covers an entire spectrum of advice for crafting compelling fiction. At one end is using good scene structure, which is similar to novel structure and may seem complex. At the other end are simpler guidelines, such as not starting too many sentences with the same word and not using too many stand-alone lines. And in the middle are craft intricacies, such as writing with pleasant cadence and knowing how to paragraph correctly.

Without further ado, let's delve deeper into how good writing mechanics can take a mediocre story and make it unforgettable.

Editor:
Rachel Starr Thomson

Scene Structure as a Mini Novel

Back in Fatal Flaw #2, we talked about the need to open scenes in the right place. The general rule is to open *in media res*—that is, while something is happening. On the other hand, it's generally best to bow out while things are *still* happening: close the dinner conversation with the last line of dialogue, not after everyone has fallen silent, gotten up from the table, washed the dishes, and gone to bed.

To put that succinctly: "Come late; leave early."

We've also looked at various elements of a great scene: action, pacing, description, dialogue, POV, the many ways to show and not just tell your story. Put all these things together, and you get a story—but that story still needs to come together within a structure. Once we get into a scene, what do we do there? What does a scene need to accomplish?

Plot structure as a whole is beyond the scope of this book. But *scene* structure follows plot structure in ways many readers may not realize. Getting the mechanics of a scene right can make the difference between a scene with impact and one that just drags or fades away.

The Miniature Novel

We've already established that it's best to come late. But once we've arrived in a scene, what do we *do* there? Let's look at a couple of different passages.

Example 1:
Honey felt a tug on the line.
"Reel 'er in slow," Grandpa said.
It was a slow, lazy afternoon on the river, the kind Honey loved. Grandpa was in a chatty mood, and they whiled away the hours fishing—sort of—while he shared memories from the past.

"Grandma and me used to come do this," he said. "The other girls thought it was strange that she liked to fish, but I guess she did. Or else she just liked to spend the time with me."

Honey smiled. She understood her grandmother. There was nothing nicer than spending time with someone you loved on a sunny day on the river, feeling the cool breeze and the splash of the water when you tried to bring a fish in. Not that it ever seemed important to really catch one.

"Well, I guess it's time we go home and get dinner," Grandpa finally said.

This example is not even a scene. It's a snapshot, a vignette (and even then, it's an incomplete one). Although it opens well enough—in *media res*—and ends with a sense of closure, it goes nowhere in between.

Scenes are the building blocks of a story. If you were to cobble together a hundred snapshots like the one above, you would not have a story at the end of it.

In fact, a scene is not just a building block *for* a novel; it's something of a novel in miniature. Scenes follow the same general path a novel does: they begin with a status quo, move through an incident that changes that status, and then build to *something*—a reveal, a confrontation, a climax of some kind. Often they will dip down into a resolution as well, though not always.

Scene structure mirrors that of any drama:

- Status quo

- Inciting incident

- Challenge(s)

- Climax

- Resolution (Optional—since scenes are only smaller parts of a bigger story, they can end in cliffhangers, whereas a novel cannot.)

If Honey had caught a fish (inciting incident), and then struggled hard to land it (challenge) but finally won out (climax to resolution), we would have a scene.

If Grandpa's conversation had turned into something deep and meaningful, such that he revealed a secret about Honey's past, or professed love for his family for the first time in his life, or admitted that he had cancer, we would have a scene.

If their fishing trip was interrupted by aliens descending on the river, and then Honey and Grandpa hid in the woods and managed to escape, we would have a scene.

A good scene has forward motion—not only in the sense that something actually happens action-wise but also in that it moves the whole story forward. By the end of a single scene, something has changed, whether the change is to characters or to circumstances. The story world is not the same as it was before that scene happened.

Let's take a look at this scene from my novel *Abaddon's Eve*.

Example 2:
Rechab awoke early and started her chores before the first light of dawn. To please her father she dressed herself in finer clothes than usual, veiled her face and chose earrings of silver, and went into the market to haggle for the day's allotment of fresh fruit and corn.

When she returned to the house midmorning, she was so startled to hear the voice emanating from her father's reception room that she nearly dropped the basket of melons she was carrying.

It was Flora.

She could not make out the words, but the imperious and determined tone was unmistakable. As was her father's mix of annoyance and admiration. Nadab had always appreciated anyone who would stand up to him and drive a hard bargain; Flora might be a woman and unusual, but the novelty of being faced by such a one might only heighten Nadab's admiration in the end.

Rechab set down her basket and lingered by the door, which burst open only moments later. Her father's enormous form stood in the doorway.

"Rechab!" he bellowed.

"I am here, Father," she said.

"Come inside. There is a most unusual woman here with a most unusual request."

Rechab entered as commanded. The sight of her visitor took her breath away. Flora had come in state. She wore silks dyed purple and scarlet, and a veil of linen so fine as to be transparent. Golden bracelets encircled her wrists, six on either hand, and gold earrings called attention to the striking beauty of her green eyes. *She might have been a goddess*, Rechab thought. No wonder her father admired her—as clearly he did. Her presence was awe inspiring, and Rechab wondered that she had stood in the same room with this woman and talked with her face-to-face just last night, without ceremony or fear.

Flora's face betrayed no recognition now, although Rechab thought she saw a twinkle in her eyes. She stood still as Flora looked her over with a haughty air.

"Yes, she'll do nicely," Flora said, turning her head back to Nadab. "I trust you can afford to dress her a little more appropriately?"

"Of course," Nadab said, shooting his daughter a look that said "I told you so."

"Then I am well pleased. Girl, your father says you are trained to deal with merchants and hold your head up proudly. Can you do that?"

"Yes," Rechab stammered.

"Convince me," Flora said.

Rechab straightened her shoulders and steadied her voice. "Yes."

"Look me in the eye."

Rechab did. There it was—an unmistakable twinkle. A promise.

Her heart leaped at the sight of it.

This woman might have been intimidating in every respect, but she was a *friend*, and she had come here as a friend.

Rechab didn't think her father could see that. The look in Flora's eye was strictly a two-way communication.

She kept Flora's gaze, and with shoulders still straight and her tone easy, she said, "Yes, I can do as you say. You wish me to represent you?"

Flora smiled now, and the smile took in Nadab as though to say she was thrilled with him. "The very thing. I am in this town to do business with merchants from the desert and the city, and I need someone who can greet them, put them at their ease, and speak for me when I do not wish to speak for myself. I know it is not usual to have a woman in that position, but then, it is not usual for a woman to conduct her own business dealings either. I feel you will represent me better than a man could do."

Flora stood, vacating the chair Nadab had offered her, and servants scurried out of the room's quarters to stand ready to assist her. She ignored them and addressed Nadab instead. "The praise I heard was not amiss. Let your daughter come to me at the nearest hour, washed and dressed. I will send you the payment we discussed straightaway."

She smiled at Rechab as she exited the house, and spoke with her voice lowered. "Come to me as quickly as you can. There is much to be done."

Scenes Are All about Change

The scene begins with the status quo: Rechab, the daughter of a greedy merchant named Nadab—who, to fill in a little of the story from a prior scene, has just made clear his intentions to sell her in marriage—wakes up in a normal day with little hope that anything will change. But an inciting incident happens in the arrival of Flora Laurentii Infortunatia, a devout and charismatic businesswoman whom Rechab briefly met the previous night.

The scene moves through a few obstacles—primarily convincing Nadab to let Rechab go temporarily without tipping him off to their prior connection—on its way to the climax, where Rechab is hired, and her life, in that moment, changes.

Move the Story Forward

In the scheme of things, this particular climax is nothing major. But it moves the story forward. The inciting incidents and climaxes within a particular scene do not have to be high-level events: they might be the tug of a fish on a line, a set of keys found, a minor confession made, a friendship struck up. But they must *change* something—something that ultimately builds the whole story by one more block.

Great description, snappy dialogue, and beautiful characterization will not craft a story all by themselves. Scenes that use dramatic structure within themselves and then link together to create the larger dramatic structure of the novel are what truly make a story come together. This is writing mechanics writ large.

Editor:
Linda S. Clare

Avoiding the "I" Trap and Other Irritants

As we wrap up our last fatal fiction flaw, let's examine how repetitive pronoun/proper name use and other small mistakes can weaken fiction and what we can do to strengthen our work.

Get Out of the "I" Trap

In the Julia Roberts/Brad Pitt movie *The Mexican*, Roberts leans out a window, hurling all Pitt's possessions on him. He protests, "But I ...I..."

She yells back. "I, I, I, I, I. It's always about you, Jerry." She then throws something else onto his head.

When writers overuse pronouns in their fiction, I think of this scene. Every writer faces the same challenge: how to communicate the story without boring readers by repeating pronouns at the beginning of sentences.

If you look at a scene you've drafted and see (or hear) nothing but I, I, I, the passage might read better if you rearrange or revise. Many people have an aversion to hearing "I" repetitively (or "he" or "she" or "it"). My solution is to draft the sentences any way they come but later revise or rearrange at least half of them.

Before:

I pressed my knuckles against my mouth after the teacher reprimanded me. I couldn't believe he'd dress me down in front of the whole class! I hadn't done anything wrong, unless you count that lit firecracker on his chair. I was determined to get revenge, even if it took all semester. I smiled at the real culprits—Tommy and Jack, those evil twins. I was always getting in trouble thanks to those two apes. I'd find a way to get even.

In the Before example, every sentence begins with "I." It does seem egocentric and, frankly, dull. Let's see how the paragraph can be reworked.

After:

> After the teacher reprimanded me, I pressed my knuckles against my mouth. He'd dressed me down in front of the whole class! I hadn't done anything wrong, unless you count that lit firecracker on his chair. Even if it took all semester, I'd get revenge. I smiled at the real culprits—Tommy and Jack, those evil twins. Thanks to those two apes, I was always getting in trouble. I would get even.

To avoid beginning every sentence with "I," I rearranged a few words, putting the end phrase at the beginning. More importantly, the new arrangements put the important part of the sentence where it has the most impact—at the beginning or the end. If you allow the important part of a sentence to languish in the middle, it tends to get lost.

Emphasize the important stuff where it will have a greater impact—beginning or end—as that's what readers tend to remember most easily. Plus, you solve the "I" problem.

There! It! Is!

Writers who begin sentences with "there" or "it" can almost always strengthen those lines by revising. *There was* or *there were* indicates weak construction that would be better if replaced by an active verb. We covered this in our look at Fatal Flaw #3: Weak Construction.

Example: *There was an old brick building at the end of the dirt road.* Better: *An old brick building sat at the end of the dirt road.* Not only do you eliminate *there* and *was*—two words that can mean many things—you also put the important words at the sentence's beginning.

In much the same way, "it" buys a writer relatively little in terms of communicating. Plus, the word *it* tends to refer to the last noun written. Example: *It was the neighbor's dog, prowling around under the window. It growled, then ran off yelping.*

To remedy the unfortunate growling window, you could write: *Under the window, the neighbor's dog prowled around. It growled, then ran off yelping.*

Writing skills begin with mechanics. Learn how to vary the openings, handle pronouns well, and use strong, specific words. Master these and other areas of writing mechanics to help rework so-so fiction into unforgettable fiction.

To Paragraph or Not to Paragraph

Let's talk about another type of structure in fiction: paragraph structure. Earlier in this book, we discussed why white space is important, but to use white space well, we need to understand when to start and end a paragraph.

Here are some basic guidelines for paragraphing in fiction:

- *Begin a new paragraph anytime the speaker changes.* By starting a new paragraph, the reader will automatically know a different character is talking.

    "Good morning, Joe," John said from the next cubicle. "Hey, John." Joe sat down at his desk.

- *Keep individual characters' actions, thoughts, and speech in one paragraph.* Character actions, also known as action beats (e.g., "He smiled" or "She crossed her arms"), allow the reader to "see" what's going on in the scene and also provide a great alternative to repeated dialogue tags (e.g., "he said").

    Jenna grabbed a bottle of orange juice from the refrigerator case and checked her watch as she headed for the register. *Late again.* She forced a smile at the cashier. "Good morning."
    "How's it going?" He nodded at her drink. "That all for today?"

- If keeping a character's actions, thoughts, and speech together results in a very long paragraph, consider shortening the paragraph by either adding another character's interaction in a new paragraph or breaking the paragraph in two at a logical place.

- When conveying action involving more than one character, (in most cases) allow each character his or her own paragraph.

> Colleen started down the aisle of the nearly full bus, glancing over the riders. Jim said he'd save her a seat. Hopefully he had.
> Near the back of the bus, a hand went up.
> She hurried back and dropped onto the seat next to him. "Thanks."

- Start a new paragraph with a change in time or place.

> Amanda closed her locker. "I'm going to the library. You coming?"
> "I'll catch up with you there." Jana said. "I have to stop by Mrs. Patterson's classroom first."
> Twenty minutes later, Jana finally walked into the library.
> Amanda waved her over to where she sat at a computer. "What took you so long?"
> She sighed as she pulled a chair beside her. "Mrs. Patterson could talk the teeth out of a saw."

- As in nonfiction, begin a new paragraph whenever the main idea of the paragraph changes.

- Start a new paragraph to offset a sentence or two for emphasis. Paragraphing so that one sentence (or two) stands alone can provide extra punch to the sentence(s) and even the scene. Just be sure not to overuse standalone sentences, because the repetition will diminish the effect.

With these guidelines in mind, let's take a look at how both faulty and appropriate paragraphing affect a scene.

Before:

> My chest tightened as Mother and Daddy's car drove out of the parking lot late that afternoon. My first day at Covington Hall had gone much better than I'd expected, but the reality of my parents going home unsettled me. Strange. How many

times over the last few years had I wished they'd give me some space? Now I was getting plenty. Forty-minutes'-drive worth of space to be exact. Daddy always did say to be careful what you wish for. Shoving my hands into my hoodie pockets, I drew a breath and let it out. What now?

"Hey, Cassie!"

I turned to find Ashley and a girl I hadn't met coming across the parking lot. Connor, Landon, and another guy followed, joking among themselves. Ashley grinned as they neared.

"We're about to go get dinner. You want to come along?"

Sure. Except that I couldn't bear the thought of eating the cafeteria food—or in the cafeteria. Let the awkwardness begin.

"Uh . . . I have my own food. It's in our room."

Landon held up the insulated lunch bag he carried. "Me too. Allergic to milk, eggs, beef, and chicken." At least I wasn't the only one with food issues.

"But I'm not real good with cafeteria smells either."

Connor shrugged. "No biggie. We eat out on the terrace when the weather's nice anyway." Maybe this wouldn't be so bad after all.

"Sounds good to me." We started toward the dorms, and Landon stepped into pace beside me. "You have allergies too?"

I forced myself to look at him, and the sincere kindness of his expression eased my apprehension a bit. "Well . . . mine are aversions."

He nodded. "We've got something in common then. My body's allergic to some foods, and your mind's allergic to some foods. Right?" Oh, this guy was awesome. I smiled.

"I've never heard it put that way before, but yeah, that pretty much covers it."

I stopped and looked at Ashley as we reached the path to our dorm. "I have to grab my food. You can go ahead and get your dinner. I'll meet you on the terrace."

"I try not to go in the cafeteria," Landon said. "Mind if I walk with you instead?"

Did I mind if the only guy I'd ever met who made me feel remotely comfortable—well, besides Daddy—walked with me? "Nope." Not a bit.

After:

My chest tightened as Mother and Daddy's car drove out of the parking lot late that afternoon. My first day at Covington Hall had gone much better than I'd expected, but the reality of my parents going home unsettled me.

Strange. How many times over the last few years had I wished they'd give me some space? Now I was getting plenty. Forty-minutes'-drive worth of space to be exact. Daddy always did say to be careful what you wish for.

Shoving my hands into my hoodie pockets, I drew a breath and let it out. What now?

"Hey, Cassie!"

I turned to find Ashley and a girl I hadn't met coming across the parking lot. Connor, Landon, and another guy followed, joking among themselves.

Ashley grinned as they neared. "We're about to get dinner. You want to come along?"

Sure. Except that I couldn't bear the thought of eating the cafeteria food—or in the cafeteria. Let the awkwardness begin. "Uh . . . I have my own food. It's in our room."

Landon held up the insulated lunch bag he carried. "Me too. Allergic to milk, eggs, beef, and chicken."

At least I wasn't the only one with food issues. "But I'm not real good with cafeteria smells either."

Connor shrugged. "No biggie. We eat out on the terrace when the weather's nice anyway."

Maybe this wouldn't be so bad after all. "Sounds good to me."

We started toward the dorms, and Landon stepped into pace beside me. "You have allergies too?"

I forced myself to look at him, and the sincere kindness of his expression eased my apprehension a bit. "Well . . . mine are aversions."

He nodded. "We've got something in common then. My body's allergic to some foods, and your mind's allergic to some foods. Right?"

Oh, this guy was awesome. I smiled. "I've never heard it put that way before, but yeah, that pretty much covers it." I stopped and looked at Ashley as we reached the path to our dorm. "I have to grab my food. You can go ahead and get your dinner. I'll meet you on the terrace."

"I try not to go in the cafeteria," Landon said. "Mind if I walk with you instead?"

Did I mind if the only guy I'd ever met who made me feel remotely comfortable—well, besides Daddy—walked with me?

"Nope."

Not a bit.

The wording of the Before and After are identical. The only difference is in the paragraphing. Chances are, there were a few places in the Before passage that confused you. Did you ever wonder who was speaking? In the After passage, the use of appropriate paragraphing makes the speaker obvious. As well, the standalone line at the end of the excerpt emphasizes how Cassie feels about Landon's kindness.

Paying attention to writing mechanics is important for clarity and ease of reading. You may write beautiful sentences and plot out riveting stories with compelling characters, but if your mechanics are flawed, you might experience novel failure. So be sure to put this last fatal flaw on your checklist of things not to ignore when writing fiction.

The 12 Fatal Flaws of Fiction Writing

Editor:
Robin Patchen

Searching for the Poetry in Story

If your readers wanted poetry, they'd pick up a Robert Frost anthology. Or perhaps Emily Dickinson or Shakespeare, right?
I don't think so.
Your readers are looking for poetry, even if they don't know it.
Well, maybe not poetry, but cadence. Readers want to hear words put together in beautiful ways. They want sentences to roll like waves or batter like bullets. They want to see alluring alliterations and evocative metaphors.
Readers long for beauty in words the way tourists seek out beauty in landscape and architecture. Perhaps they fly to Paris for the wine and cheese, but they'll admire the Notre Dame on the way to dinner, and the trip will be richer for it.
How do you use cadence to make your stories as satisfying as a great French meal and as grand as the Notre Dame? One way is to consider cadence when you write.

Cadence Is Not Just Pretty Writing

Cadence is rhythm. It's that thing that makes you need to finish a limerick or lyric. If I were to sing "The wheels on the bus," everybody in the room would say or at least think "go round and round." You can't help yourself because cadence longs to be finished. Poetry has a rhythm, and rhythm longs for completion.
Beautiful writing is about more than cadence though. It's also about choosing lovely words, choosing the right words—those that reflect the scene and mood. It's about letting people see beyond the words to the setting and characters and emotions beneath. It's hard to describe, so let's look at an example.

Before:
It was raining outside. I felt safe inside, in my living room, where it was dry. I was wearing a pair of pink pajama pants,

sweatshirt, and a pair of thick socks. I made myself a cup of hot chocolate. I cuddled up in front of the fireplace with my cat, who was named Mrs. Boots. The cat snuggled her head into my elbow. Everything was good in the world, and I felt content. But then I heard a noise outside, where there was some kind of a bump, and I got scared.

Technically, there's nothing wrong with the above paragraph. The words and punctuation are being used correctly. But does that paragraph have any rhythm? Any cadence? Does it evoke any emotions?

Before we look at the After paragraph, let's analyze this one a little.

Learning and Redundancy

The first sentence is boring and tells us very little. Is it a gentle rain or a hard rain? A warm rain or a cold rain? Is it daytime or night? Or is it daytime but dark because of the rain? Are there thunder and lightning? How long has it been raining? How long is it going to rain? That first sentence, while technically correct, tells us next to nothing.

The second sentence—"I felt safe inside, in my living room, where it was dry."—irritates me on multiple levels. First, it *tells* us this person felt safe. But in fiction we're supposed to show, not tell. Also it uses the word *inside* and *in* back-to-back. And really, isn't it safe to assume it's dry inside? That last phrase is redundant and unnecessary.

Parallelism

Think about the third sentence: "I was wearing a pair of pink pajama pants, sweatshirt, and have a pair of thick socks." You always want to write with parallel structure. In that sentence, you can't have "a pair of" a sweatshirt, though. We could fix it like this: "I wore pajama pants, a sweatshirt, and thick socks." That's better, because the cadence flows. Read it aloud and hear what I mean.

Another option: "I wore my favorite pink pajama pants and my blue Red Sox sweatshirt." I like the extra detail of the "Red Sox," and I think it gives us a little clue about the character. Do we need the socks? If so, then we'd need to work that information in another way.

Identification

The next sentence is blah but not worth parsing. These two are next: "I cuddled up in front of the fireplace with my cat, who was named Mrs. Boots. The cat snuggled her head into my elbow." The word *cat* is used twice back-to-back. Is "who was named" necessary? What about: "I cuddled in front of the fireplace. Mrs. Boots jumped onto the sofa with me and nudged her furry body in the crook of my elbow. She looked at me with her big gold eyes and purred until I scratched her behind the ears." Better, I think, and I didn't use the word "cat" once.

Inelegance

The next sentence isn't worth mentioning. The final thought: "But then I heard a noise outside, where there was some kind of a bump, and I got scared." Aside from the obvious telling—"I got scared"—this sentence is clunky and inelegant. The reader won't get nervous because of that noise, though he might cringe at the bad writing.

So the sentences taken alone aren't good, and when you read them together, they make the whole thing worse. There is no cadence or rhythm to that paragraph, no poetry, no imagery. Just flat words on a page. Let's look at the After passage.

After:

The rain streamed down the window and plopped in puddles on the back porch. I squinted in the darkness and could barely make out the trees bent and whipping in the wind. I snuggled in my favorite Red Sox sweatshirt, grabbed a steaming cup of hot chocolate, and headed for the living room. The fire I'd lit earlier was already warming the downstairs, drawing the dampness away. I'd turned off the TV when the satellite went out, which was right after the weatherman promised the storm would pass by morning.

I set my mug on the coffee table, lifted my novel, and settled into the corner of the sofa. Mrs. Boots, never one to miss an opportunity, climbed onto my lap. She implored me with those big brown eyes, her purrs louder than the thunder rumbling in the distance. "Okay, settle down." I scratched her behind the ears, and she laid her head on top of her furry paws with a look of pure contentment.

With one hand petting the cat, I lifted my book again. I had just finished a chapter when something startled me. I paused and listened. Surely nobody would venture this far from town on such a dark and treacherous night, but after a moment, I heard the sound again. A bump, then a scraping. And the noises were coming from the back porch.

I hope you agree that's better. I attempted to lull the reader into a sense of comfort and security, because that is how the main character feels. But I also wanted to hint at the impending danger with the thunder rumbling in the distance. Frankly, that's a subtle hint, and it's not important to me that the reader pick up on that. If the reader feels content and then surprised by the bump, then the reader feels what the heroine is feeling, and that's the objective.

Mastering the Art of Poetry

Think about each word. Is your character feeling content? Then the rain might pitter-patter on the deck. Is the mood darker? Then the rain could pound against roof. Same situation, but the word *pound* conveys a very different feel than the whimsical pitter-patter. Many words convey some sort of emotion, not just in their meaning but in their sounds. For instance, is it any wonder that the word *beautiful* is much more commonly used than its synonym *pulchritudinous*. There is nothing beautiful about that word. And while *comely* may mean pretty, it's too close to its antonym *homely* to be used very often. So the words you choose and their sounds matter.

One great way to discover if there's rhythm in your prose is to read it aloud. Hear the words you've chosen and listen to their sounds. Hear the rhythm, the cadence. Ask yourself if it sounds right, and keep working on it until it does.

Finding the poetry in the story leads not only to better writing but to fuller immersion. It's worth the extra time, and like so many of our fatal flaws, it may be difficult at first to get a handle on it, but as you work on it, your prose will naturally become more poetic.

Editor:
C. S. Lakin

The Truth about Writing Mechanics

I suppose it's only to be expected that in a book written by editors someone would mention the obvious: to present flawless writing, a writer needs to learn how to write grammatically correct sentences.

Don't panic—this isn't going to be a grammar lesson. If you want to take the time to learn about grammar, there are plenty of books and blogs that can help (especially *Say What? The Fiction Writer's Handy Guide to Grammar, Punctuation, and Word Usage*, another book in The Writer's Toolbox Series).

But really, every writer should spend time learning the tools of his trade. We use words, and we use them in abundance. We should wield them both creatively and correctly.

We've all heard it said that before you can break the rules, you need to master them. I agree, for the most part. Some writers have a wonderful style that doesn't adhere to a whole lot of grammar rules. Some of those writers bring the flavor of ethnicity to their prose, or reflect a lack of proper education to their first-person narrator (consider Mark Twain's characters, for example). There are times when deliberately breaking those rules works.

But a whole novel with fractured or chaotic sentence structure is going to give most readers a headache.

The sentence, to me, is the foundation of all prose. I love a beautifully crafted sentence. I love to be surprised by an unusual, unexpected word. The placement of each word in a sentence can be carefully decided for a specific impression or impact. Moving one word to the beginning or end can change the feel or sentence meaning, even if subtly. For this last section in our discussion, let's go beyond grammar and talk about using words *well*.

Making Every Word Count

The one-eyed witch in my novel *The Unraveling of Wentwater* warned, "Take care with your words. They have consequences." Every time the witch receives a word in payment for a spell she casts, she puts it in a jar and sets it on her shelf. From then on that word no longer exists. My heroine has to stitch every word back into existence after a spell goes awry and causes the world to vanish.

Words have the power to heal and to hurt. I wonder how many wars have been started, marriages ruined, and murders committed all from the utterance of a single word? As wordsmiths, writers have a serious charge. Maybe you don't see yourself in such a capacity, but what if you did? What if you made every word count, instead of counting words?

Writers these days seem to be all about counting words. Quantity over quality. Pounding out a minimum word count each day instead of searching for the perfect word or working on crafting the perfect sentence.

Something feels flawed to me when a writer pushes to get five thousand words down on paper or the computer screen in record time—all so she can feel a sense of satisfaction (or post her great accomplishment on Facebook).

Slow Down and Smell the Words

I'd like to encourage writers to slow down. As we barrel along at breakneck speed in our daily routine, it takes (sometimes gargantuan) effort to slow our brains to a crawl. We need to crawl if we are going to notice our world. Maybe even come to a complete stop, to a place of utter stillness, to *really* notice. How can we write about anything if we don't take the time to experience life through our senses? That sensory detail—the things we observe, smell, taste, touch—gets processed, chewed up, and digested as fodder for creativity.

I remember hearing lines like "You're too young to write a novel. You haven't lived long enough or experienced enough *life* to have anything significant to say." Now that I'm well past the midpoint of my life, I get that. But just because we may be old, doesn't mean we've been paying attention.

Writing can be a lot like life. We get used to certain things, we fall into routine, we like comfort and don't challenge ourselves. We don't want to take risks or stretch ourselves too much as we age. We like that ratty old chair. We vacation in the same place every year. We like familiarity.

But this can filter into our writing and affect our creativity. With an attitude of "I have to hurry and write a lot of words" because our writing time is limited or our lifespan feels too short, or an attitude of "I'm too comfortable and settled in my style and don't want to push myself," our writing can start to fossilize.

Attitude and Writing Mechanics

So, really, my focus in this chapter on writing mechanics has to do with our attitude. Are you always in search of the perfect word? The perfect sentence? Is your goal centered on making sure you meet a target word count or is it on writing the best story you can?

Attitude greatly affects writing mechanics. If we approach our writing time with a sense of impatience and word-count expectations, how likely is it we'll write well?

Some people, like me, work best under deadline. I self-impose ridiculous deadlines for my projects. I won't get my books written and published if I don't. I think that's a carryover from all the newspapers I worked on. Many nights I had editors breathing down my neck—literally—as I stood rolling the waxed pieces of paper onto the board as the clock ticked down till press time (I worked in composing, which was the department that "composed" the newspaper back in the day before computers). But even though I put that deadline pressure on myself, I never rush the writing.

Rushing and Gushing

Again, it's attitude. There's nothing wrong with gushing out a scene, getting it all down before the ideas slip out your ears. Sometimes that feels like rushing instead of gushing. But there's a difference. Writers rush to finish a draft, rush to publish before taking time to carefully go over every sentence and question every word. In their rush they don't bother to edit, don't bother to look up the correct use of a word, don't bother to have readers give constructive feedback. Sure, go ahead and gush, but don't *rush*. Go back, slow down, and start sifting through your words.

I see this a lot with my editing clients. Some want to get on the publishing bandwagon yesterday. They'll inform me their book is already up for sale on Amazon, but they didn't have the time or money to edit it. Other clients come to me with a proverbial tail between their legs, admitting they did the aforementioned and after few sales and negative reviews (mostly about how sloppy the writing was), they now want to slow down, get help, and learn how to write the perfect sentence and the perfect book (in a manner of speaking).

How much better it would have been if they had ignored word count and focused on words. Ignored the whistling wind urging them to hurry and just plopped down on the ground and closed their eyes and listened to the timbre of the wind. Then they would be in a much better place to be able to describe the wind—and everything else.

I don't have any Before or After passages in my section of this fatal flaw. Instead, I'd like to have you think about your own Before and After—when you sit down to write during that block of time you've set aside and when your time is up and you're finished for the day.

Don't look at the clock. Don't count words. Make your words count. That is the heart of writing mechanics.

In Conclusion . . .

Words, sentences, paragraphs, and scenes. Those are the components of story. As with any profession, it behooves writers to learn to wield and master the tools of their trade. Work on becoming a proficient wordsmith. Language is our realm, and words are the building blocks of every tree, flower, and character.

Spend time reading beautifully written novels, poems, and short stories. Slow down and taste words; roll them around in your mouth. Show words the honor they deserve and work with them respectfully. Take time, too, to learn the mechanics of writing so you say what you mean and don't say what you don't mean. Aim for excellence, precision, creativity. Don't settle on the first things that gush onto the page. Go back and make them better. Perfect, if possible.

Often the difference between a good writer and a great one is in the writing mechanics. Don't let laziness or a lack of interest in grammar and word usage cause you to succumb to this fatal flaw of fiction writing. You owe it to yourself and your readers to master this one.

Fatal Flaw #12 Checklist

Go through your scenes and look for these culprits that show flawed writing mechanics:

- Too many sentences starting with the same word(s)

- Too many sentences beginning with weak construction, such as "it was" and "there were"

- Passages that lack writing cadence or euphony

- Too many paragraphs starting the same way

- Too many paragraphs of the same length

- Overly long paragraphs

- Improper use of paragraphing

- Too many stand-alone lines

- Scenes that lack good structure, failing to build to a key moment

Your Turn: Try to spot and fix all the areas that show flawed writing mechanics in this passage. An example of a revision is on the next page (no peeking!). There isn't one correct way to rewrite a passage, so your final version may be different from the revision provided. The key is to test yourself to see if you've nailed Fatal Flaw #12.

It was 7:53.

I had arrived at work right on time. I had arrived early, in fact. I placed my bagel and OJ on the desk and looked over the surrounding cubicles. They were all empty except one. Two cubicles over, Jennifer sat at her computer typing with one hand while downing coffee with the other. She could do just about anything with one hand, since she had a six-cups-a-day habit. The air smelled differently today. "Morning, Jen," I said.

She turned. "Oh. Hi, Samantha." She looked at the clock and smiled. "You're the early bird today. What's up with that?"

"I didn't hit one traffic light driving in. I don't think that's ever happened before." I set my purse under my desk and joined her. "What time do you get in every day?"

She sipped her coffee and shrugged. "Usually around 7:40. I like to ease into my day."

"Are you drinking something different?"

She held up her Styrofoam cup. "Pumpkin spice latte. It is October now, you know. Of course, I'll be back to coffee when this is finished."

I grinned. "Of course."

"You never drink coffee, do you?"

"No. I drink tea in the winter sometimes, but I don't really like hot drinks."

As I walked to my cubicle, Paul and Mike rounded the corner. There was a large insulated mug in Paul's hand, and there was ceramic mug in Mike's hand. Was I the only one who didn't drink coffee?

"Morning, guys," I said.

Paul saluted. "Hi, Samantha." Mike added, "Hey. You're in already?"

I dropped into my chair as they went to their own desks. "Yep. Time to get to work."

Revision of the Previous Passage:

It was 7:53. For once, I arrived at work right on time. In fact, not only on time—*early*.

I placed my bagel and OJ on the desk and looked over the surrounding cubicles. All were empty except one. Two cubicles over, Jennifer sat at her computer typing with one hand while downing coffee with the other. The girl could do just about anything with one hand, courtesy of her six-cups-a-day habit. Although today the air held a distinctly different aroma.

"Morning, Jen," I said.

She turned. "Oh. Hey, Samantha." A glance at the clock brought a smile to her face. "You're the early bird today. What's up with that?"

"I didn't hit one traffic light driving in. Don't think that's ever happened before." I set my purse under my desk and joined her. "What time do you get in every day?"

She sipped her coffee and shrugged. "Usually around 7:40. I like to ease into my day."

"Are you drinking something different?"

She held up her Styrofoam cup. "Pumpkin spice latte. It is October now, you know. Of course, I'll be back to coffee when this is finished."

I grinned. "I'll let you get back to work."

"Hey, Samantha." Her whisper stopped me before I'd taken four steps toward my cubicle.

I turned around, and seeing the seriousness of her expression, moved toward her.

She looked around before turning her attention back to me. "There's a rumor going around that lay-offs are coming again—and this time, they'll involve our department. Have you heard anything?"

I hadn't, though I wasn't surprised. We all knew the company had seen better days. I tried to smile. "I don't think you have too much to worry about. Everyone knows how well you perform and how conscientious you are. No one else is here at 7:40."

She nodded. "And I'd think you're safe too. You know this job better than any of us."

"Besides, sometimes rumors are just that—rumors. No use worrying about something that might not happen, right?"

"Right." She grinned. "Thanks."

I returned to my cubicle and booted my computer. While I waited, I reached for my bagel, but I couldn't get more than one bite down. The thought of lay-offs completely nixed my appetite. Chances were that Jen and I would be the last of the department to be let go, but the whole situation was still unsettling. I did do my job well, but I could still improve in some areas.

Perhaps I needed to make more of an effort to get to work on time every day.

Conclusion

There's nothing worse for a writer than reading reviews (or agent rejection letters) filled with comments such as "The writing was wordy" and "There was too much backstory, so I couldn't get into it" and "I was so bored. The scenes dragged, and the dialogue was corny and unbelievable."

Many writers are shocked and disheartened by such words, and rightly so. But the shock comes from not having learned how to identify the fatal flaws of fiction writing. We hope that you won't ever have to suffer such feedback. Or if you already have, maybe you won't ever have to again. By applying all you've learned in this book, you'll be able vanquish the twelve fatal flaws of fiction writing, and when your books are published, you'll get raving—not scathing—reviews.

It can be overwhelming to tackle these flaws, so just take on one at a time. What is the weakest point in your writing? Study the chapter on that flaw and work on identifying the culprits contributing to it, then apply the insights and techniques to your writing. Share your revisions with a critique partner or group. Or hire a fiction-savvy editor to read and respond to your material. In time, with practice and feedback, you can best all twelve of these fatal flaws.

Your short story or novel is something you should be proud of. Take the time to make it the best it can be. Keep reading writing craft books, attending workshops and conferences, and getting professional editing help to polish your story for a world of readers. Read great novels and study how the authors wield language and compose passages.

No one need suffer novel failure. You don't have to be uniquely brilliant or talented to write fiction well. You just need to be forewarned and forearmed. We hope this in-depth exploration of the twelve fatal flaws of fiction writing will serve you long and well on your writing journey.

Happy writing!

Meet the Editors

C. S. Lakin is the author of more than a dozen novels and the writing craft books in The Writer's Toolbox Series, of which this book is a part. She writes suspense, mystery, fantasy, women's fiction, YA sci-fi, and historical Western romance. She loves throwing her characters into trouble and pushing them to the limits of their sanity, then tossing them a lifeline. Characters are at the heart of all her stories, but she loves a strong plot.

Her award-winning blog, Live Write Thrive, gives weekly instruction and encouragement to writers. She specializes in manuscript critiques and loves to help writers see their books get published and garner rave reviews.

Susanne lives in the San Francisco area with her husband, Lee, and loves to read, camp, hike, and play with her dogs and cats. Summers you can usually find her hiking the PCT or on the beach at Lake Tahoe, throwing the stick for her ginormous lab, Coaltrane. Between editing, writing blog posts, and watching her adorable grandson, she has little time to write novels, but since she feels sleep is highly overrated, she often crams in time and eats a lot of chocolate to stay awake.

Susanne also loves to teach workshops. Contact her if you'd like her to speak to your writers' group or at your local writing conferences. Just make sure there's chocolate!

Linda S. Clare is the author of two women's fiction novels and three nonfiction books. Her first love is writing fiction that speaks to the wounded heart in all of us, with stories of characters searching for their place to belong. She has also published dozens of poems, essays, and short stories, one of which was nominated for a Pushcart Prize.

Linda presently teaches college creative writing courses in Oregon. She facilitates a weekly face-to-face critique group and blogs at

Linda Clare's Writer's Tips. She coaches and edits other writers and her students regularly win awards for their work.

She and her husband, Brad, have four grown children and three terrible cats, and make their home in Oregon's Willamette Valley. When she's not writing and teaching, she loves to sneak away to her flower garden or act silly with her three grandchildren.

Linda is a frequent speaker at writers' conferences, book clubs, and other groups. She's also the alter ego of humorist Miss Writerly Crankypants and the criminal Cranky Cat. Whether you're looking for a speaker, editor, coach, or instructor, she brings her own blend of encouragement, expertise, and crankytude!

Christy Distler edits for publishing houses and also provides freelance editing and proofreading through Aspire Editing Services. Her short fiction, nonfiction, and poetry have been published in

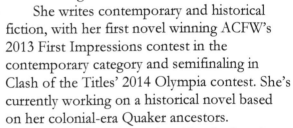

denominational periodicals, literary magazines, and anthologies.

She writes contemporary and historical fiction, with her first novel winning ACFW's 2013 First Impressions contest in the contemporary category and semifinaling in Clash of the Titles' 2014 Olympia contest. She's currently working on a historical novel based on her colonial-era Quaker ancestors.

Obsession with words aside, she lives in Pennsylvania with her husband, two small children, a large black Lab who thinks she's a lap dog, and an ever-changing number of amphibians. She considers dark chocolate a food group and a daily requirement. When not writing and editing, she can be found reading, giving thumbs-ups at gymnastics practice, and involved in family, church, and school activities.

Robin Patchen is the author of four novels—two women's fiction and two with a strong element of suspense, including her latest full-length suspense, *Finding Amanda*. When she's

not writing, she works as a freelance editor specializing in fiction. After serving as an editorial assistant at Wayside Press, she opened her freelance doors in 2013. Today, Robin works with people at every level in publishing, from the newest writers still honing their skills to veteran multipublished authors stepping into hybrid publishing. She is also the freelance line editor for Redbud Press.

Robin is married and has three teenagers, so her life is a whirlwind of activity. She loves to travel, and though her days are busy with writing and editing, she reads fiction when she has time. She also loves to teach writing courses to new and experienced fiction writers and is available to speak at writers' conferences.

Rachel Starr Thomson is a freelance editor and founder of Independent Publishing Solutions, a publishing one-stop shop for

writers. She's also the author of numerous books, both fiction and nonfiction, including The Prophet Trilogy, The Oneness Cycle, and The Seventh World Trilogy. Over the years she has poured herself into teaching as well as writing, coaching hundreds of students in person and online. She transitioned into full-time editing in the early 2000s. Rachel lives in the Niagara region of Ontario, Canada, but

spends much of her time on the road as a speaker and spoken-word artist for 1:11 Ministries. In her free time she reads fantasy novels, hikes the Bruce Trail, dreams up business ventures, and drinks too much coffee.

Want to become the best novelist you can be?
The Writer's Toolbox Series will give you all the tools you need to write terrific, well-structured stories that will stand the test of time and scrutiny.

If you benefited from this book, be sure to check out these other books in the series:

• *Say What? The Fiction Writer's Handy Guide to Grammar, Punctuation, and Word Usage* is designed to help writers get a painless grasp on grammar. You can buy the expanded second edition in print or as an ebook, available in all formats on all online venues.

• *Writing the Heart of Your Story: The Secret to Crafting an Unforgettable Novel* will teach you how to mine the heart of your plot, characters, themes, and so much more. If you want to write a book that targets the heart of readers, you need to know the heart of your story. Buy it online in print or as an ebook, available in all formats on all online venues.

• *Shoot Your Novel: Cinematic Techniques to Supercharge Your Writing*—an essential writing craft guide that will teach you the art of "show don't tell" using time-tested cinematic technique. In this era of visual media, readers want more than ever to "see" stories unfold before their eyes. By utilizing film technique and adapting the various camera shots into your fiction, your writing will undergo a stunning transformation from "telling" to "showing." In print and ebook for all formats.

• *The 12 Key Pillars of Novel Construction*: An essential writing craft guide that provides clear, simple, and concise instruction how to structure any novel using twelve key pillars. "Inspection Checklists" are provided for each pillar, to help you examine your novel structure to make sure it is sound and will stand the test of time and scrutiny! A fresh and innovative method that takes the mystery and confusion out of building a novel. Buy it online in print or as an ebook, available in all formats on all online venues.

• *The 12 Key Pillars of Novel Construction Workbook*—A step-by-step in-depth guide to help you develop your novel. Includes hundreds of prompts, worksheets, sample mind maps, and exercises to ensure your novel is structured well and will stand up to time and scrutiny. Available in paperback.

Made in the USA
Lexington, KY
28 December 2015